DATE DUE

			PRINTED IN U.S.A.

DEC 1 9 2012

Music and Twentieth-Century Tonality

Routledge Studies in Music Theory

1 **Music and Twentieth-Century Tonality**
Harmonic Progression Based on
Modality and the Interval Cycles
Paolo Susanni
and Elliott Antokoletz

Music and Twentieth-Century Tonality

Harmonic Progression Based on
Modality and the Interval Cycles

Paolo Susanni and Elliott Antokoletz

Routledge
Taylor & Francis Group
NEW YORK   LONDON

First published 2012
by Routledge
711 Third Avenue, New York, NY 10017

Simultaneously published in the UK
by Routledge
2 Park Square, Milton Park, Abingdon, Oxon OX14 4RN

*Routledge is an imprint of the Taylor & Francis Group,
an informa business*

Library of Congress Cataloging-in-Publication Data
Susanni, Paolo, author.
    Music and twentieth-century tonality : harmonic progression based on
modality and the interval cycles / Paolo Susanni and Elliott Antokoletz.
        pages cm — (Routledge studies in music theory ; 1)
    Includes bibliographical references and index.
    1. Music—20th century—Analysis, appreciation. 2. Musical
analysis. I. Antokoletz, Elliott, author. II. Title. III. Series:
Routledge studies in music theory ; 1.
    MT6.S87 2012
    780.9'04—dc23
    2011049874

ISBN: 978-0-415-80888-0 (hbk)
ISBN: 978-0-203-11929-7 (ebk)

Typeset in Sabon by IBT Global.

Printed and bound in the United States of America on sustainably sourced
paper by IBT Global.

To the Susanni and Antokoletz families

Contents

Tables and Figures

TABLES

Preface

The vast majority of those who study western art and popular music from an early age are first schooled in the fundamental principles that underlie the music of the traditional tonal system. The journey commences with the study and application practice of the major and minor scales, which form the core of this system. This entails the identification and building of intervals, primary triads, and the more complex tertian constructions such as seventh chords. These triads and larger tertian constructions represent the principal harmonic elements of the system. Once these are mastered, the study of traditional harmonic function harmony is undertaken. Students spend most of the time allotted to music theory studies, learning the principles of harmonic function and concepts of voice-leading that dictate all pitch relations in traditional tonal music. The subject is taught in the minutest of details and is still considered the core of essential musical knowledge.

In typical western musical education, the contrapuntal modal music of the Middle Ages and Renaissance is given little priority in comparison to that given to the music of the common practice era. It also is usually reserved for special studies at an advanced educational stage. This *non sequitur* is at odds with the actual historical sequence of developments from modality to major/minor tonality. Most often, the principles that underlie the music of the common practice era are given little if any historical context, that is, that which underlies the changes in the perception of such musical concepts as consonance and dissonance.

20th century music is dealt with in much the same way as that of the Middle Ages and Renaissance, even though so much of it has become part of the standard musical repertoire and the subject of intense theoretical and musicological scrutiny. Only a small fraction of the total time spent in the study of musical theory and harmony is devoted to it. Most performers and scholars leave the university with only a marginal knowledge of 20th century music.

No amount of in-depth study of traditional tonal music such as that of Bach, Beethoven, and Brahms can prepare one for the analysis of music as wide-ranging in style as that of Debussy, Stravinsky, and Ligeti. The music of the latter composers cannot be analyzed using the canons of the traditional tonal system. The traditional scales of the common practice period are part of an open system of transpositions and modulations, their interactions forming the core of analytic methods that theorists and composers used in their work. The new musical language is based on a new conception of the identity and structure of scales and their interactions. In contrast to the openness of the traditional major/minor system, the scales used in 20th century music tend to represent closed entities (discrete and contrasting structures), and their interactions differ from those found in traditional major/minor scales.

A short explanation of some of the fundamental differences between traditional tonal music and modal or scalar based 20th century music might highlight the difficulties encountered in the analysis of the music of the latter category.

In traditional tonal music based on the major/minor scale system and tertian harmony, each degree of the major or minor scale occupies a particular position that indicates the known functions such as tonic, subdominant and dominant, and the notion of a leading tone. In this music, individual scale degrees play different melodic and harmonic roles in creating motion. In the sphere of traditional tonal progression, each note fulfills a specific tonal function relative to its contextual position. The level of musical tension and function of each note in the tonal composition creates a hierarchical system based primarily on these two aspects. Traditional tonal hierarchy is largely created by the unequal subdivision off the octave into the major and minor modes as well as their triadic substructures. At the end of the 19th century and beginning of the 20th century, the weakening and eventual dissolution of tonal hierarchy led to the equalization of the twelve tones. Thus, tonality relies on the unequal subdivision of the octave while the dissolution of tonal function relies on the equal or symmetrical subdivision of the octave.

Traditional tonal music is limited to a single type of harmonic structure (i.e., the triad derived exclusively from the major and minor scales), whereas the works by 20th century composers are often based on diverse types of harmonic constructions derived from a host of different scalar formations that include the seven diatonic modes, special non-diatonic modes, hybrid modes, and the system of interval cycles. The new harmonic structures tend to weaken and even obliterate tonal function.

The harmonic or vertical aspect of traditional tonal music represented by a functional progression of triads and chords is, for the most part, clearly distinguishable from the melodic level that is based only on linear thematic statements. In many works of the 20th century, the intervallic cell, a small collection of pitch classes defined by its intervallic content, replaces the triads of the traditional tonal system. These intervallic cells can operate simultaneously on both harmonic and melodic levels without differentiation, thus radically altering common perception and understanding of previously held notions of melody and harmony.

Many music teachers and scholars still believe that there is no theory capable of deciphering 20th century music pitch relations in a manner comparable to that of the traditional tonal system that draws together all pitch formations under one unified set of principles.

There are attempts to unlock the manifold compositional materials and processes of modal or scalar based 20th century music. Some scholars have tried to analyze 20th century music using Schenkerian methodology. This is not plausible because the Schenkerian approach can only be applied to music that is based on functional triadic structures. The application of PC-Set theory has also been attempted. PC-Set analysis is perhaps applicable to atonal music such as that of Schoenberg. It does not work for music based on the modes or scales, however abstract they may be. We are therefore left with a vast repertoire of modal and scalar based 20th century music that remains undecipherable if we attempt its analysis using the *a priori* assumptions of the traditional major/minor system or the mathematical reductionism employed in PC-Set theory. The complicated numerical formulae that arise from these kinds of analyses are so far removed from any form of simple musical terminology that they tend to further alienate prospective students and teachers.

20th century music analysis is superficially represented in most core curricula and standard texts. Consequently, both the quantity and quality of instruction are diminished. Most texts that deal with 20th century music analysis include only the identification of the music's basic scalar and harmonic formations without any inquiry into how pitch relations generate tonal progression. As a result, a student might be able to identify a small number of musical structures but not explain how these structures interact to generate tonal progression and form. While major/minor system analogies used in many of these texts are helpful in explaining the elements common to both music of the traditional tonal system as well as some aspects of 20th century music, they are encased in traditional terminology that cannot describe the pitch relations and musical materials of the vast bulk of 20th century music.

This list of problems would seem to indicate that a simple yet comprehensive study of 20th century music remains either beyond the reach of most musicians and accessible only to the most specialized in the field. Nothing could be farther from the truth.

The discovery of a larger system of pitch relations in Bartók's music was revealed by Elliott Antokoletz in his 1975 Ph.D. dissertation. He found that pitch relations in Bartók's *Fourth String Quartet* are primarily based on the principle of equally subdividing the octave into the total complex of interval cycles. He also discovered that the functions and interactions of basic symmetrical pitch cells were significant in the generation of these cycles and played a fundamental role in the establishment of central pitch areas by means other than traditional tonal functions.

This new system analysis has a long and complex history. Many composers, music theorists, and musicologists have contributed to the development of certain basic principles of symmetrical pitch construction since the beginning of the 20th century. The need for analytical tools that could be used to decipher pitch relations of the new musical language was already felt at the turn of the 20th century. The German theorists Bernhard Ziehn[1] and Georg Capellen[2] recognized that traditional systems of analysis could not account for many aspects of tonal progression in the ultra chromatic language of the late 19th and early 20th centuries, but they recognized the significance of symmetrical pitch constructions.

Capellen's reduction theory was able to justify a host of then "inexplicable" dissonant harmonies, paving the way for Schoenberg's "emancipation of the dissonance."[3] Ziehn's studies of strict contrapuntal inversion in Renaissance polyphony led him to a new notion of tonal centricity based on an axis of symmetry. Many aspects of Ziehn's technique of symmetrical inversion, formulated in the late 19th century, foreshadowed Schoenberg's technique of inversion.

In the 1930s, American composer/theorist George Perle began to develop a new theory of tonality based on inversional symmetry and the interval cycles.[4] Perle's 1977 book *Twelve-Tone Tonality* represents the culmination of his theory that he had been developing since the 1930s as composer and theorist.

In 1947, Nicolas Slonimsky published the *Thesaurus of Scales and Melodic Patterns* that systematically laid out any scale that can be derived from the chromatic spectrum in musical notation.[5] The *Thesaurus* became a significant practical source for composers, performers, and scholars alike.

Thirteen years later, another American composer/theorist, Howard Hanson, published his harmonic treatise *Harmonic Materials of Modern Music: Resources of the Tempered Scale*. While Hanson's treatise does not pretend to systematize tonal progression, it demonstrates how one may generate pentatonic, modal, and synthetic scales by overlaying a sequence of like intervals.[6]

Antokoletz's post-1975 studies have revealed the existence of a vast array of modal/cyclic relationships that show how all the modes, diatonic, nondiatonic, and hybrid, are inextricably connected to the system of the interval cycles. In *The Music of Béla Bartók: A Study of Tonality and Progression in Twentieth-Century Music*, Antokoletz showed these principles to be fundamental to Bartók's music. His *Twentieth-Century Music* demonstrates how these principles are relevant to a larger body of post-tonal music.

In the late 19th and early 20th centuries, changing musical aesthetics led to a significant number of diverse developments in pitch relations that altered nearly all aspects of the art. Since musicians are generally schooled in the analytical principles of common practice era, it is vital that theoretical links be established to facilitate analytical techniques of a broader range of evolving harmonic principles. It seems more feasible to comprehend new analytical perspectives using familiar musical structures as a point of departure for an evolving musical language.

This book is designed to describe the structure of pitch collections that make up the web of modal/cyclic pitch relations and how they interact to generate a new kind of tonality and harmonic progression.

The first chapter provides an overview of the most basic issues of evolving compositional practice. All the material and concepts that are examined in the book are introduced from the outset. Chapter 1 proposes only to familiarize the reader with the global web of pitch relations that make up the new twelve-tone language in the first decade of the 20th century.

Certain contemporary pitch structures that were imminent during the common practice era are discussed as an adumbration of new "functional" schemes that could only become possible with the new principles of voice leading in post-tonal music. Contextuality versus pre-compositional assumptions allow the reader to understand how the functions of the hierarchy of tonal function was gradually replaced by the equalization of the twelve tones. It is also helpful in bridging the gap between that which is familiar and that which is foreign. When appropriate, conventional musical terminology is used alongside newer terminology designed to describe new concepts. There are, however, certain concepts that can only be described by using the new terminology. In this case, these will be introduced by using simple analogies that relate them to subjects (physical science, mathematics, etc.) other than music.

Pitch collections are laid out individually and systematically in order of complexity. They are exemplified in tables and musical fragments drawn from 20th century music literature. Once a certain class of pitch sets, for example, all the interval cycles, is identified and its component members listed, the pitch relations that exist between the members are examined in detail. Each class of pitch sets yields a specific set of pitch relations that are used differently by various composers to articulate different means of tonal progression. To demonstrate individual kinds of pitch relations, a number of short musical extracts are analyzed. There are, however, a small number of pieces in which a multiplicity of pitch relations and compositional techniques are used. Complete analyses of a small number of these works are placed at the end of chapters to draw together aspects of the global web of pitch relations that exist in those works.

The sixth chapter is perhaps the most significant because it draws together the pitch relations that exist between different modal and cyclic collections. It details the mutual transformations of these two collection types and, because of their common source, the chromatic continuum, shows them to be reflections of one another. It is in this chapter that the global network of pitch relations that constitutes the unordered twelve-tone system is clarified.

The prospective 20th century music scholar may regard this study as a complete set of analytical tools that can be used equally well by both the experienced scholar and inexperienced student.

Acknowledgments

With gratitude, I should like to acknowledge my co-author, teacher, and friend, Elliott Antokoletz, for his belief in and support of this volume. His work has become one of the cornerstones of 20th century music studies, and his profound musical knowledge has been a source of inspiration for countless music scholars.

We would like acknowledge Cem Ercelik for his electronic engraving of all the musical examples.

For permission to reprint copyrighted material, acknowledgement is gratefully made to the following:

C. F Peters Corporation, New York, NY, for George Crumb's *Makrokosmos* Vol. I No. 12 "Spiral Galaxy."

Boosey and Hawkes, Inc, New York, NY, for excerpts from Bartók: *Études* Op. 18, *Suite* Op. 14, *Sonata for Piano*, *Mikrokosmos*, *Out of Doors Suite*, and *Bagatelles* Op. 6; Stravinsky: *Sérénade en La*; Copland: *The Cat and the Mouse*; Ginastera *Piano Sonata* No. 1.

G. Schirmer Inc. New York, NY, for excerpts from Adams: *Phrygian Gates*; Muczynski: *Toccata* Op. 15; *Étude* No. 1.

MGB Hal Leonard -Italy for excerpts from Messiaen: *Le baiser de l'Enfant-Jésus.*

Edwin F. Kalmus & Co., Inc., for excerpts from Lutoslawski: *Melody.*

Editio Musica, Budapest, for excerpts from Bartók: *Bagatelles* Op. 6, No. 2; Kodaly *Valsette.*

Polskie Wydawnictwo Muzyczne S. A. PWM Edition, Kraköw, Poland, for excerpts from Lutoslawski: *Étude* No 1, and *Melodie.*

Chester Music, Ltd., London, for excerpts from Lutoslawski: *Étude* No. 1, and *Melodie*.

European American Music Distributors, LLC, New York for excerpts from Ligeti: *Études* Vol. I; Penderecki: *Threnody for the Victims of Hiroshima*; Takemitsu *Rain Tree Sketch*; Bartók: *Sonata for Piano*; Webern: *Piano Piece* Op. Posth.; Schoenberg: Op. 11, No. 1.

Alfred Music Publishing, CA., for excerpts from Krzysztof Penderecki Threnody for the Victims of Hiroshima.

Carl Fischer, LLC. New York., for excerpts from Charles Ives Psalm XXIV.

1   General Concepts

Music: Joseph Haydn *Sonata* in C, Hob XVI
Claude Debussy *La Cathédrale engloutie*
Frederick Chopin *Prelude* in C minor, Op. 28 No. 20
Anton Webern *Piano Piece* Op. Posthumous
Oliver Messiaen *Le baiser de l'Enfant-Jesus*
Arnold Schoenberg *Three Piano Pieces* Op. 11, No. 1
Franz Liszt *Après un Lecture de Dante*
Béla Bartók *Mikrokosmos* No. 121, *Étude* Op. 18, No. 2
Darius Milhaud *Corvocado.*
Samuel Barber *Church Bell at Night* Op. 29, No. 2
Wolfgang Amadeus Mozart *Sonata* K331
Igor Stravinsky "Tilim-bom"
George Crumb *Spiral Galaxy*

THE AURAL AND VISUAL EXPERIENCE

Unfortunately, most musicians start to cultivate their analytical approach
to music long after they have experienced it in its most direct manifesta-
tion, sound. Remarkably, the aural experience of music is hardly ever used
as an analytical tool, even though it is the one that ignites all our responses
be they emotional, spiritual, or intellectual. Though the language of much
20th century music differs greatly from that in which most musicians are
schooled, it too relies on the same basic principles upon which all music
is based, that is, repetition and variation. On a fundamental level, even
the untrained ear is able to perceive these two things. The ear discerns
musical changes and organizes them into intelligible formal structures. It
can detect repetition and variations in melody, harmony, tempo, meter,
dynamics, and register, as well as timbre and articulation. This common
human ability allows us to distinguish between the chorus and the verse
of a song. The more the musical ear is trained, the more it is able to detect
all manner of changes in a musical texture. For all the reasons stated
as well as for the fact that the average musician has a good ear or aural
instinct, listening to a piece of music that is to be analyzed is perhaps the
first and most important step of the analytical process. While listening
to a new piece of 20th century music may make one feel a little like the
audiences who first experienced Stravinsky's "Rite of Spring," repetition
of the aural experience will allow the ear to unravel and sort that which is

new, unfamiliar, or foreign. Eventually, the ear will allow for the creation of a general aural image that has a perceived formal structure. While the accuracy of the perceived formal structure depends entirely on the level of aural skills and musical expertise of the listener, the aurally created "sketch" provides an advantageous analytical starting point.

Much analytical information can also be obtained from a visual inspection of the score. Nowhere is this truer than in 20th century music. In the analysis of traditional tonal music, the predominant focus of study is how the relationship between motive and functional harmonic progression perpetuates musical motion and generates musical form. It is possible and even desirable to reduce an entire movement of a Beethoven sonata to a succinct formal outline underpinned by a succession of Roman numerals without ever mentioning changes in musical factors such as tempo, meter, articulation, dynamics, and register. Little attention is paid to these factors because in the context of traditional tonal music, they are perceived to play a lesser roles in the generation of musical structure and tonal progression. While motif retained its structural relevancy in much 20th century music, functional harmonic progression ceased to play any significant role in both the creation of musical structure and generation of tonal progression. In 20th century music, musical parameters deemed secondary in traditional tonal music play significant roles in tonal progression and, therefore, the generation of musical form. It is for this reason that familiarizing oneself visually with new scores is as important as listening to the music.

Because of the many innovations in musical language, 20th century musical scores can be subdivided into two broad categories: that which uses traditional notation and that which uses newly invented notation best suited for the specific compositional goals and performance demands of the piece. Music of the second category is easily recognized given its use of symbols rather than its use of traditional music notation that represents the fundamental musical parameters of every note, that is, meter, pitch, duration, articulation, and dynamics. Music notated in this manner is usually issued with a set of instructions that explains how the symbols are to be interpreted. Music of the former category may at first glance look like traditional tonal music, but upon closer inspection, the differences begin to emerge. While it is difficult to list all the visual differences between traditionally notated 20th century music and traditional tonal music, it is true to say that the changes in the musical language of the last century gave rise to a host of diverse compositional processes that translate directly into scores of different visual characteristics. If one were to consider the types of harmonic constructions of the music of the two periods, one could immediately see that the shape of the tertian harmonic constructions of the common practice era look nothing like the harmonic constructions of the 20th century that are mostly based on intervals other than the third. The common use of constantly changing and asymmetrical meters in 20th century music is also in stark contrast to the metrical uniformity of traditional tonal music. The simultaneous use of different key signatures occurs frequently in 20th century music, while it never occurs in its traditional counterpart. These are but a few of the many factors that render the visual appearance of 20th century scores different from those of the traditional tonal system. These and many more differences will be described in detail during the course of this chapter.

Listening to music with a score in hand is, of course, the optimum initial step because seeing the aural unfolding of music creates a powerful integral experience.

FROM THE CHURCH MODES TO THE TWELVE-TONE SCALE

Nearly all of western art music is based on pre-compositional, fixed-interval scalar collections. These include the diatonic, non-diatonic, hybrid forms of the old church modes in their modern context, folk modes, the major and minor scales of the traditional tonal system, and the simple and compound cyclic collections found in a large portion of 20th century music. In order to understand the evolution of western musical language, one must understand the gradual changes in conception of the structure and identity of scales and their interactions.

Western music from the early Christian era to the early Baroque period was based on the system of diatonic church modes. Each of these modes is constructed according to a specific and fixed succession of whole and half steps that render each mode unique. The fundamental note or modal tonic is given pitch class priority and referential status. All modal pitch relationships are perceived and understood as relative to the tonic. A mode cannot be altered without it losing its identity. If notes foreign to the mode are temporarily introduced into the musical texture, they will be heard as chromatic intrusions and understood as embellishments not belonging to it. These intrusions do not threaten modal integrity due to their rhythmic disposition, but rather serve to embellish the diatonic-modal tones. If, however, the structure of the mode is permanently altered, that is, the modal element is altered, then a change of mode takes place. This is known as a *true modulation*.[1] Modulation can be seen as a change of modal identity. In the modal system, modulation can only occur between modes that belong to that system. In early modal music, modulation can only occur linearly because the music can only be based on one mode at a time.

Tonal music, from the Baroque to the late Romantic era, is based on major and minor scales. The major scale is primary since the melodic and harmonic forms of the minor scale are diatonic only by analogy. Like the modes, the structure of the major scale is a fixed succession of whole and half steps that cannot be altered without compromising the tonal integrity of that scale. Unlike the modes of the early modal system, each scale degree of a major or minor scale is assigned and fulfills a specific functional role.

Each role has its place within a larger system based on a tonal hierarchy. In the traditional tonal system, the tonic represents the tonal center or key of the music. Temporary alterations of the scalar structure of major and minor scales are also perceived as chromatic intrusions. The only true modulation that can occur within the tonal system is that of a switch from major to minor, or minor to major mode. Modulation from major to minor and vice versa entails the alteration of third and sixth scale degrees and has no effect on tonal function. However, the permanent alteration of other scale degrees, such as the leading tone, would result in the complete collapse of the tonal hierarchy because functions such as that of the leading tone are those that generate progression in tonal music as part of the dominant or leading tone chord. This can be adequately demonstrated using the opening measures (mm. 1–4) of Haydn's piano Sonata in C, Hob XVI. The melodic material of these measures is accompanied by only two harmonic functions, the tonic and the dominant. In the V7–I6/4–V progression (mm. 3–4), the melodic leading tone moves by the required half step to resolve to the tonic. If this leading tone were to be chromatically flattened, its relationship to the tonic would be changed and it would lose its functional properties.

As in the old modal system, "modulations" in the tonal system can only occur linearly between major and minor modes because the music can only be based on one or the other mode at any given time. Toward the end of the common practice era, exemplified by Wagner and Bartók, an ever-increasing number of chromatic alterations began to weaken tonal function so essential to traditional tonal progression. This was compounded by the incorporation of modes and scales that could not generate functional pitch relationships. As a result, the twelve chromatic tones were equalized, and a new conception of the identity of the chromatic scale was achieved. The chromatic scale supplanted the major and minor scales of the crumbling tonal system as the prime or basic pitch collection of the modern era. This change of conception had far-reaching implications. A seemingly limitless realm of new tonal relationships was unveiled. These relationships could now be based on newly established sets of rules. The new tonal relations would generate new means of tonal progression. It also meant that all existing scalar formations, now viewed as subsets of the chromatic continuum, could be used in new ways.

Compositions based on the system of twelve equal tones can be viewed in two broad categories: 1) the twelve tones as "theme" or contextually ordered entity as in the twelve-tone serial works of the Second Viennese School, and 2) as scale, or contextually unordered source of the harmonic materials as in the non-serial works of Bartók, Stravinsky, Ligeti, and Tower.

In serial twelve-tone composition, the chromatic scale is completed by an ordered succession of all twelve tones. The order in which the twelve tones are cast is chosen by the composer for each individual composition. The thematically "ordered" chromatic scale becomes the fixed compositionally determined source. It is from this device that systematic transformations of the original order, that is, inverted and retrograde forms and their transpositions are derived. No matter how the derived forms of the row are used in the music, chromatic completion will always occur because it is preordained by the system. Every note within the system has equal value, which precludes any allusion to traditional tonality.

The opening measures of Webern's *Piano Piece* Op. Posth. (Figure 1.1) show how all the musical material, whether horizontal or vertical, is arranged according to the row A–Bb–B–G#–G–C#–D–Eb–F#–F–E–C.

In the unserialized twelve-tone languages of Debussy or Stravinsky, the complete chromatic collection as scale is a pre-compositional premise, that is, it can serve as the common source for any number of different compositions. Since it is not made to follow any prearranged order, it may be used in any number of ways. In a large portion of 20th century music the chromatic spectrum is partitioned into subset pitch collections. These can include segments of the chromatic scale itself, complete or incomplete diatonic and non-diatonic modes, and complete interval cycles or segments thereof. All may be used either singly or in simultaneous combinations. Since the chromatic scale is the primary source for the pitch materials of 20th century music, common subcollections of the various modes and interval cycles serve as the basis for mutual transformation.

In the unordered twelve-tone system, the identity of any or all subcollections can be changed without ever breaching the integrity of the system because the chromatic continuum is the all-encompassing source. The pitch

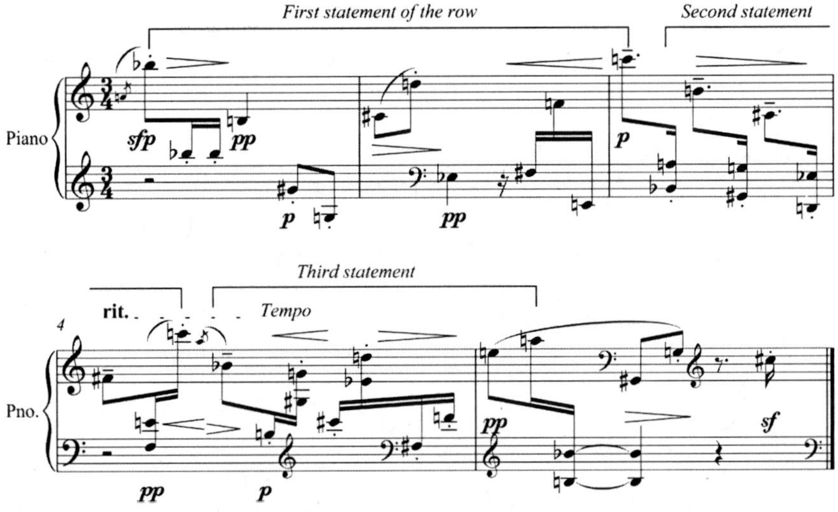

Figure 1.1 Webern, *Piano Piece* Op. Posth. (mm. 1–5). Webern Piano Piece Op. Posth. Copyright © 1966 Universal Editions A.G., Wien/UE13490 © Renewed. All rights reserved. Used by permission of European American Music Distributors LLC, US and Canadian agent for Universal Edition A.G, Wien.

content rather than order is essential to the pivotal function of pitch collections. This means of assigning a tonal center in 20th century music no longer relies on pre-compositional assumptions and fixed interval relations. This new musical perspective effected drastic changes not only in pitch relations but in almost all other aspects of music as well.

A preliminary study of Debussy's prelude for piano, *La Cathédrale engloutie*, will serve to introduce the mechanics of the new musical context described.[2] The chords of the opening measure consist entirely of perfect fifths and fourths moving in parallel motion that contravene all rules of traditional tonal function. This technique is often referred to as *planing*. While this term accurately describes the musical motion it says nothing about the pitch relations that generate tonal progression. If the perfect fifth chords of the right hand [G–D, A–E, and E–B] were to be written out horizontally, a symmetrical sequence or chain of perfect fifths [G–D–A–E–B] would result. Any chain of identical intervals is known as an *interval cycle*.[3] While at first this may seem meaningless, further inspection reveals that this cyclic segment generates the first complete scalar collection of the piece, that is, the G pentatonic scale [G–A–B–D–E], unfolded horizontally by the right-hand chords (Figure 1.2).

The pentatonic collection is therefore simply a reordering of the cyclic segment [G–D–A–E–B = G–A–B–D–E]. This reordering, if one remembers, is made possible because both the interval cycle and the pentatonic collection are but different expressions of a certain pitch content derived from the chromatic scale. Debussy confirms that the perfect fifth cycle indeed generates the pentatonic scale toward the end of the first formal section where the same right-hand chords of the first measure reappear (mm. 14–15). This time, however, the accompaniment consists exclusively of two purely cyclic harmonic (perfect fifth) constructions [G–D–A and A–E–B]. These two chords again unfold and confirm the pentatonic pitch content of the opening measure [G–D–A–E–B].

A reexamination of the opening reveals that the dotted whole-note chords of the upper and lower-most registers (mm. 1–4) participate to extend the pentatonic pitch content to a diatonic one. While the initial whole-note chord [G–D] forms part of the pentatonic pitch content, the

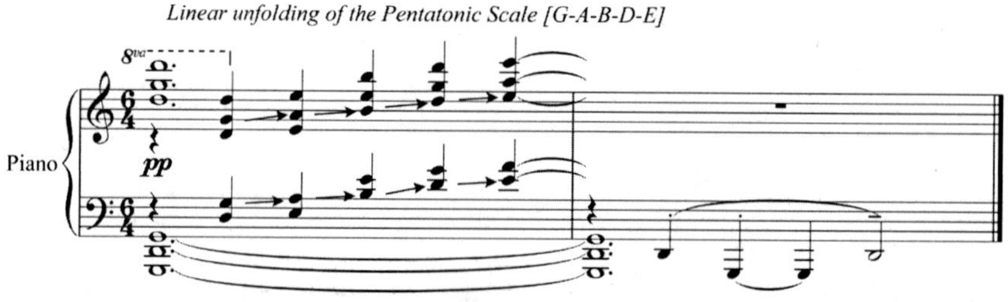

Linear unfolding of the Pentatonic Scale [G-A-B-D-E]

Figure 1.2   Debussy, *La Cathédrale engloutie* (mm. 1–2).

second one (m. 3) adds a new perfect fifth [F–C]. Expressed as a perfect fifth cyclic segment, the complete pitch content of the third measure is F–C–G–D–A–E–B. Rearranged in scalar order this will yield the complete F Lydian mode [F–G–A–B–C–D–E–F]. In extending the perfect fifth cycle the pentatonic pitch content is transformed into a diatonic one. This modal pitch content is finally expressed in its scalar order in the subsequent passage (mm. 23–24) where it is rotated several times before the entry of the central theme.[4]

A different kind of transformation occurs in the "codetta" of the central theme. The pitch content of the final measures of the central theme (mm. 38–41) is ʾC Ionian [C–D–E–F–G–A–B–C], the modal tonic being asserted in every measure as a pedal tone. At the end of this passage (mm. 42–47), however, the dyad [D–C] in the high register of the upper part is extended by whole tones in the octaves of the lower part to outline a four-note segment of the whole-tone interval cycle [D–C–Bb–Ab]. At the beginning of the next formal section this whole-tone segment is again extended by one note to yield an incomplete whole-tone or interval two cycle [E–( )–D–C–Bb–Ab]. By cyclic extension of part of the C Ionian mode, Debussy achieves a new kind of transformation known as the *cyclic extension of modes.*[5] This too is made possible by the unordered twelve-tone system.

It is interesting to note that in the measures during which this transformation occurs, both whole-tone [C–D–E–( )–Ab–Bb] and contrasting Ionian [C–D–G] chords exist simultaneously but are kept apart by their different registral placement until the central chords that represent the Ionian mode drop out to bring the whole-tone collection to the fore. This example not only demonstrates the transformation of an asymmetrical diatonic mode into a symmetrical interval cycle,[6] but also how register can be made to effect fundamental structural changes.

The unordered twelve-tone system accommodates various forms of tonal centricity based on the use of pentatonic and diatonic collections that establish tonal centers as a matter of course or the symmetrical arrangement of tones such as the whole-tone cycle of the Debussy example that have no tonal center. The example also demonstrates that whereas in the "ordered" twelve-tone system, the chromatic scale is always in the foreground, in the non-serial twelve-tone system it acts as a background scalar referent from which one can draw different elements to the fore.

The "codetta" passage mentioned previously demonstrates how composers started to emphasize the role of musical parameters such as register as primary in assisting tonal progression in 20th century music. In this music, the parameters of dynamics, articulation, rhythm, and reregister are no longer just ornamental but become functional in the generation of musical structure and tonal progression. This forces the prospective analyst to look at music from completely different perspectives, regarding these musical parameters as integral and not incidental.

HARMONIC CONSTRUCTION AND PITCH CELLS

Traditional tonal music is limited to a special set of tertian harmonic structures (i.e., triads and seventh chords derived exclusively from the major and minor scales). These harmonic structures progress one to another according to the principles dictated by tonal harmonic function and voice leading. For the most part, the only latitude left to composers of tonal music is the choice of individual chords they use to fulfill an otherwise predetermined succession. This kind of harmonic succession moves from an initial tonic function and will ultimately resolves back to the tonic.[7]

In contrast to this, 20th century works are often based on diverse types of harmonic constructions derived from a host of different scalar formations. These include the diatonic, non-diatonic, and hybrid modes as well as the system of interval cycles. The new harmonic structures tend to weaken and even obliterate tonal function. In these works, the manner in which one harmonic structure moves to the next is determined not by function but by compositional choice. While it is easier to observe this phenomenon when composers use nontertian harmonic constructions, it may become more difficult when the harmonies imitate or mimic their tertian counterparts.

The opening chords of *Le baiser de l'Enfant-Jesus* from Messiaen's *Vingt Regards* (mm. 1–2) seem to outline a chromatically colored tonic-to-dominant progression. The second progression (mm. 2–3), though similar in construction, reverses the functional direction from dominant to tonic. Together they outline a complete I–V–I progression in the key of F# major. While we might interpret these progressions as being purely tertian, we discover that this is a mere illusion if we consider that the entire pitch content is derived exclusively from a compound cyclic collection known as the octatonic scale. It is only when these same two progressions appear in the second part of the piece that their true identity is revealed, even though the note spellings betray their actual octatonic rather than tertian diatonic source. All the pitches of the first progressions are derived not from a chromatically colored F# major [F#–G#–A#–B–C#–D#–E#] but from the octatonic-1 compound cyclic collection [C#–D#–E–F#–G–A–A#–B#] while the pitches of the second progression are derived from the octatonic-2 compound cyclic collection [D–E–F–G–G#–A#–B–C#]. This highlights the fact that progressions that seem tonal can be derived from what are considered to be abstract scales in which the constituent pitches do not create any sort of tonal hierarchy.

At the beginning of the Modéré passage (mm. 80–82), the same octatonic-1 collection that generated the seemingly tonal progression of the first two measures now generates a highly dissonant harmonic progression based on completely different type of harmonic structures. The first three chords of each of these measures constitute a series of parallel octatonic clusters that are based on mixed intervals (seconds, thirds, and fourths).

Opening chord progressions accompanied
by octatonic cycles from which they are
derived

Figure 1.3 Messiaen, *Le baiser de l'Enfant-Jesus* (mm. 39–44). Copyright © 1944 *Durand Editions Musicales, Paris. Reproduced by kind permission of MGB Hal Leonard–Italy.*

These chords, such as E–A–C#–D#, F#–A#–D#–E, and G–B#–E–F# (m. 75), do not generate any form of functional harmonic progression, the theme chords together merely outlining an ascending octatonic scale E–F#–G–A–A#–B#–C#–D#.[8]

In this passage, Messiaen, like Debussy, uses register and rhythm to separate out the different pitch collections used to create the three different layers of musical activity. The first three sixteenth-note chords notated on the lower two staves, outline the octatonic collection. These are placed in the lowest register and occur at the beginning of each measure. They are followed by chords that sound Messiaen's specially designed themes such as the "Thème d'accords." The "thematic" chords are placed in the highest register and are punctuated by whole-tone dyads that start to (m.f. 76) outline a descending chromatic scale. This short passage clearly demonstrates that two or more different pitch collections can exist simultaneously within the unordered twelve-tone collection.

The harmonic or vertical aspect of traditional tonal music represented by a functional progression of triads and chords is, for the most part, clearly

distinguishable from the melodic level, which is based only on linear thematic statements. In many works of the 20th century, the *pitch cell*,[9] a small
collection of pitch classes that is defined by its intervallic content, replaces
the triads of the traditional tonal system. These intervallic cells can operate
simultaneously on both of the harmonic and melodic levels without differentiation, thus radically altering common perception and understanding of
previously held notions of melody and harmony. This creates a completely
new analytical perspective.

Perhaps the most frequently analyzed pitch cell is formed by the first
three notes [B–G#–G] of Schoenberg's *Three Piano Pieces* Op. 11, No. 1.
The cell is first unfolded melodically (mm. 1–2) and consists of a minor third
and a semitone (Ex. 1.4). When calculated in semitones, these two intervals
create an interval ratio of 3:1. A transposed version of the cell [A–Bb–Db]
is unfolded harmonically immediately after (m. 3). In these same measures
the intervallic structure of the original cell is changed to produce two new
intervallically expanded variants. The first [F–Gb–B], with and interval
ratio of 1:5, appears as a vertical structure (m. 2), while the second (E–F–
A), of interval ratio 1:4, is unfolded melodically (mm. 2–3).

The original cell and its variants are responsible for the simultaneous
generation of both the horizontal and vertical activity of the piece. At times
it is arranged in such a way that it fuses the melodic and harmonic aspects
of the music to generate a texture where these two elements become indis-
tinguishable from one another. Nowhere is this clearer than toward the
end of the development section (mm. 46–47) where inverted forms of the
original cell in the upper part are punctuated by pitches of the lower part
that unfold a new transposition of the original cell.[10]

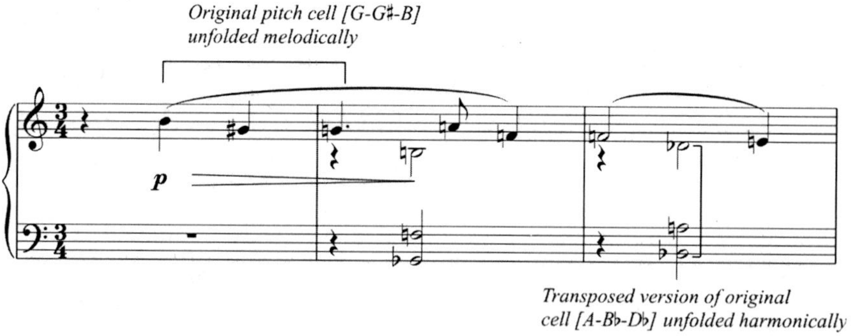

Original pitch cell [G-G#-B]
unfolded melodically

Transposed version of original
cell [A-Bb-Db] unfolded harmonically

Figure 1.4   Schoenberg, *Three Piano Pieces* Op. 11, No. 1 (mm. 1–3). *Schoenberg
3 Piano Pieces, Op. 11 Copyright © 1938 Universal Editions A.G., Wien/UE 2991.
© Renewed. All rights reserved. Used by permission of European American Music
Distributors LLC, US and Canadian agent for Universal Edition A.G, Wien. Used
by permission of Belmont Music Publishers, Los Angeles.*

TONALITY AND CENTRICITY

Conventionally, the tonal center or key denotes mode and transpositional level of the scale used at any given moment in the composition. For the most part, the primary key of a tonal piece is established at the outset and may be revisited during the course of the piece returning after a selected number of modulations at its end. In many multi-movement works of the common practice era, the first and last movements are generally in the primary key of the work.

In the highly chromatic works of the late 19th century, however, the question of key becomes a more complex issue because during this period an increase in the degree of chromaticism effected a loosening of functional tonal relationships. The high degree of chromaticism allowed composers to move between distantly related chords and keys with greater latitude in choosing harmonic direction. It also meant that they could move between different tonal areas in very rapid succession. Establishing an initial key was no longer of primary importance. In many late romantic works, the real tonal center emerges some time after the opening and sometimes only at the end of the piece.

The opening of Liszt's *Après un Lecture de Dante* consists of a sequence of phrases that each start with a series of descending tritones that are followed by harmonic progressions that establish the keys of Ab major (m. 6), B major (m. 12), and finally G minor (m. 24). The real tonal center of D minor is unambiguously established (mm. 33–34) when its dominant and leading tones (A and C#) are sounded. Of the three keys established in the opening the first two are remotely related to the primary key, only the third being closely related to it.[11]

The rapidity of shifts between remote keys is clearly outlined by the *agitato* passage (mm. 202–211) in which a C dominant seventh chord [C–E–G–Bb] resolves to Db instead of F, a D dominant seventh chord [D–F#–A–C] resolves to Eb instead of G, and a final E dominant seventh chord [E–G#–B–D] that resolves to a new progression of fully diminished seventh chords completely destroying any sense of key.[12] Ultimately, the extreme use of chromaticism, like that of the preceding example, contributed to severely weakening the tonal system.

In 20th century idioms, we can no longer speak about key when the pitch relations in a piece of music are no longer based on the functional tonal hierarchy. The terms tonal center, or tonal centricity, are more apt. The establishment of tonal centers within 20th century works may be achieved in several different ways. If a piece is in a particular mode such as D Dorian or B-flat pentatonic, then it means that its modal center is represented by its modal tonic. In such a case, the analysis of pitch relations presents few problems given the definitive modal context.

In many 20th century pieces, however, composers use modal combinations that make simultaneous use of two or more different modal and or cyclic pitch collections. The terms bimodal (two) and polymodal (more than two) are frequently used to describe these combinations. Bimodal combinations are of two varieties. The first consists of two different modes that share a common tonic (D Dorian and D Phrygian). In this case, the modal center is also determined by the first modal degree even though the modes are different. Often, this kind of combination yields chromatic discrepancies that generate what is known as *polymodal chromaticism*. These discrepancies can be used to generate new melodic or harmonic pitch collections that may or may not be modal. Polymodal chromaticism is a significant aspect of Bartók's *Mikrokosmos* No. 121, "Two Part Study."[13]

The first phrase opens with a single D in the lower part, establishing the primary tonal center of the work. To ensure the primacy of this tonal center, the D is asserted several times during the course of the piece and is also used as the concluding sonority. Immediately after the sounding of this initial pitch, the upper part enters with a single E initiating the two-part texture. In the following measures (mm. 2–3), the parts combine to unfold an incomplete modal pitch content containing an A/A# discrepancy that implies the presence of at least two different modes, an incomplete D Lydian mode [D–E–(F#)–G#–A–B–(C#)][14] and an incomplete non diatonic mode [D–E–(F#)–G#–A#–B–(C#)].

In the first part of the second phrase (mm. 4–6), the A# disappears allowing for the now nearly complete Lydian mode [D–E–F#–G#–A–( )–C#] to emerge. In the final section of the piece (mm. 17–25), a new bimodal combination is unfolded. The upper part outlines the incomplete D Aeolian mode [D–( )–F–G–A–Bb–C] while the lower part once more unfolds a D Lydian mode [D–E–F#–( )–A–B–C#].

There are, of course, pieces in which the modal combination consists of two or more modes that do not share a common tonic (D Dorian and E Phrygian). One must evaluate their relevancy within the overall musical context. If the two modes of a bimodal combination remain distinct and independent of one another, then one must assign two separate modal centers. Such is the case with the opening measures of "Corcovado," a movement from the *Saudades do Brasil* cycle.

The opening melody (mm. 1–4) clearly outlines the pitch content of the D Ionian mode [D–E–F#–G–A–B–C#–D]. The accompaniment of the same measures consists exclusively of two alternating harmonies [G–B–D and D–A–C] that suggest an incomplete mode [G–A–B–C–D–( )–( )] rooted to the initial G triad. The chromatic C/C# discrepancy between bitonal (D/G major) melody and accompaniment (m. 2), together with the insistence of the G triad, creates a distinct bitonal combination in which each mode generates its own tonal center.[15]

There are, however, instances where for various reasons one of the modes of the combination is heard, or analyzed, to be predominant over the other. In that case, the modal center of the predominant mode will be considered primary. Just as was the case with the common tonic combinations, modal combinations that do not share a common tonic also give rise to discrepancies that can be used to generate new pitch collections.

Polymodal combinations (i.e., when more than two modes are used) should be viewed in the same way as the bimodal combinations where the two different modes do not share a common tonic.

Unlike in traditional tonal music, where even a transitory tonal center is a direct result of harmonic function, there are many instances in 20th century music where the pitch collections that are being used give no clear indication of a tonal center. This is especially true when composers use symmetrical pitch collections such as the interval cycles or polymodal combinations. In this kind of 20th century music, the harmonic ideal is most often not one of tonal center but of harmonic color. Polymodal combinations and interval cycles produce their own individual kind of sound and are especially chosen to this end. While their pitches are still important in the generation of tonal progression and formal structure, their individual tonality is of secondary importance.

In a texture where tonal centricity is ambiguous, the composer can assert it in different ways. He or she may choose to repeat a single note or chord that represents the desired tonal center in a prominent registral or metric position. Ostinato chords or registrally isolated pedal points can be used to anchor the overall texture to a fixed element that acts as a tonal center. This technique is similar to the use of pedal points in traditional tonal music where a single chord tone underscores the contrasting musical activity that occurs above it. A note or harmonic structure that represents a particular tonal center can also be placed at important formal junctures of a work in the same way that cadences are used in traditional tonal music.

In traditional tonal music, the tonal center is almost always unambiguously established at the beginning of a composition. Many 20th century compositions, however, rely on the principle of emergent tonality. What this means is that the musical elements provided at the beginning of a movement or of a formal section are insufficient or too ambiguous to give a clear indication of a tonal center. These insufficiencies are gradually filled in by newly supplied musical elements that complete the prerequisite set of properties of the desired tonal center. In this way, the tonality is gradually allowed to emerge. This phenomenon indicates that it is important to first see what happens at the end of a piece or formal section in order to clarify the compositional techniques that enable this kind of tonal process.

In Barber's second song from the song cycle Op. 29 "Church Bell at Night," the "A" tonality is rendered ambiguous by several different factors. While the opening melodic statements of the vocal line (mm. 1–4) seems to affirm an A tonality in which the tonic (A), and the fifth (E), are embellished by their respective leading tones (G# and D#). However, the melody does not end on the tonic at all. The final melodic G# and D# that had served in their appropriate functional roles are weakened by their total lack of resolution at the ending. Nevertheless, the complete melodic pitch content [A–( )–C/C#–D#–E–F–G#] does gives rise to a compounded A mode.

The non-functional pairs of chords that accompany the melody are not tertian constructions and seem not to help in the establishment of a clear tonal center. The pitch content of the first chord [B–G#–C–E–F#–A#–D#], which appears on most of the prominent metric points as well as the beginning and at the end of the piece, is in direct contrast to the assumed tonic because of the presence of the A#. It is, nevertheless, counterbalanced by the second chord of the pair [C–F–E–A] that neutralizes the A# of the first chord of the pair. This second chord is immediately followed by a pedal tone that tonicizes A. Nevertheless, a clear tonal center remains elusive.

In the middle portion of the song, the melodic line, chords, and pedal tones of the accompaniment come together to elucidate the tonal center. The G# and D# used to embellish the tonic and fifth of the melody in the opening measures, are now used harmonically to fulfill their leading tone roles by resolving repeatedly to the tonic and fifth (A and E). The pedal tones of these measures [A–C–Db(C#)] anchor the entire accompaniment and melody to an A tonic. It is also at this point (m. 4) that the melody unfolds a fifth to tonic progression. The A tonality thus emerges in the central portion of the song only to be rendered once more ambiguous by the closing measures in which an expected A tonic is not sounded as the final note.

Tonal centricity based on inversional symmetrical collections around an axis of symmetry is yet another way of establishing tonal centers. The underlying principle is that pitches are symmetrically arranged around an axis. This axis acts as the tonal fulcrum or center. The shift from one axis to another is much like modulating form one key to another in traditional tonal music. Axially based tonal centricity is one of the most significant systems of tonal progression devised in the 20th century.

In the *Tempo giusto* section of Bartók's second *Étude* Op. 18, the pitch content of the contrary motion arpeggios which are placed metrically between the melodic octaves [F–C#–A–E and Eb–Bb–Gb–D] is neither tertian nor cyclic. While the arpeggiated content seems almost random, their arrangement reveals that every note of the upper arpeggio is mirrored literally by a note of the opposing lower arpeggio.[16] Each pair of opposing notes is equidistant from an axis of symmetry, as represented, in this case by an Eb/E dyad.

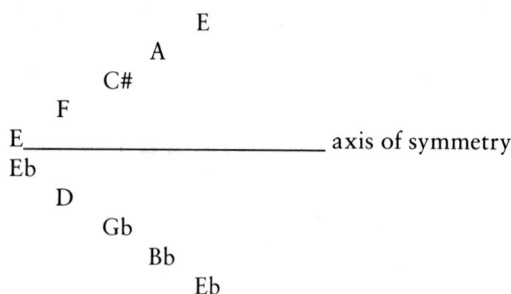

```
                        E
                   A
              C#
          F
E_____ axis of symmetry
Eb
     D
          Gb
               Bb
                   Eb
```

During the course of the *Étude*, different sets of pitches are symmetrically arranged around shifting axes of symmetry.

FORMAL STRUCTURES

Phrasal and periodic structures in traditional tonal music can be broadly defined by two principles: the first is the presentation and repetition of specific thematic material, the second, and just as significant, is based on the different kinds of cadences that are used to demarcate important junctures of these formal structures. We know, for example, that a parallel period consists of a repeated four-measure phrase where the first phrase ends in a cadence that is relatively weaker than the cadence found at the end of the repeated phrase. The first cadence tells us that the period is incomplete, while the second cadence closes off the formal structure.

The opening of the first movement of Mozart's Sonata K331 is based on such a formal structure. The regularity of the thematic repetition in the second four-measure phrase and that the open half cadence (m. 4) is counterbalanced by the perfect authentic cadence at the end of the parallel period (m. 8).[17]

While some phrase and period structures in 20th century music mimic those found in traditional tonal music, others are determined by different theme types and repetition. A simple rest at the end of a phrase can mark its conclusion and a sudden change of texture can signal the beginning of a new phrase. Sometimes, the music is not even based on phrases or periods but is measured in units of time.

The first period (mm. 1–10) in Stravinsky's children's song "Tilim-bom" from the song cycle *Histoire pour enfants* is underscored by an unchanging ostinato bass line pattern, which is in no way functional and is not discontinued to permit a cadence. It is the melody and the upper part of the piano accompaniment that generate the formal structure. The vocal melody is a slightly irregular form of the "Sentence" where the thematic material of the second part of the continuation (mm. 5–10) contrasts with that presented in the first part (mm. 1–4). Since there are no cadences in the piano part, Stravinsky demarcates the phrase sequence [4+4+2] with a distinct change of texture in the right-hand part of the accompaniment. In this way he is still able to delineate the phrases without the use of cadence.[18]

Cadences may be replaced by cadential patterns that are also now more reliant on other contextual factors such as metric placement of the chords or even the completion of a pitch-set basic to the composition. Since the referent pitch collection of much 20th century music is the chromatic scale, its completion often signals the end of either small or large formal structures.

SYNTHESIS

A more comprehensive study of George Crumb's first *Makrokosmos* allows not only for a formal analysis based on entirely new formal criteria but also serves to demonstrate the many ways in which the chromatic scale of the unordered twelve-tone system can be expressed. The piece consists of a series of five unmeasured sound blocks, some separated by pauses. The change and repetition of different textures determine the formal structure of this piece because there are no themes or cadences. A formal analysis based solely on contrasting musical textures or sound blocks yields an A–A–B–C–B formal structure. The "A" section texture is obtained by the strumming and plucking of the strings inside the soundboard of the instrument. The "B" textures consists of rapid ostinato scalar patterns played on the keyboard, while the "C" texture consists exclusively of cluster chords also played on the keyboard.

The first two "A" sound blocks are not unlike the first two phrases of a traditional period. However, it is not only the repetition of similar textures that generates the formal pattern. The unfolding of the pitch content of these two sound blocks is also fundamental in the creation of form. The pitch content of the first block is unfolded by the perfect fifth cycle that generates two cyclic segments [A–E–B–F#, notated on the main staff, and C#–G#–D# notated above the main staff] (Figure 1.5)

The second sound block unfolds two new perfect fifth cyclic segments [Eb–Bb–F–C, notated on the main staff, and G–D–A, notated above the staff]. When combined, the cyclically unfolding pitch content of the two sound blocks generates the complete perfect fifth cycle [A–E–B–F#–C#–G#–Eb–Bb–F–C–G–D–A], which can also be interpreted in scalar order [A–Bb–B–C–C#–D–Eb–E–F–F#–G–G#–A] to yield the complete chromatic scale. Thus, the opening "period" is articulated by two sound blocks, each of which unfolds half of the perfect fifth cycle. Together, they complete the chromatic spectrum before the commencement of a new and contrasting formal section.

The first "B" section (Figure 1.6) is introduced by three grace-note dyads [D–E, Bb–D#, and A–Cb]. While at first it seems that only the first and third dyads seem to be related, both being harmonic whole-tones, it is the second and only melodic dyad that reveals the pitch relations that bind together these grace notes. The first harmonic E–D dyad is immediately followed by the D# of the second dyad while the Bb of the same dyad is sounded immediately before the A–Cb of the third dyad. This creates a six-note symmetry [E–D#–D–( )–( )–Cb–Bb–A] around a C/C# axis. The symmetrical process is continued throughout the remainder of the section. While the right-hand ostinato pattern unfolds an incomplete pentatonic scale [A–B–D–E], the left hand simultaneously unfolds a similar pentatonic scale a semitone lower [Ab–Bb–Db–Eb]. When combined, these two pentatonic sets generate a chromatic pitch collection [Ab–A–Bb–B–( )–Db–D–Eb–E] that is symmetrical around a C/C axis.

The chromatic cluster chords of the "C" section (Figure 1.7) move in contrary motion from the outer extremes of the keyboard to create a mirror effect that once more suggests some form of symmetry. This is verified by the symmetrical arrangement of the pitch content of the individual clusters as well as the larger symmetries generated by the cluster chord combinations. The first right-hand chord [D#–E–F–F#–G–Ab], a symmetrical chromatic

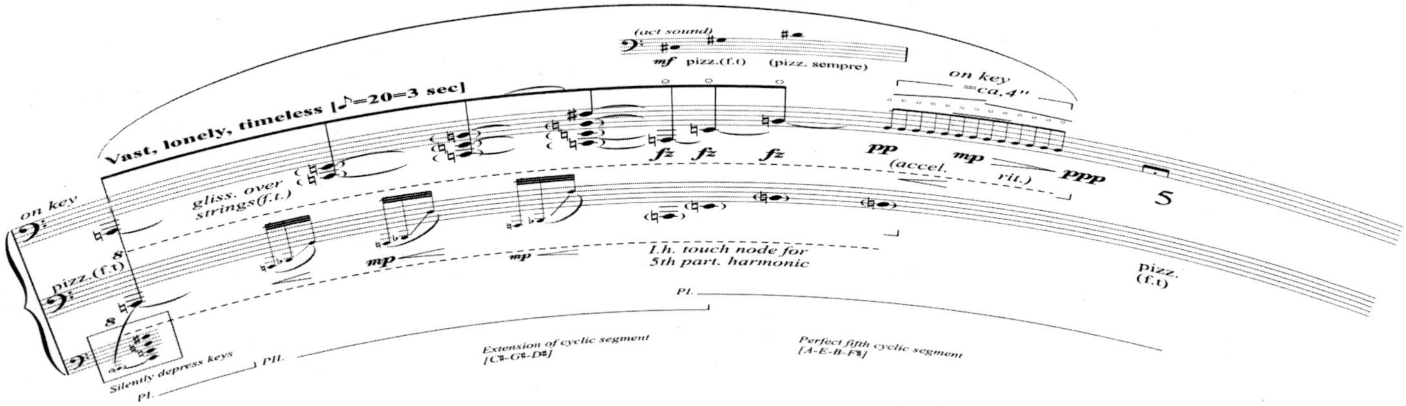

Figure 1.5 Crumb, *Spiral Galaxy* first "A" section. Copyright © 1973 by C.F. Peters Corporation. All Rights Reserved. Used by Permission.

Figure 1.6   Crumb, *Spiral Galaxy* first "B" section. Copyright © 1973 by C.F. Peters Corporation. All Rights Reserved. Used by Permission.

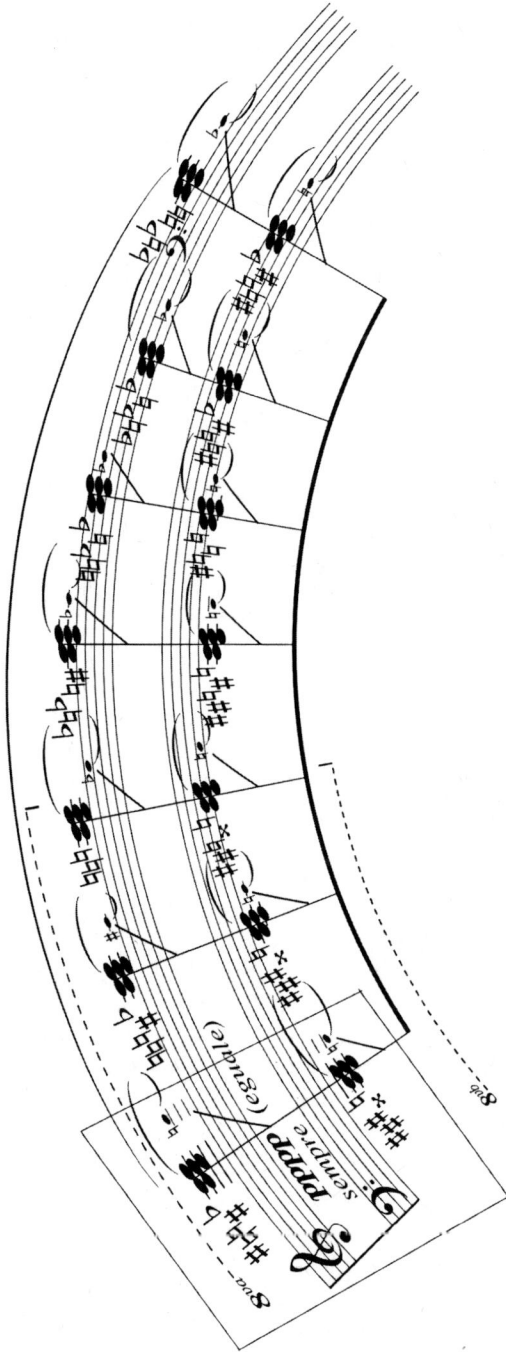

Figure 1.7 Crumb, *Spiral Galaxy* "C" section. Copyright © 1973 by C.F. Peters Corporation. All Rights Reserved. Used by Permission.

cluster, is mirrored by a simultaneous left-hand chromatic cluster [Gx–A#–B–B#–C#–D]. Together they produce all twelve notes [Gx–A#–B–B#–C#–D–D#–E–F–F#–G–Ab–( )], symmetrical around a D/D# axis. The axis is manifested in the top tone of the left-hand cluster and the bottom tone of the right-hand cluster. This axial relationship exists between all right- and left-hand clusters of the passage, which unfolds a series of seven axes [D\D#, G\G#, C\C#, F\F#, Bb\B, Eb\E, and Ab\A] that shift cyclically by perfect fifth. This formal section is undoubtedly the most revealing of all the sections because it synthesizes the perfect fifth cycle of the combined "A" sections and the chromatic cycle, the two cycles being intrinsically related to each other. The only difference between them is the sequential order of the elements.

The second of the two "B" sections is identical in structure to the first, except that the new incomplete pentatonic collections are transposed. The right-hand collection [D–E–G–A] is combined with the left-hand collection [Db–Eb–Gb–Ab] to generate a new pitch collection [Db–D–Eb–E–( )–Gb–G–Ab–A], symmetrical around an F/F axis. It is interesting to note that the axes of symmetry of the two "B" sections are also related by the perfect fifth [F/F–C/C]. This merely confirms that the pitch content of the entire piece is underpinned by the perfect fifth cycle even though the musical textures of the sections diverge from each other significantly.

Crumb also makes use of register to aid in the development of form. The "A" sections move from the extreme lower register to the central register. The "B" sections occupy the middle register, while the "C" sections move from the extreme high register to the upper end of the low register. The focus on different registers lends a spatial dimension to the formal plan. Though this piece has no key, time signature, melody, cadences, phrases, or any other of the markings, we usually use to analyze form in music, the formal structure of the work could not be more clearly articulated. Crumb articulates musical form by synthesizing pitch relationships based on interval cycles and axial symmetry with different timbres and different registers.

The new concepts detailed in this chapter provide some of the indicators that the analyst must consider when studying a 20th century work. Since so much of this music remains unanalyzed, many of its aspects remain unknown. It is therefore important that a prospective analyst look at a new work from as many different perspectives as possible. While this book does not aim to cover all aspects of 20th century music, it provides the essential concepts and materials necessary to unveil a unified system of analysis for music that uses the unordered twelve-tone system as its basis. While this idea is considered by many to be unattainable, an overwhelming number of analyses based on cyclic pitch relationships have proven otherwise. Analyses of this kind are both practicable and provable. The ensuing chapters are dedicated to the primary goal of analysis, which consists of determining the pitch relations that generate tonal progression. Detailed explanations and musical examples will help to elucidate the actions and interactions of a host of different pitch-sets that generate different modes of tonal progression.

2 The Interval Cycles

Music: Ludwig van Beethoven *Piano Sonata* Op. 111
Franz Liszt *Gnomenreigen*
Wallingford Riegger *Major Seconds*
György Ligeti *Cordes à vide*
Charles Ives *Psalm XXIV*
Béla Bartók *Étude* Op. 18, No. 1, *Suite* Op. 14, No. 2
Witold Lutoslawski *Étude* No. 1

In much of the music of the 20th century, the octave is subdivided symmetrically. Each interval class (M2/m7, m3/M6, etc.) that subdivides the octave contains two intervallic differences that add up to an octave.[1] For example, interval-1 (C–C#) and interval-11 (C#–C) form the interval class 1/11. In each interval class, the smaller of the two intervals generates a interval cycle that subdivides the octave equally.[2] The *interval cycle* can therefore be regarded as a chain of identical intervals, the sequence of which is completed by the return of the initial pitch at the octave. Since interval cycles are generated by a regular succession of single intervals, they maintain an equal and constant *interval ratio*.

The interval ratio represents intervallic proportions and is mathematically expressed by two or more numerals that denote the size of the component intervals. The numerals stand for the number of semitones. The interval ratio of any major triad, for example, is 4:3 because there are four semitones between the root and the third and three semitones between the third and the fifth. The interval ratio of the chromatic (1/11) cycle is always 1:1 because the intervallic space between each successive pair of notes is always the semitone.

The total number of interval cycles consists of one cycle of minor seconds (1/11), two cyclic partitions of major seconds (2/10), three cyclic partitions of minor thirds (3/9), four cyclic partitions of major thirds (4/8), and six tritone cyclic partitions (6/6). The perfect fourth cycle (5/7)[3] is unique in that it does not generate a cycle that subdivides the octave symmetrically because it must pass through several octaves before reaching the initial pitch class.

Most of the interval cycles can be interpreted in more traditional terms. The interval-1/11 cycle is the chromatic scale, the interval-2/10 cycles the two whole-tone scales, the interval-3/9 cycles the three fully diminished

Table 2.1   Complex of Interval Cycles*

0/12	1/11	2/10	3/9	4/8	5/7	6/6
C	C				C	
C	B				E#	
C	Bb				A#	
C	A				D#	
C	G#				G#	
C	G				C#	
C	F#	C C#			F#	
C	F	A# B			B	
C	E	G# A	C C# D		E	
C	Eb	F# G	A Bb B	C C# D Eb	A	
C	D	E F	F# G G#	G# A A# B	D	C C#D Eb E F
C	C#	D D#	Eb E F	E F F# G	G	F# G G#A A# C#
C	C	C C#	C C# D	C C# D Eb	C	C C#D Eb E F

* For the sake of legibility, only the first half of the table is presented. The second half would be the mirror image of the first: 6/6–7/5–8/4–9/3–10/2–11/1–0/12.

seventh chords, and the interval-4/8 cycles the four augmented triads. The interval-5/7 cycle is taught us in the order of sharps and flats and is commonly known as the *circle of fifths*. The interval-6/6 cycles are the six tritones. We do not, however, want to retain too much of the traditional terminology because the music in which the cycles are found to interact has little or nothing to do with the music of the common practice era.

CYCLIC STRUCTURES IN THE TRADITIONAL TONAL ERA

Symmetrical cyclic constructions such the fully diminished seventh chord and the augmented triad have been used by the vast majority of composers of the traditional tonal era and especially those of the Romantic and Late Romantic periods because the symmetrical properties of these chords could easily be used to render ambiguous the tonal direction of a given harmonic sequence, to obfuscate the establishing of key, and even to suspend functional tonal progression. A single, fully diminished chord, for example, can be resolved in a number of ways. When these cyclic chords are used in their leading-tone seventh chord capacity, any of the four chord tones can become the leading tone.

C–Eb/D#–F#–A

C–Eb–F#–A where C, as the leading tone, resolves to Db–F–Ab
C–D#–F#–A where D# as the leading tone, resolves to E–G#–B
C–D–F#–A where F# as the leading tone, resolves to G–B–D
C–Eb–Gb–A where A as the leading tone, resolves to Bb–D–F

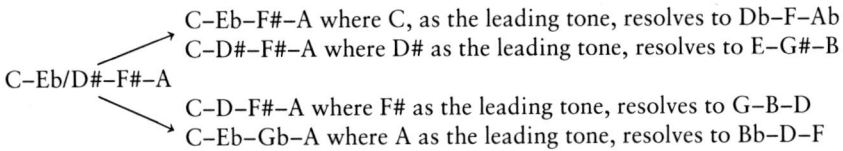

This shows how the symmetrical properties of the diminished chord can be used to produce it tonal ambiguity by bestowing upon each chord tone an equivalent function.

The immediate leading-tone seventh to tonic resolution mentioned already can be further delayed by lowering any of the four constituent tones of the diminished seventh chord to obtain four different dominant seventh chords that also resolve to four possible tonic chords.

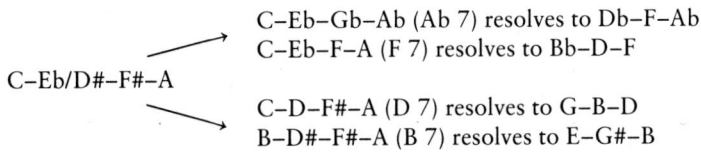

C–Eb/D#–F#–A

C–Eb–Gb–Ab (Ab 7) resolves to Db–F–Ab
C–Eb–F–A (F 7) resolves to Bb–D–F
C–D–F#–A (D 7) resolves to G–B–D
B–D#–F#–A (B 7) resolves to E–G#–B

This equality places the resolution of the chord in the hands of the composer, who decides among four equally plausible tonal outcomes. Symmetrical structures in the tonal context leads to the equalization of the twelve tones.

Beethoven's experimentations with such principles often lead him to purposely avoid establishing a tonic key at the beginning of a work. In his final piano sonata in C minor Op. 111, Beethoven demonstrates how the symmetrical properties of the cyclic diminished seventh chord can be used to confound the establisment of a tonic.

The piece opens with three short thematic statements, each of which begins with a leading-tone diminished seventh chord. The first (m. 1) is the leading-tone seventh chord [F#–A–C–Eb] of the dominant [G–B–D]. It resolves momentarily to that chord, creating the impression that G might be the principal tonality of the work. This notion is reinforced by the asser-tion of the G major chord on both the strong beats of the resolution mea-sure (m. 2). The second diminished seventh chord [B–D–F–Ab], the true diminished seventh of the tonic [C–Eb–G], resolves not to the tonic but to the diminished seventh of IV or subdominant [F–Ab–C] on the downbeat, suspending the arrival of the C minor tonic triad. It then resolves to the subdominant, which is only then followed by a major version of the tonic chord [C–E–G]. A third diminished chord, the diminished seventh [E–G–Bb–Db] of the already stated subdominant, is instead resolved to a minor vii [Bb–Db–F] harmony that completely derails the arrival of the tonic key, which emerges several measures later.[4]

In this opening passage, Beethoven clearly demonstrates how the sym-metrical properties of the chord can be used to make tonal direction completely unpredictable and to suspend the establishment of a key. What is even of greater significance is the fact that the three diminished chords are cyclically ordered [Eb–Ab–Db]. Ordering of tonal areas according to cyclical patterns foreshadows a commonplace 20th century technique.

While the use of tonally ambiguous fully diminished seventh chords is common throughout the tonal era, the use of other cyclic chordal constructions such as the augmented triad or interval-4/8 cycle only came into vogue during the Late Romantic period. Composers such as Liszt started to make extensive use of this cyclic construction because of its unique color and its tonally ambiguous symmetrical properties. In the tonal context, the symmetrical augmented triad can be resolved in several different ways by chromatically raising or lowering different combinations of its chord tones.

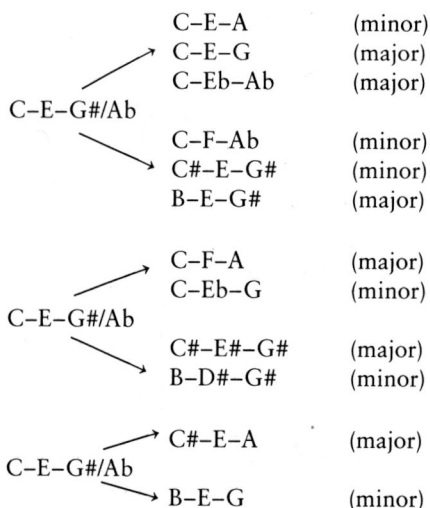

	C–E–A	(minor)
⟋	C–E–G	(major)
	C–Eb–Ab	(major)
C–E–G#/Ab		
	C–F–Ab	(minor)
⟍	C#–E–G#	(minor)
	B–E–G#	(major)

⟋	C–F–A	(major)
	C–Eb–G	(minor)
C–E–G#/Ab		
⟍	C#–E#–G#	(major)
	B–D#–G#	(minor)

⟋	C#–E–A	(major)
C–E–G#/Ab		
⟍	B–E–G	(minor)

Thus, this cyclic construction can suspend tonal function for as long as is desired.

In the concert étude *Gnomenreigen* (mm. 110–121), Liszt exploits this tonal ambiguity in a lengthy series of augmented triads that leads to the finale of the work. In the first triad of the progression [A–C#–E#], the two upper notes are resolved upward [A–D–F#], giving the impression that one might be moving to the key of D . However, this is immediately followed by chromatic transposition of the same gesture that initiates an ascending series of unresolved augmented triads that ends on the two-octave transposition of the first triad [A–C#–E#]. This, however, the two outer notes are resolved upwardly [A#–C#–F#], establishing the F# major tonality of the finale.[5]

While this passage is indicative of the ambiguity and unpredictability of chromatic harmonic function in the Romantic era, it shows how the incorporation of symmetrical cyclic chords, in cyclic sequence, reinforced precisely the aforementioned concepts. Like the chord tones of the fully diminished seventh chord, the chord tones of the augmented triad can each be assigned the same function to render them equivalent.

Toward the end of the 19th and beginning of the 20th centuries, the cyclic concept began to pervade many aspects of musical composition. The interval cycles themselves began to be used alongside traditional scales and modes. Composers soon realized that cycles and modes shared many common elements that permitted transformation between them. Many interval cycles can be reordered to generate common scales and modes.[6] The interval-7/5 cycle is perhaps the most musically significant because it can be employed either in its entirety or in part to produce a plethora of pentatonic, diatonic, or nondiatonic modes that abound in the music of the unordered twelve-tone system. For example, any seven-note segment of the interval-7/5 cycle can be cast in diatonic modal order.

Interval-7 cyclic order: F–C–G–D–A–E–B
Diatonic scalar order: C–D–E–F–G–A–B

This means that the diatonic pitch content can be expressed in two different ways. The determination of order is in the hands of the composer and no longer a pre-compositional or a priori assumption. The interval cycles and compound cyclic pitch collections replaced the major and minor scales of the tonal era as the source materials for a vast quantity of 20th century musical idiom. Because tonal progression no longer relied on the tonal hierarchy generated by the order of pitches of the major scale, pitch content and the pitch relations within it superseded scalar sequence. The identity of scales and modes was inexorably changed. Function-based tonality could not accommodate symmetrical pitch relations that generate their own form of tonal progression. In the late 19th century, works based solely on the interval cycles began to make their appearance. In some of these pioneering works, the new cyclic pitch relations erased all commonly held notions tonality. As the 20th century progressed, symmetrical pitch relations generated by the interval cycles became the basis for a large portion of western art music.

CYCLIC RELATIONS GENERATED
BY SINGLE CYCLIC PARTITIONS

While it may seem probable that basing an entire musical composition solely on a single interval cycle may cause problems with invariance of musical color, it seems not to be the case. The potential to generate multiple cyclic-interval relationships is inherent in each individual cycle because the placement of more than two pitches in the time and space of a musical context will generate pitch relations between the first two notes and all the ones that may follow. If, for example, we unfold the three pitches of any tritone cycle [C–F#–C], then tritone relationships will be created between the F# and the two Cs, and an octave relationship will be created between the two Cs. While there are many musical works based exclusively on single interval cycles, the pieces that seem to offer the clearest examples of basic cyclic relationships tend to be didactic works like études or character pieces. The reason for this is that these kinds of works are explicitly formulated to showcase the colors generated by cyclic sonorities and, in the case of études, designed to teach new technical skills necessary for the execution of new cyclic musical textures.

Though not nearly as extensive and comprehensive as Bartók's *Mikrokosmos*, Wallingford Riegger's (1885–1961) series of children's pieces explores the unique sounds generated by the cycles. To this end, he gave his set of miniatures simple, self-explanatory titles such as *The Augmented Triad* and *The Tritone*. The *Major Second*, as its title suggests, consists solely of two pairs of whole-tone dyads [Db–Eb/D–E and Gb–Ab/G–A] that represent and juxtapose dyads from the two whole-tone or interval-2/10 cycles. The complete pitch-class content of the miniature is unfolded in the opening four measures. The opening whole-tone 1 dyad[7] [Db–Eb] of the left hand is immediately contrasted by the whole-tone 0 dyad [D–E] of the right hand (mm. 1–2). Together, these two dyads generate a chromatic tetrachord [Db–D–Eb–E] that suggest that the chromatic (interval-1/11) cycle is being equally subdivided into its two whole-tone partitions.[8] The process is confirmed when the second set of dyads [Gb–Ab and G–A] are subjected to the same treatment (mm. 3–4), generating a transposition of the opening chromatic tetrachord [Gb–G–Ab–A]. This time, however, the whole-tone 0 dyad is in the left hand while the whole-tone 1 dyad is in the right hand.

The switching of the two whole-tone cycles between the two hands generates a second relationship between the whole-tone dyads and the perfect fifth (7/5) cycle that is expressed linearly by the individual right-hand and left-hand parts. In the right hand, the D–E dyad is followed by the G–A dyad. Together they generate a four-note segment of the perfect fifth cycle [G–D–A–E] in juxtaposition with another four-note segment of the same cycle [Gb–Db–Ab–Eb], generated linearly by the left-hand dyad pair [Db–Eb and Gb–Ab]. The pitch relations generated in this small piece encompass the relationship between the two extremes of the cyclic realm, the *chromatic*, represented by the interval-1/11 cycle, and the *diatonic*, represented by the interval-7/5 cycle. The chromatic (1/11) and the perfect fifth/fourth (7/5 or 5/7) interval cycles are the only two cycles that generate all twelve pitch classes and therefore express the same pitch content. The only difference between the two cycles is that of sequential order. If we lay out the complete perfect fifth cycle and partition it in exactly the same way that we did the chromatic cycle, we will obtain the same two whole-tone cycles from the partitioning of the chromatic cycle.

C–G–D–A–E–B–F#–C#–G#–D#–A#–E#
                  ↗ C–D–E–F#–G#–A#

                  ↘ G–A–B–C#–D#–E#

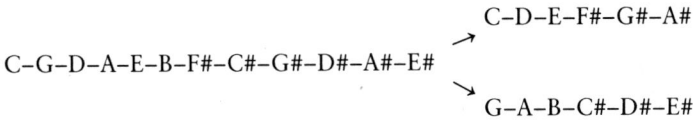

The whole-tone cycles can therefore be seen as the gateway between *diatonic* and *chromatic* spheres of music and it is these cycle that create the binding relationship between the semitone and perfect fifth cycles. This is made even clearer if the two cycles are aligned with one another.

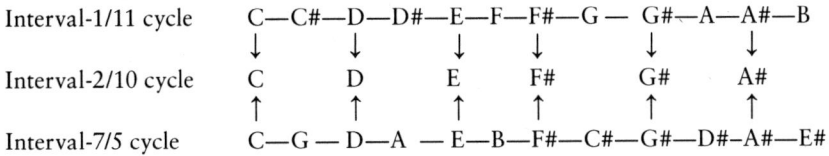

Interval-1/11 cycle	C—C#—D—D#—E—F—F#—G — G#—A—A#—B
	↓ ↓ ↓ ↓ ↓ ↓
Interval-2/10 cycle	C D E F# G# A#
	↑ ↑ ↑ ↑ ↑ ↑
Interval-7/5 cycle	C—G — D—A — E—B—F#—C#—G#—D#–A#—E#

The second of Ligeti's piano études, *Cordes à vide* (1981), is based exclusively on the interval-5/7 cycle. The closest meaningful English translation of the French title is "Hollow Chords." The meaning of this title is directly reflected by the continuous stream of perfect fifths outlined by both upper and lower parts that generate a purely intervallic texture that has no clear melody and an accompaniment that is missing the rich harmonic sonority characteristic of complete chords. The basic compositional technique used in this piece is the linking of segments of the perfect fifth (7/5) cycle in loops or spirals that are themselves linked to one another by either perfect fifth or semitone.

The upper part consists of paired musical figures that either unfold the perfect fifths in strict cyclic order (figure (a)], or that interlock the perfect fifths at the semitone [figure (b)]. In the opening measures (mm. 1–2), the first figure unfolds a descending three-note segment of the perfect fifth cycle [A–D–G]. This figure is chromatically linked to the second figure, which consists of two chromatically adjacent perfect fifths [Bb–Eb/Cb–Fb]. The chromatic linking of the two figures occurs between the first fifth of the first figure [A–D] and the first fifth [Eb–Bb] of the second figure (Figure 2.1).

The procedure is repeated (mm. 2–3) with a restatement of the first figure [A–D–G] that is linked to a transposed version of the second figure [C#–F#/D–G/Eb–Ab] via its second fifth [D–G]. This pairing occurs two more times at different transpositional levels (mm. 4–7). The accompaniment of the opening measures (mm. 1–4) consists of three interval-5 cyclic segments that are linked by perfect fifths that generate a closed cyclic loop that begins and ends on the same pitch class [Bb–Eb–Ab–Db–Gb–Cb → B–E–A–D–G–C → F–Bb] unfolding the complete interval-7/5 cycle. Since the *moto perpetuo* quality of the texture lacks any of the traditional structural markers, the completion of the cycle in the fourth measure is significant because it heralds the end of a traditional four-measure phrase in much the same way that a cadential pattern would in a tonal work.[9]

Figure 2.1 Ligeti, *Cordes à vide* (mm. 1–4). *Ligeti Études Pour Piano, Book I. Copyright © 1986 Schott Music GmbH & Co. KG, Mainz—Germany. All Rights reserved. Used by permission of European American Music Distributors LLC, sole U.S. and Canadian agent for Univeral Edition A.G, Wien.*

The accompaniment to the second phrase (mm. 4–7) is made up of two intertwining interval-5 cyclic strands that coil around one another like a DNA double helix. Ligeti achieves this by subdividing each cyclic strand in an alternating pattern.

Strand 1: C#–F#–B–E–A–D   G–C–F–Bb–Eb
Strand 2: D#–G#–C#–F#–B   E–A–D–G–C–F

The upper part of the third phrase (mm. 7–8) commences with an inverted version of the original figure (a) that outlines a four-note cyclic segment [Db–Ab–Eb–Bb]. This is linked by fifth to a second (a) figure [F#–B–E]. These two (a) figures are followed by three (b) figures, the second and third of which articulate a new ordering of the chromatically adjacent fifths. The first of these two figures outlines a series of chromatically ascending fifths [F–C, Gb–Db, and G–D] while the second figure outlines a descending series [E–B, Eb–Bb, and D–A]. If these two series were to be aligned against one another, they would describe an inversional symmetrical progression in which every note is equidistant from an axis of symmetry.

```
                            D
                        G
                    Db
                Gb
            C
        F
        _____  D/D Axis of symmetry
        B
            E
                Bb
                    Eb
                        A
                            D
```

In the context of this piece, this particular disposition of the fifths describes a new way in which cyclic elements can be arranged, while also making evident how one set of symmetrical pitch relations (those of the cycle itself) can generate secondary pitch relationships in the form of axes of symmetry. These axes can be used as the basis for the generation of both cyclic and modal pitch collections or as a new means of tonal progression. The concept of axial symmetry, for example, is used in many 20th century works as a means of establishing a new kind of tonal centricity where the axes operate in much the same way as do traditional tonal centers in traditional tonal works.[10] The closing of the opening section (mm. 11–13) is marked by the appearance of the first dyad chords that become the characteristic feature of the second section of the piece. Noticeably, both parts end the first section by unfolding the same fifth that begins the piece, D–A in the upper part and Ebb–Bbb in the lower part. This symbolizes not only the end of the section but the closing of the interval-7/5 cyclic loop as a formal marker.

At the beginning of the second section (m. 14) the D–A dyad, now at the center of the texture is cyclically extended in opposite directions by both the upper [D–A–E] and lower [A–D–G] parts creating a cyclic link between the formal sections.[11] This shows that the cycle plays a role in the formal layout of the work. This principle is confirmed by the link that exists between the second section and the modified recapitulation (m. 26), where the last dyad of the former section [E#–B#] is cyclically extended by the first dyad of the upper part [F–Bb] of the recapitulation.

The second formal section of the piece (mm. 14–26) is based on varied forms of the original (a) and (b) figures which are now often combined, often blurring their individual identity. The (a) figure often appears as vertical perfect fifth dyads rather than arpeggiated fifths, while the (b) figure is gradually extended. Alternating (a) figures partition the chromatic spectrum into "white note" and "black note" cyclic collections. The first (a) figures (mm. 14–15) outline a white-note segment of the perfect fifth cycle [C–G–D–A–E], followed immediately by a new (a) figure that outlines a black note segment [Gb–Db–Ab–Eb–Bb]. Chromatic completion by the fused figural pairs becomes more frequent and occurs in progressively shorter time frames. The fusion of figures achieved by interlocking cyclic dyads becomes one of the most prominent aspects of the section. The (a) and (b) figures (mm. 15–16) are now strictly linked by perfect fifths [C–G–D + Gb–Db–Ab–Eb–Bb and F–C + D–A–E–B–F#–C#] to the point that the chromatically adjacent fifths unfold all twelve tones (mm. 15–16), creating yet another complete loop. [12]

This piece clearly illustrates the binding relationship between the perfect fifth and chromatic cycles, the one being a different ordering of the other. Both the Ligeti and Riegger case studies also illustrate that in music based purely on cyclic pitch relations, the different dispositions of a single cycle within a musical texture automatically generates other cycles. The specific disposition of the whole-tone dyads in the Riegger example generates both perfect fifth and chromatic cyclic segments. Within a cyclic musical context, an individual cycle is but a single expression of the entire system of interval cycles. In a certain sense, the entire system of interval cycles is inherently present in any single cycle.

The formation of multiple cycles and resultant intercyclic relationships that occur in the works discussed thus far were generated by single interval cycles. There are, however, a large number of works in which cyclic relationships are created by the concurrent use of more than one cycle. This does not mean that the cyclic relationships in these works are any different from those found in the former category of pieces. What it does mean is that different intervallic properties of one cycle are simultaneously expressed by another present cycle. It also means that the number of simultaneous cyclic relationships may be greater because of the presence of a larger number of cycles.

CYCLIC PARTITIONING AND INTERLOCKING

Having demonstrated some of the most fundamental relationships that exist between individual cycles, it is now possible to show how interval cycles can be used to generate other cycles and an even larger palette of pitch relations. The simplest process to uncover these relationships is to partition the complete interval-1/11 or chromatic cycle into sequentially shorter cycles with increasingly larger interval ratios. The first partitioning of this kind yields the two mutually exclusive whole-tone or interval-2/10 interval cycles.

$$C–C\#–D–D\#–E–F–F\#–G–G\#–A–A\#–B \quad \nearrow \quad \begin{array}{l} C–D–E–F\#–G\#–A\# \\ \\ C\#–D\#–F–G–A–B \end{array}$$

This principle is used as the basic compositional process in the first of Bartók's *Études* Op. 18 (1920). The study opens with a four-note segment of the chromatic or 1/11 cycle [F–Gb–G–Ab], which is referred to as "Cell X."[13] It is registrally subdivided into two semitone interval couples [F–Gb/G–Ab]. Any symmetrical tetrachord can be partitioned into three discrete interval couples[14]—here, two semitones [F–Gb/G–Ab], two whole tones [F–G/Gb–Ab], and an axial interval couple of semitone and minor third [Gb–G/F–Ab]. At the beginning of the *Study* (mm. 1–2), the cell is partitioned according to its registral and linear orderings. Registrally, it is partitioned into its semitonal interval couples [F–Gb/G–Ab] and linearly in its two axial interval couples [Gb–G/F–Ab].[15] After a brief occurrence of one of its transpositions [Db–D–Eb–E], also based on the same partitioning as the original cell, a new transposition of the same tetrachord

[C–Db–D–Eb] yields a new interpretation of the component interval couples. The cell is now registrally presented in its whole-tone interval couples [C–D and Db–Eb], both of which are extended by a series of alternating notes to C–D–E and Db–Eb–F. This event signals the partitioning of the chromatic cycle into its two mutually exclusive whole-tone cycles that are eventually reunited or interlocked, as discrete entities, toward the end of the piece (mm. 110–114).[16] While new expansions to noncyclic pentatonic and diatonic structures occur during the course of the piece, the purely cyclic transformation from the chromatic to the whole-tone remains the core process. The middle stage of this process occurs in the central portion of the study (mm. 42ff), where a new chromatic tetrachord [B–C–C#–D] is registrally partitioned into its whole-tone interval couples, B–C# and C–D. This time, however, only the B–C# interval couple is extended, not by a series of alternate notes, but by a continuous series of four pitches that form a whole-tone tetrachord [Eb–F–G–A] which completes one of the two whole-tone cycles [C#–Eb–F–G–A–B]. This tetrachord has been referred to elsewhere in Bartók's music as "cell Y."[17]

The whole-tone 1 collection is briefly reabsorbed (mm. 43–46) into the chromatic continuum represented in these measures by a new chromatic tetrachord [E–F–F#–G] that initiates a chromatic ascent (mm. 47–48), in which both whole-tone cycles unfold in alternation. While this is the first complete whole-tone partitioning of the chromatic cycle in the piece, it occurs only as an accompanying figure.[18] It is only at the climactic conclusion of the work (mm. 110–114) that the full extent of this process is revealed by the entire texture in which both whole-tone cycles are unfolded in canonic inversion (Figure 2.2).

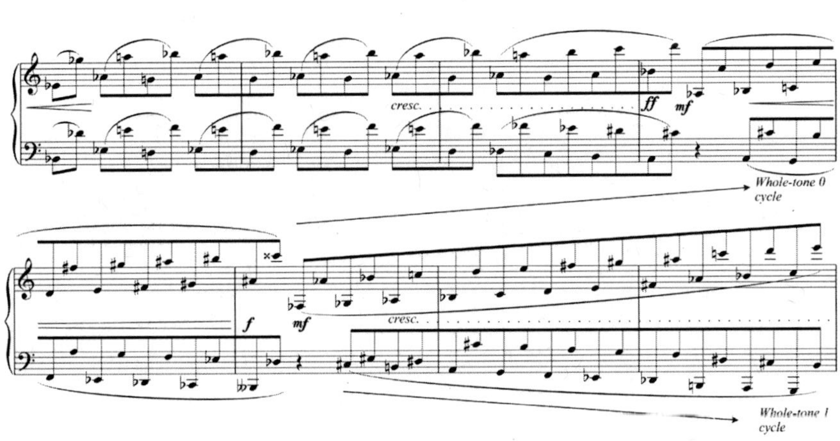

Figure 2.2 Bartók, *Study* No. 1 (mm. 107–114). *Étude from Three Studies Op. 18 by Bela Bartok.* © *Copyright 1920. Hawkes & Son (London), LTD. Reprinted by Permission.*

If we were to partition the interval-2/10 cycles in the same way Bartók partitioned the chromatic cycle, we would discover that each of the whole tone cycles is made up of two interval-4/8 cyclic segments. We can also partition the whole tone cycle to obtain three interval-6/6 cyclic segments.

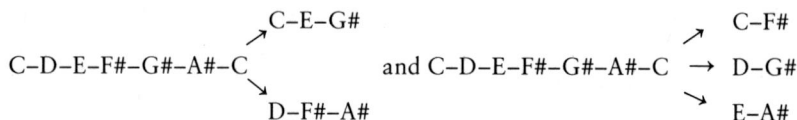

$$
\begin{array}{ll}
& \nearrow\; C–E–G\# \\
C–D–E–F\#–G\#–A\#–C & \\
& \searrow\; D–F\#–A\#
\end{array}
\qquad
\begin{array}{ll}
& \nearrow\; C–F\# \\
\text{and } C–D–E–F\#–G\#–A\#–C \;\to\; & D–G\# \\
& \searrow\; E–A\#
\end{array}
$$

The reverse process of partitioning is one in which like cycles of larger interval ratios are interlocked to create cycles of smaller interval ratios. Interlocking of cycles can occur at different intervallic distances. With the two whole-tone cycles this is not possible because the only way these two cycles can be fused is at the semitone.

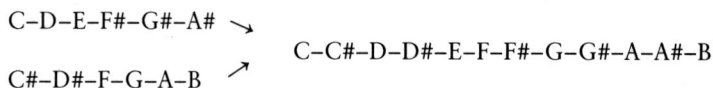

$$
\begin{array}{l}
C–D–E–F\#–G\#–A\# \searrow \\
\qquad\qquad\qquad\qquad C–C\#–D–D\#–E–F–F\#–G–G\#–A–A\#–B \\
C\#–D\#–F–G–A–B \nearrow
\end{array}
$$

In the second of the four movements of Bartók's *Suite* Op. 14, the interlocking of interval-4/8 cyclic segments to generate both interval-2/10 (whole-tone) cycles is the driving force behind the tonal progression of the piece. In the opening thematic statement (mm. 1–4), the interlocking of the interval-4 cyclic segments is articulated in alternating sequence of even and odd measures (Figure 2.3). The complete whole-tone 1 cycle [Db–Eb–F–G–A–B] is generated by the two interval-4/8 cyclic segments [G–Eb–B in m. 1 and F–Db–A in m. 3] while the incomplete whole-tone 0 cycle [C–( )–E–( )–Ab–Bb] is produced by two other interval-4/8 cyclic segments [C–Ab–E in m. 2 and Bb–( )–( ) in m. 3]. The second statement of the theme (mm. 5–8) is identical to the first in all respects except that it ends by adding a new note to the last interval-4/8 cyclic segment [Bb–F#–( )] so that the whole-tone 0 cycle remains incomplete [C–( )–E–F#–Ab–Bb].

In the next two thematic statements, the order of the two whole-tone cycles is reversed so that the complete whole-tone 0 cycle is unfolded in the odd measures (mm. 9, 11, 13, and 15) while the now incomplete whole-tone 1 cycle unfolds in the even measures (mm. 10, 12, 14, and 16). In the ensuing measures (mm. 17–20) both whole-tone cycles, now in their complete form, are unfolded sequentially in adjacent measures [B–D#–G–A–C#–E# in mm. 17–18 and F#–A#–D–E–G#–B# in mm. 19–20].[19]

The interval-4/8 cycles that are interlocked at the whole-tone to generate the whole tone segments can themselves be partitioned into smaller tritone or interval-6 cyclic segments. If the interval-6 cyclic segments are interloked at the minor third (interval-3) instead of the whole-tone, they will generate an interval-3/9 cyclic segment.

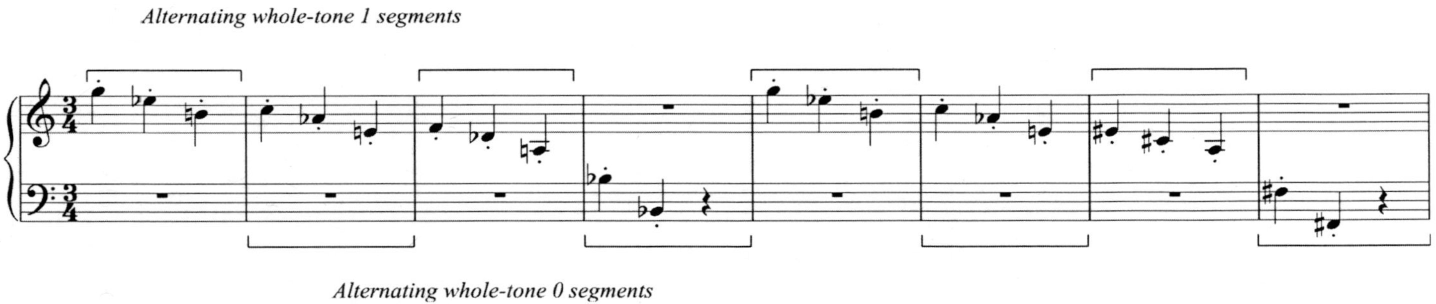

Alternating whole-tone 1 segments

Alternating whole-tone 0 segments

Figure 2.3 Bartók, *Suite* Op. 14 (mm. 1–8). *Suite, SZ62, Op. 14 by Bela Bartok.* © *Copyright 1918 by Boosey & Hawkes, Inc. Reprinted by Permission.*

C–F# ↘

        C–Eb–F#–A

Eb–A ↗

The tritone, therefore, is directly related to both the whole-tone cycles and the interval-3/9 or minor third cycles. This indicates that there is a relationship between the whole-tone and minor third cycles. Each interval-3/9 or minor third cycle is made up of two tritones that are each representative of one of the two whole-tone cycles.

              ↗ C–F# from whole-tone 0 [C–D–E–F#–G#–A#]

C–Eb–F#–A–C ‹

             ↘ Eb–A from whole-tone 1 [Db–Eb–F–G–A–B]

The relationship between the minor third cycles and the whole-tone cycles is of vital importance to the understanding of the relations that exist between the interval cycles and compound cyclic constructions.

In the Bartók example, the two interval-4/8 cyclic segments were interlocked at the whole-tone to obtain a whole-tone or interval-2 cycle.

C–E–G# ↘

        C–D–E–F#–G#–A# (whole-tone 0 scale)

D–F#–A# ↗

If, however, we interlock the same segments at the minor third, we will have created a *compound cyclic-interval construction*.[20]

C–E–G# ↘

        C–Eb–E–G–G#–B (augmented scale)

Eb–G–B ↗

In compound cyclic-interval constructions, the interval ratio is constant but not equal. For example, the preceding scalar segment has a constant interval ratio of 3:1 because of the sequential alternation of minor thirds and semitones. This particular construction is also known as the *augmented scale*. Perhaps the most common compound cyclic interval construction of the 20th century is the octatonic scale. If we interlock two interval-3/9 partitions at either the whole-tone or semitone, we will obtain an octatonic collection.

C–Eb–F#–A ↘

        C–D–Eb–F–F#–Ab–A–B (octatonic-0 scale)

D–F–Ab–B ↗

C#–E–G–Bb ↘

        C#–Eb–E–F#–G–A–Bb–C (octatonic-1 scale)

Eb–F#–A–C ↗

D–F–G#–B ↘
               D–E–F–G–G#–A#–B–C# (octatonic-2 scale)
E–G–A#–C# ↗

The interlocking of sequential segments of single interval cycles can generate a host of new compound cyclic collections. Interval cycles and compound cyclic collections can also be used to generate all diatonic, nondiatonic, pentatonic, and hybrid modes.

While the two Bartók examples are each demonstrative of one of the two processes, either partitioning or interlocking, there are many works that employ both processes. In the opening measures (mm. 1–3) of Lutoslawski's first *Étude* for piano, segments of three different interval cycles are presented simultaneously. In a sequence of perfect fourths and fifths, the right hand (mm. 1–2) unfolds a seven-note segment of the interval-7/5 cycle [Ab–Eb–Bb–F–C–G–D] while the left hand (mm. 2–3) unfolds a five-note segment of the interval-1/11 cycle [C–Db–D–Eb–E], and a four-note segment of the interval-2/10 cycle [C–Bb–Ab–Gb] (Figures 2.4a and 2.4b).

(a) mm. 1-3

(b) mm. 5-6

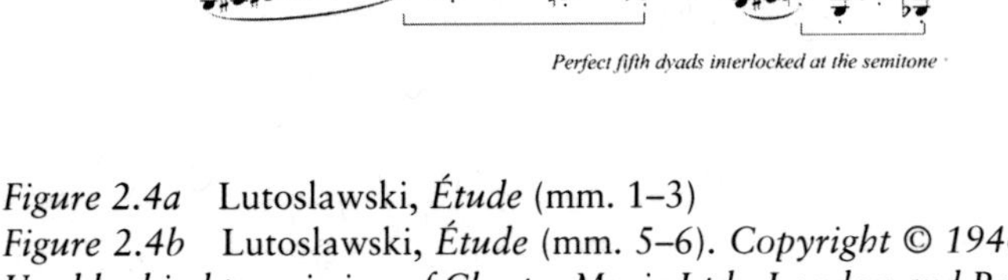

Figure 2.4a Lutoslawski, *Étude* (mm. 1–3)
Figure 2.4b Lutoslawski, *Étude* (mm. 5–6). *Copyright © 1946 by PWM Edition. Used by kind permission of Chester Music Ltd., London and Polskie Wydawnictwo Muzyczne S.A., Kraków.*

The chromatic cyclic segment is presented in terms of both semitones and whole tones. The first group of four sixteenth notes of the left hand [C–Db–Eb–E] of interval ratio 1:2:1 is chromatically filled in by the second group of sixteenth notes [D–E–Eb–Db] of the opposite interval ratio 2:1:2 to generate a completely chromatic segment. The presence of whole tones seems to imply that the chromatic scale is being presented in terms of its two component whole-tone cycles. This is partially verified by the unfolding of the whole-tone segment mentioned previously. The three interval cycles generated by the single interval-2/10 cycle of the Riegger piece are simultaneously presented as separate entities in this piece.

The final left-hand segment [Db–C–Bb–Ab–Gb] that links the second and third measures is the most revealing in terms of the chromatic and whole-tone cycles because it consists of a central whole-tone segment [C–Bb–Ab] that is circumscribed by a semitone [C–Db] on one end and a whole-tone [Ab–Gb] on the other. This segment can be seen as the superimposition of the whole-tone tetrachord previously mentioned [C–Bb–Ab–Gb], and a diatonic tetrachord [Ab–Bb–C–Db]. It is the latter kind of tetrachord that is projected into both left- and right-hand parts of the ensuing measures.

In these measures (mm. 3–4), the diatonic tetrachords of both upper and lower parts are arranged in pairs in which the second tetrachord of each pair is joined to the first by semitone. In the upper part, for example, the perfect fourths (or fifths) that encompasses the tetrachords [G–F#–E–D/Db–C–Bb–Ab] create two perfect fourth dyads interlocked at the semitone [D–G/Ab–Db]. This process is mirrored in the lower part [Db–Gb/G–C]. The interlocking of perfect fourth (fifth) dyads at the semitone becomes the basis of the accompaniment figure at the end (m. 6) of the first phrase (Figure 2.4b).

The perfect fifth cycle is also used to link the pitch content of individual measures. In the upper part (mm. 2–5), the last note of each measure and the first two notes of the next outline three-note segments of the perfect fifth cycle [F–C–G, Bb–F–C, and Eb–Bb–F]. Together, these outline a five-note segment of the perfect fifth cycle [Eb–Bb–F–C–G]. In the left-hand part of the same measures (mm. 3–5), the tetrachordal pairs follow a perfect fifth cyclic order [Db–F#–B]. The cyclic pitch relations generated in the opening phrase (mm. 1–6) are repeated at a different transpositional level in the second statement (mm. 7–11) of the opening phrase.

In the development section that follows, the perfect fifth cycle itself emerges as the primary pitch collection. The upper part (mm. 11–12), which consists of a series of fifths and fourths similar to that of the opening, unfolds three-note segments of the perfect fifth cycle interlocked at the semitone [D#–A#–E#/D–A–E and C#–G#–D#/C–G–D]. Together with the final perfect fifth dyad [B–F#], which is itself interlocked at the semitone, the upper part unfolds the interval-7/5 cycle [C–G–D–A–E–B–F#–C#–G#–D#–A#–E#]. This time (m. 12) it is not accompanied by a segment of the chromatic cycle but by pairs of perfect fifth and perfect fourth dyads in which the perfect fifths contract by semitone to become perfect fourths

[B–F# /C–F, and A–E /Bb–Eb]. As pairs, the perfect fifth dyads outline a four-note cyclic segment [A–E–B–F#] while the perfect fourth dyads unfold another four-note cyclic segment [Eb–Bb–F–C]. Together, they generate a gapped segment of the perfect fifth cycle [Eb–Bb–F–C–( )–( )–A–E–B–F#]. The notes required to fill in the gap [G–D] and complete the cycle [C#–G#] are supplied by the G pedal point (m. 12) and the chord tones on the down-beat of the subsequent measure.[21]

In the central portion of the development section (mm. 20 ff.), the whole-tone partitioning of the chromatic cycle first alluded to in the opening mea-sures is realized in a more complete and systematic manner. The ascending sixteenth-note groups of the accompaniment each outline four-note seg-ments of the two respective whole-tone (interval-2) cycles [Db–Eb–F–G and C–D–E–F#].Their semitonal sequencing is a clear demonstration of the whole-tone partitioning of the relevant interval-1 cyclic segment [C–Db–D–Eb–E–F–F#–( )].[22] The partitioning and interlocking of interval cycles at different intervallic distances is one of the compositional processes that gives rise to two phenomena common to the vast bulk of 20th century music, that is, diatonic extension and chromatic compression.

DIATONIC EXTENSION AND CHROMATIC COMPRESSION

The interval-1/11 cycle represents the *chromatic* aspect of music because it is made up exclusively of semitones while the interval-5/7 (perfect fourth) cycle, or its mirror, interval-7/5 (perfect fifth) cycle, represents the *dia-tonic* aspect of music. Both the fourth and fifth have, at different times, come to represent western man's ideal of consonance. The perfect fourth is the interval upon which the whole Greek system of tetrachords rests. It remained *nostra mollis diaphonia* "our sweet diaphony" to the 12th cen-tury, when it was supplanted by the perfect fifth.[23] The perfect fifth was not only proven to be *the* perfect consonance because of its position in the overtone series, but also played a pivotal role as circumscriber of diatonic triadic harmony. It is no coincidence that the most "dissonant" (semitone) and the most "consonant" (perfect fifth) interval cycles are but differently ordered manifestations of the same content.

Interval-1/11 cycle   C–C#–D–D#–E–F–F#–G–G#–A–A#–B
Interval-7/5 cycle   C–G–D–A–E–B–F#–C#–G#–D#–A#–E#

The two cycles merely represent the same pitch content in two different states or forms, the chromatic and the diatonic. Since the pitch content of these two extremes is identical, then there has to be a process by which one can be transformed into the other.

To describe this kind of transformation within his own music, Béla Bar-tók coined the terms *diatonic expansion* and its counterpart *chromatic compression.* What these terms denote is that the component intervals of all musical structures within a texture are either large or small and that they can be transformed through either expansion or compression. This principle can be diagrammatically represented in the following manner:

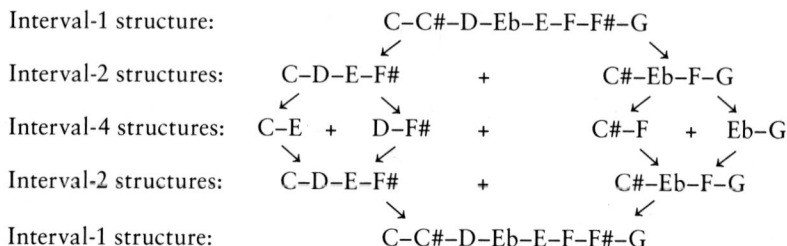

Interval-1 structure:		C–C#–D–Eb–E–F–F#–G	
Interval-2 structures:	C–D–E–F#	+	C#–Eb–F–G
Interval-4 structures:	C–E + D–F#	+	C#–F + Eb–G
Interval-2 structures:	C–D–E–F#	+	C#–Eb–F–G
Interval-1 structure:		C–C#–D–Eb–E–F–F#–G	

The repeated partitioning of the chromatic segment into structures with increasingly larger interval ratios followed by the consequent interlocking of the resulting partitions can be made to represent five chronological stages in a musical composition. Each successive stage would sound entirely different from the preceding one because of the expanding and contracting intervallic makeup of the component structures and, as already pointed out, without a single change to the pitch content. This process does not apply solely to interval cycles but can also be extended to include a host of scalar pitch collections.

THE CYCLIC SIGNIFICANCE OF NONCYCLIC PITCH COLLECTIONS

The common practice conception of the "white key" collection, C–D–E–F–G–A–B–C, is a tonal one, exploited not for its symmetrical properties, but rather for its functional ones. Within the realm of the traditional tonal system, the scale is seen as a fixed succession of tones from which one derives functional triadic harmonies. The 20th century conception of the same white key scale is entirely different because it is the *pitch content of the scale that is of primary importance*, whereas the ordering of the pitch content depends entirely on the musical aims of the individual composer.

With this in mind, we can view the complete pitch content of our white key collection from a cyclic perspective. From this position, one can see how it is possible to generate noncyclic pitch sets using interval cycles. We can generate the pitch content of the white key collection [C–D–E–F–G–A–B] using the interval-7/5 cycle to obtain the same pitch content either in cyclical order [F–C–G–D–A–E–B] or in modal diatonic order. If we extend the 7/5 cyclic segment by another perfect fifth [F–C–G–D–A–E–B–F#], we generate two superimposed modes in scalar order.

F–G–A–B–C–D–E (F Lydian)

F–G–A–B–C–D–E–F#

G–A–B–C–D–E–F# (G Ionian)

As can be seen, the first of these is the white key diatonic collection in Lydian mode. If desired, this mode can be rotated six more times so as to obtain the complete set of diatonic modes on the white keys. This cyclically generated combination is but one of the many types of simultaneous modal combinations found in bimodal and polymodal music of the 20th century. Together with the primary regard for pitch content rather than scalar order, the cyclic-interval reordering of noncyclic scalar sets changes the identity of all diatonic, pentatonic, and some non-diatonic and hybrid modes. These scalar collections and the interval cycles are mere substructures of a much larger unordered twelve-tone system where the chromatic continuum is the referent. In this music, composers view diatonic, non-diatonic, hybrid modes, simple and compound interval cycle sets as different interpretations of one another.

SYNTHESIS

The cyclic pitch relations generated in the pieces discussed thus far have been based on either a single or a small number of interval cycles. Such works are relatively common in the 20th century musical repertoire. However, works that systematically and purposefully use all the interval cycles are most rare.

Psalm XXIV "The Earth is the Lord's" by Charles Ives is based on just such a principle. In addition to the systematic layout of the cycles, Ives unfolds them in strict inversion which has the effect of creating a new set of pitch relations that generate not only interval cycles but also compound cyclic collections as well as complete pentatonic and diatonic ones.[24] The inversional unfolding of the cycles begins on the first unison chord of the hymn. The soprano and bass collectively unfold the complete interval-1 cycle (m. 3) in contrary motion, creating a literal expansion. The expansion is buttressed by the simultaneous generation of an interval-3/9 cycle (C–D#–F#–A–C and its inversion C–A–Gb–Eb–C) on the downbeats of these same measures (Figure 2.5). This cycle is completed (m. 6) at the first fermata.

The initial harmonic progression (mm. 1–2) also contributes to the expansion process. The harmonies outline an expansion from the interval-0 chord [C], to an interval-1 [B–C–C#] chord followed by interval-2 [Bb–C–D] and interval-3 [A–C–D#] chords. The F (m. 2) and the G of the perfect fifth chord at the fermata (m. 6) seem not to be part of this systematic expansion process. Nevertheless, their symmetrical placement around C seems to indicate that further cyclic expansion will occur. This ultimate diatonic expansion is later confirmed by the unfolding of the interval-7/5 cycle as the climax of the work.

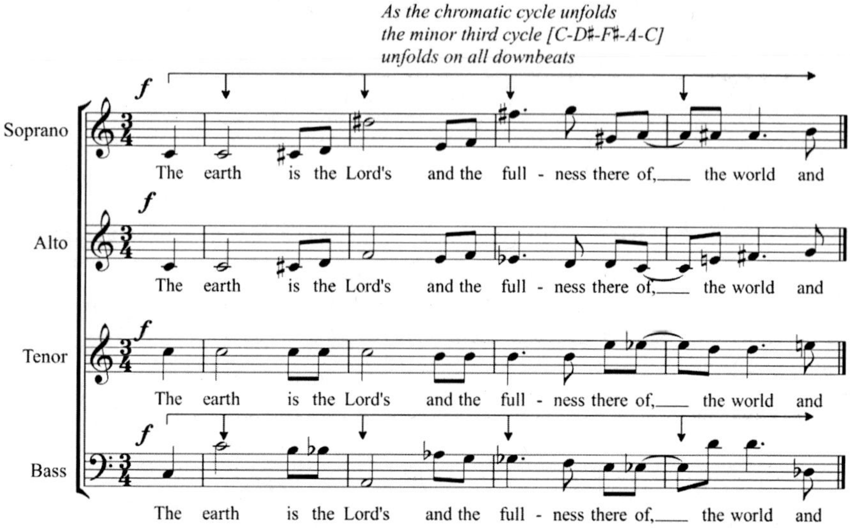

Figure 2.5 Ives, *Psalm XXIV* (mm. 1–4). Psalm XXIV by Charles Ives. Copyright © 1955 by Mercury Music Corp.International copyright secured. All rights reserved. Used with permission of Theodore Presser Company

The continued expansion is confirmed by the two phrases (mm. 6–11) that complete the first stanza. The two outer voices resume their outward contrary motion. This time however, they proceed by whole-step and complete (m. 8) an interval-2 cycle [C–D–E–F#–G#–A#–C]. The notes on the downbeats (mm. 7–10) now outline a complete interval-4/8 cycle [D–F#–A#–D], while the cadential chord at the end of the stanza (m. 11), contains five of the six notes of the interval-2 cycle [C–D–E–F#–G#]. At the beginning of the second stanza (mm. 12–14) there appears to be an interruption in the systematic unfolding of the expanding cycles. Both soprano and bass continue to move in contrary motion, but this time by whole and half steps generating the first of two compound interval cycles, namely, the octatonic cycle.[25] The unfolding of the octatonic (interval ratio 2:1) and a new interval ratio 4:3 lead to the resumption of the simple cycle generation in the third stanza, where two interval-5 segments are unfolded in the soprano measures of the third stanza. Here, the soprano unfolds a five-note segment of the interval-5/7 cycle [C–F–Bb–Eb–Ab], while the bass generates a second segment of the same cycle [C–G–D–A]. These two segments form the exclusive pitch content of the cadential chord (m. 24) at the end of the phrase (Figure 2.6). The missing notes are unfolded cyclically in the subsequent phrase, completing the interval-5/7 cycle.

Direct relationships between interval cycle and diatonic mode become evident in this passage. The aforementioned cadential chord [A–D–G–C–F–Bb–Eb–Ab] can be reordered into two complete Ionian modes [Bb–C–D–Eb–F–G–A–Bb and Eb–F–G–Ab–Bb–C–D–Eb]. Though Ives does not

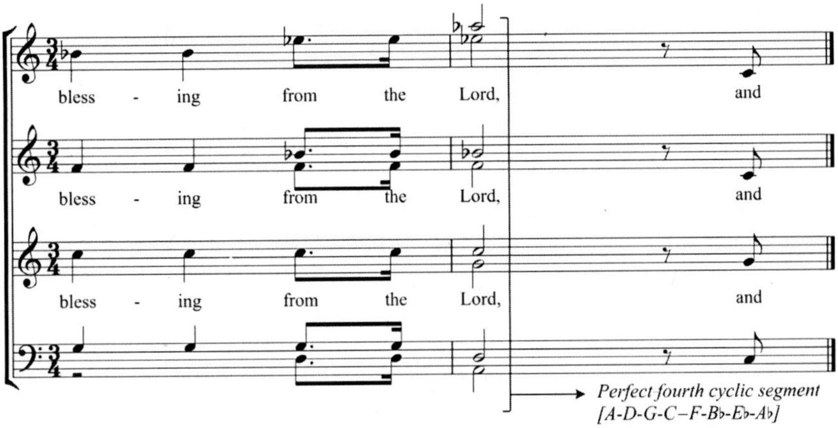

Figure 2.6 Ives, *Psalm XXIV* (mm. 23–24). Psalm XXIV by Charles Ives. Copyright © 1955 by Mercury Music Corp. International copyright secured. All rights reserved. Used with permission of Theodore Presser Company

develop these relationships, the process of generating diatonic formations from interval cycles plays an important part in the music of many 20th century composers.[26] Six interval-6/6 cyclic partitions are systematically generated in the third phrase (mm. 28–30) of the stanza. Using continuous octave displacement, the soprano generates C–F#, B–F, Bb–E, and A–D# in a chromatic descent, while the bass ascends chromatically, generating C–Gb, C#–G, and D–Ab.[27] The open fifths of the fourth stanza signal the climax of cyclic expansion. The cyclic unfolding of the interval-7/5 cycle occurs again in the outer voices. The soprano (mm. 34–41) unfolds the cyclic segment C–G–D–A–E–B–F#–C#–G#–D#. The bass completes the cycle (mm. 34–35) by unfolding the segment C–F–Bb. The pitch content of the cadential chord (m. 41) is exclusively cyclic [Bb–F–C–G–D–A]. This five-note symmetry (Bb–F–G–G–D) may be rearranged to obtain the complete pentatonic collection Bb–C–D–F–G. This phenomenon occurs again later in the stanza (m. 43). Though the melody does not confirm the formation of the pentatonic scale, the harmonic pitch content is pentatonic. The relationships between interval cycles and other scalar formations, in this case the pentatonic, are manifest for the second time. The final stanza (mm. 45–57) is dedicated to a rapid contraction of the cycles. This contraction compresses the cycles back to their "chromatic" state.

This piece combines all the materials and concepts described in this chapter. It unfolds all the interval cycles according to the principles of diatonic expansion and chromatic compression. The interval cycles of the piece generate compound cyclic collections as well as complete pentatonic and diatonic ones. The unfolding of the cycles in strict inversion creates axes of symmetry.

INTERVALLIC SUMS AND DIFFERENCES

If we think of any simple musical structure such as a seventh chord in terms of numbers, it is plain to see that it can be described in terms of sums and differences. All the component intervals generates the complete structure while the differences between the component intervals generate the specific characteristics of the structure. A minor seventh chord, for example, is the sum of three intervals of a third. The difference between the three thirds is that one is made up of four semitones while the other two consists of only three semitones. One may look at the same seventh chord in terms of interval cycles. In a cyclic musical texture, the minor seventh chord could easily be the result of interlocking of a two-note segment of the perfect fifth cycle at the intervallic difference of a minor third. In the cyclic realm, the change of intervallic sums and differences is not only responsible for the creation of different individual cycles but also for the resulting changes in pitch relations between the different cycles. All this translates directly into changes of textural sonorities.

Having examined the structure of interval cycles and having explored the most significant cyclic interrelationships, it is possible to examine how the cycles can combine to generate different compound cyclic collections that generate new pitch relationships. The aforementioned seventh chord is a fine example of how interval cycles can be used to generate such a familiar structure.

3   Compound Cyclic Collections

Music: Frederick Chopin *Sonata in Bb minor* Op. 49
       Franz Liszt *Les jeux d'eaux à la villa d'Este*
       Maurice Ravel *Jeux D'eau*
       Charles Ives *Psalm XXIV*
       Ferrucio Busoni *Sonatina Seconda*
       Alberto Ginastera *Sonata* No. 1
       Robert Muczynski *Toccata* Op. 15
       Toru Takemitsu *Rain Tree Sketch*

If the smaller of the two intervals of an interval class that generate an interval cycle were to be partitioned into two or more unequal proportions, a new composite sequence would be generated within the cycle. This composite sequence is known as a *compound cyclic collection*. Compound cyclic collections consist of repeating intervallic orders. Each order consists of a fixed sequence of two or more intervals. The intervals within an order cannot all be equal because if they were, a new simple interval cycle would be generated. Each compound-interval cycle is identified by the fixed interval ratio of its orders. The interval ratio is calculated in semitones so that the complete compound cyclic collection C–C#–F#–G–C–C#, for example, is represented by an interval ratio of 1:5 [C–C# = 1 semitone and C#–F# = 5 semitones]. For the sake of analytical symbols, the compound cyclic collection is abbreviated to c.c. (compound collection). This acronym is followed by the numerals that represent the interval ratio of an interval order. The labeling of the compound-interval cycles is best expressed by the interval ratio because identifying them in terms of interval classes would require four different numbers, double those used to identify the interval cycles (Table 3.1)

The interval ratio of a compound cyclic collection describes a number of its facets. While the interval ratio numerals describe the size and sequence of the intervals involved, their sum represents the larger interval outlined by a complete interval order. This is called the *order interval*. For example, a complete order that consists of interval-5 (perfect fourth) followed by interval-1 (semitone) will add up to a tritone. The orders outline the simple interval cycle that is being partitioned, here, the interval-6 or tritone cycle. Thus, every note pair will describe a tritone irrespective of which note one starts to measure this interval, whether it be 5 +1 = 6 or 1+5 = 6.

Table 3.1 Compound Cyclic Collections

3/9	3/9	4/8	4/8	5/7	5/7	5/7	5/7	5/7	5/7	6/6	6/6	6/6	6/6	7/5	7/5	7/5	7/5	7/5	7/5	8/4	8/4	8/4	8/4	8/4	8/4
C	C	C	C	C	C	C	C	C	C	C	C	C	C	C	C	C	C	C	C	C	C	C	C	C	C
Bb	B	A	B	C#	D	Eb	E	F	F#	B	Bb	A	Ab	F#	G	G#	A	Bb	B	B	Bb	A	G	F#	F
A	A	Ab	Ab	G	G	G	G	G	G	F#	F#	F#	F#	F	F	F	F	F	F	E	E	E	E	E	E
G	Ab	F	G	G#	A	Bb	B	C	C#	F	E	Eb	D	B	C	C#	D	Eb	E	Eb	D	Db	B	Bb	A
F#	F#	E	E	D	D	D	D	D	D	C	C	C	C	Bb	Bb	Bb	Bb	Bb	Bb	Ab	Ab	Ab	Ab	Ab	Ab
E	F	C#	Eb	Eb	E	F	F#	G	G#					E	F	F#	G	G#	A	G	F#	F	Eb	D	C#
Eb	Eb	C	C	A	A	A	A	A	A					Eb	Eb	Eb	Eb	Eb	Eb	C	C	C	C	C	C
C#	D			Bb	B	C	C#	D	Eb					A	Bb	B	C	C#	D						
C	C			E	E	E	E	E	E					Ab	Ab	Ab	Ab	Ab	Ab						
				F	F#	G	G#	A	Bb					D	Eb	E	F	F#	G						
				B	B	B	B	B	B					Db	Db	Db	Db	Db	Db						
				C	C#	D	Eb	E	F					G	Ab	A	Bb	B	C						
				C	C	C	C	C	C					C	C	C	C	C	C						
Interval Class 3/9		Interval Class 4/8		Interval Class 5/7						Interval Class 6/6				Interval Class 7/5						Interval Class 8/4					

Table 3.1 (continued)

Interval Class 11/1

10:1	9:2	8:3	7:4	6:5	5:6	4:7	3:8	2:9	1:10
C	C	C	C	C	C	C	C	C	C
B	Bb	A	Ab	G	F#	F	E	Eb	D
Db	Db	Db	Db	Db	Db	Db	Db	Db	Db
C	B	Bb	A	Ab	G	F#	F	E	Eb
D	D	D	D	D	D	D	D	D	D
Db	C	B	Bb	A	Ab	G	F#	F	E
Eb	Eb	Eb	Eb	Eb	Eb	Eb	Eb	Eb	Eb
D	Db	C	B	Bb	A	Ab	G	F#	F
E	E	E	E	E	E	E	E	E	E
Eb	D	Db	C	B	Bb	A	Ab	G	F#
F	F	F	F	F	F	F	F	F	F
E	Eb	D	Db	C	B	Bb	A	Ab	G
F#	F#	F#	F#	F#	F#	F#	F#	F#	F#
F	E	Eb	D	Db	C	B	Bb	A	Ab
G	G	G	G	G	G	G	G	G	G
F#	F	E	Eb	D	Db	C	B	Bb	A
Ab	Ab	Ab	Ab	Ab	Ab	Ab	Ab	Ab	Ab
G	F#	F	E	Eb	D	Db	C	B	Bb
A	A	A	A	A	A	A	A	A	A
Ab	G	F#	F	E	Eb	D	Db	C	B
Bb	Bb	Bb	Bb	Bb	Bb	Bb	Bb	Bb	Bb
A	Ab	G	F#	F	E	Eb	D	Db	C
B	B	B	B	B	B	B	B	B	B
Bb	A	Ab	G	F#	F	E	Eb	D	Db
C	C	C	C	C	C	C	C	C	C

Interval Class 10/2

9:1	8:2	7:3	6:4	4:6	3:7	2:8	1:9
C	C	C	C	C	C	C	C
B	Bb	A	Ab	F#	F	E	Eb
D	D	D	D	D	D	D	D
Db	C	B	Bb	Ab	G	F#	F
E	E	E	E	E	E	E	E
Eb	D	Db	C	Bb	A	Ab	G
F#	F#	F#	F#	F#	F#	F#	F#
F	E	Eb	D	C	B	Bb	A
Ab	Ab	Ab	Ab	Ab	Ab	Ab	Ab
G	F#	F	E	D	Db	C	B
Bb	Bb	Bb	Bb	Bb	Bb	Bb	Bb
A	Ab	G	F#	E	Eb	D	Db
C	C	C	C	C	C	C	C

Interval Class 9/3

8:1	7:2	6:3	5:4	4:5	3:6	2:7	1:8
C	C	C	C	C	C	C	C
B	Bb	A	Ab	G	F#	F	E
Eb	Eb	Eb	Eb	Eb	Eb	Eb	Eb
D	Db	C	B	Bb	A	Ab	G
F#	F#	F#	F#	F#	F#	F#	F#
F	E	Eb	D	Db	C	B	Bb
A	A	A	A	A	A	A	A
Ab	G	F#	F	E	Eb	D	Db
C	C	C	C	C	C	C	C

Table 3.1   (continued)

C	C	C	C	C	C	C	C	C	C
C#	D	Eb	E	F	G	Ab	A	Bb	B
C	C	C	C	C	C	C	C	C	C
1:11	2:10	3:9	4:8	5:7	7:5	8:4	9:3	10:2	11:1

Interval Class 12/0

INTERVAL CYCLES AND THEIR SYSTEMATIC COMBINATIONS

The simplest way to view a compound cyclic collection to see it as the interlocking of two equal interval cycle segments at different intervallic sums or differences (this is clearly visible in Table 3.1, where one cycle is represented in bold script, while the second of the pair is in normal script). The 5:1 compound cyclic segment C–F–F#–B can be seen as the interlocking of the tritones (interval-6) C–F# and F–B, at the perfect fourth (interval-5), indicated by the first of the two interval ratio numerals. It may also be seen as the joining of the two perfect fourths C–F and F#–B at the semitone (interval-1). If we used the second of the aforementioned ratios, that is, 1:5, we would still have the interlocking of two interval-6 cyclic segments, except that this time it would be interlocked at the semitone and would therefore yield the cyclic segment C–C#–F#–G. The tritone can also be subdivided using interval ratios 2:4 and 4:2. This shows that there are multiple ways of subdividing the order intervals.

The number of compound cyclic collections that can be obtained from a single order interval depends entirely on the number of unequal interval ratio permutations allowed by that interval. The tritone, for example, can be partitioned into four unequal interval ratio permutations (1:5, 2:4, 4:2, and 5:1) allowing for the generation of four compound cycles. The perfect fifth, on the other hand, allows the generation of six cyclic collections because it can be partitioned into six different, unequal interval permutations (1:6, 2:5, 3:4, 4:3, 5:2, and 6:1). The larger the order interval, the greater the number of obtainable compound cyclic collections.

Like the simple cycles, compound cyclic collections can be classified according to different criteria. In terms of pitch content, compound interval cycles fall into two categories: those that contain all twelve tones and those that do not. Any compound interval cycles that interlock perfect fourths (interval-5) or perfect fifths (interval-7), for example, will contain all twelve tones because both the interval-5/7 and interval-7/5 cycles also contain all twelve tones.

While all but the interval-5/7 and interval-7/5 cycles subdivide one octave symmetrically, the space that different compound cyclic collections subdivide varies greatly. The range of a compound cyclic collection depends on two factors: the size of the interval that is being partitioned and the interval ratio into which it is compounded. Like the interval cycles, there are compound cyclic collections that are completed by the repetition of the two initial pitch classes[1] at the interval of an octave and those that have to cycle past that octave interval to end with the same two pitch classes of the first order to attain completion. Strictly speaking, all compound cyclic collections must cycle past the octave because the octave is defined by the repetition of single pitch classes at an exact distance.

In c.c. 2:1 or octatonic-0 cycle [C–D–Eb–F–F#–G#–A–B–C–D], for example, the C–D pairs at the beginning and end of the collection are an octave apart whereas the 1:8 cycle [C–C#–A–Bb–F#–G–Eb–E–C–C#] must cycle past three octaves in order to attain completion. Unlike the interval cycles, compound cyclic collections cannot symmetrically subdivide the musical space in which they exist because they are made up of unequal composites.

COMPLEMENTATION AND INVERSION

Like the interval cycles, each compound cyclic collection has its complement. In the octatonic cycle, for example, the order interval of the minor third can be subdivided in two different ratios, 1: 2 or 2:1. The complementary interval of the minor third, the major sixth (interval-9), will yield four pairs of complementary cycles (1:8/8:1, 2:7/7:2, 3:6/6:3, and 4:5/5:4)

While inversionally complementary, compound cyclic collections are obtained in the same manner as inversionally complementary interval cycles, the results of the inversional complementation of compound cycles are somewhat different in that the pitch content will change. Any simple interval cycle, like the interval-2/10 cycle, will remain identical in terms of pitch content.

Whole-tone 0	C—D—E—F#—Ab—Bb—C—D—E—F#—Ab—Bb—C
Interval ratio:	2 2 2 2 2 2 2 2 2 2 2 2

However, when inverted, any compound cyclic collection, like c.c. 2:1 or octatonic-0 will generate a new compound cycle of the same interval order size but of inverse interval ratio—in this case, the 1:2 ratio cycle also known as octatonic-1.

Octatonic 1: C–C#–D#–E–F#–G–A–Bb–C–D–Eb–F–F#–G#–A–B–C Octatonic 0
Interval ratio: 1 2 1 2 1 2 1 2 2 1 2 1 2 1 2 1

This phenomenon will hold true for any compound-interval cycle that does not contain all twelve tones. If a compound-interval cycle contains all twelve tones, then the mirrored cycle will replicate them, making the pitch content of the two inversionally related cycles identical. Just as is the case with the interval cycles, the pitch content of many compound cyclic collections can be rearranged in scalar order to generate entire pentatonic and diatonic collections. In certain cases, the rearrangement of the pitch content is not even necessary. The first five pitches of c.c. 2:3 [C–D–F–G–Bb], for example, constitutes a complete pentatonic rotation in scalar order. It can be rotated to yield its more easily recognizable [F–G–Bb–C–D] form. The first nine pitches of the same 2:3 cycle [C–D–F–G–Bb–C–Eb–F–Ab] can be rearranged in scalar order [C–D–Eb–F–G–Ab–Bb–C], unfolding the complete C Aeolian mode. While this may seem surprising, it must be remembered that c.c. 2:3 is the interlocking of two interval-5/7 cycles, each of which can be used to generate complete diatonic collections. The pitch content yielded by a compound cyclic collection, however, is determined not only by the kind of interval cycles that are being interlocked, but also the intervallic distance at which they are interlocked. While c.c. 2:3 will, for example, yield a diatonic pitch content, c.c. 1:4 will yield a more chromatic pitch content because of the sequential occurrence of semitones dictated by the interval ratio (see Table 3.1). Nevertheless, the possibilities for generating pentatonic and diatonic collections are doubled when using compound-interval cycles. While complete pentatonic and diatonic collections can only be generated by simple interval cycles 5/7 and 7/5, those same collections can be generated by the four compound-interval cycles 2:3, 3:2, 3:4, and 4:3.

A HISTORICAL PERSPECTIVE

While it is difficult to know when the first use of compound cyclic collections was made, we know that their usage increased as the functional hierarchy of the traditional tonal system gradually disintegrated and was replaced by the equalization of the twelve tones. There exists, nevertheless, a number of unusual musical examples in which composers of the early romantic era used compound interval cycles within a tonal context. Just as Schubert used the symmetrical qualities of the simple interval-3 cycle to suspend harmonic progression in his *Wanderer Fantasy*,[2] so Frederic Chopin uses the complete octatonic cycle to achieve the same end in the concluding passages to both the exposition and recapitulation of the first movement of his *Sonata in Bb minor* (1839). The octatonic collection used in the exposition [A#–B–C#–D–E–F–G–G#] occurs at the end of a highly chromatic passage (mm. 91–92). It suspends the resolution of a dominant seventh to its tonic, both quarter-note chords, for an entire measure. This suspension of a functional tonal progression is created because the octatonic cycle is a nonfunctional structure that creates a momentary tonal ambiguity. The manner in which the cycle is created is of great interest because it shows that it is the result of traditional musical conventions rather than revolutionary ones. The entire chordal passage, of which this octatonic cycle is the conclusion, is made up of chromatically resolving two-note slurs. By preceding each constituent chord tone of the primary diminished seventh chord [B–D–F–G#] with chromatic lower neighbors [A#–C#–E–G], Chopin generates two diminished seventh chords that are interlocked at the semitone. This combination creates a complete octatonic 2 collection.[3]

The generation of octatonic collections through the interlocking of two interval-3 or minor third cycles at either the semitone or whole-tone became a standard procedure in a large body of 20th century music. Though we do not think of them as such, major and minor triads and seventh chords are, in effect, compound cyclic collections.

Major triad	C–E–G	interval ratio of 4:3
Minor triad	C–Eb–G	interval ratio of 3:4
Major seventh chord	C–E–G–B	interval ratio of 4:3
Minor seventh chord	C–Eb–G–Bb	interval ratio of 3:4

In traditional tonal music these chords cannot be interpreted as cyclic constructions because the underlying referential pitch collection from which they are derived is not a compound interval cycle but a major or minor scale. Furthermore, each chord tone obeys the rules of tonal harmonic function that governs its succession. It is a widely accepted fact, however, that the use of extended tertian constructions such as ninth, eleventh, and thirteenth chords, some of which are cyclic, helped to weaken the tonal system. One of the main reasons was that tertian extension of simple triads or seventh chords creates tonally ambiguous chords. The reason for this is that the chord tones that make up their upper extensions create new chords that may have contrasting functions to the root, third, and fifth of their lower part. For example, a tonic ninth chord in C major [C–E–G–B–D] is the combination of the tonic function I triad [C–E–G] and dominant function V triad [G–B–D]. If this chord is inverted to any position where the root is not clearly audible as the primary function, its resolution can become more a matter of choice rather than sequential functional order. In the early stages of their use, these extended tertian constructions were anchored to a functional bass line and treated as "coloristic" sonorities that still obeyed the rules of traditional harmonic progression.

In the opening measures of Liszt's *Les jeux d'eaux à la villa d'Este* (1883), the bottom half of each arpeggio outlines a fully functional seventh chord or triad, while the top half extends these harmonies to respective coloristic ninth chords. The basic harmonic progression described by the bottom part of the arpeggios (mm. 2–3) is a standard dominant to tonic progression (V7-I) in the key of F# major.[4]

However, the top half of the same arpeggios (C#–E#–G#–B–D# and D#–F#–A#–C#–E#) describes a dominant to submediant (V9–vi9) progression creating a dual authentic/deceptive progression simultaneously. The reasons why the vi9 is heard as a tonic and not as a submediant chord are that it contains all the pitches of the tonic seventh chord (F#–A#–C#–E#), making the D# sound like an added note. Also, the vi9 chord is anchored to a tonic triad outlined by the bottom half of the arpeggio and is therefore heard as an extension of it. The chord itself is nevertheless a blend of both the tonic seventh (F#–A#–C#–E#) and the submediant seventh (D#–F#–A#–C#) chords that gives rise to a cyclic harmonic construction (interval ratio 3:4) that is neither I nor vi. Extended harmonic constructions made up of contrasting chords of similar or varying functions, tend to create functional ambiguity that affected an initial loosening and the eventual breakdown of the strict rules that dictate traditional harmonic progression.

In the late 19th and early 20th centuries, a period of tumultuous musical change, composers grounded in the tonal tradition began to experiment with new forms of tonality that included not only tertian harmonies but also harmonic constructions derived from modes and abstract pitch collections such as the whole-tone and octatonic scales. The result was a hybrid musical language that uses extended tertian harmonies along with cyclically derived ones. In this newly formed tonal context, Roman numeral analysis can only be applied to tertian constructions if and when they follow the rules of tonal function. It cannot, however, account for tertian constructions that do not follow tonal harmonic progression nor can it account for the harmonic constructions derived from cycles. Both interval cycles and compound cyclic collections can generate pitch collections that sound much like traditional tonal ones though they are not.

Since compound cyclic collections arise from the intercalating of simple interval cycles, they too are directly related not only to one another, but also to pentatonic, diatonic, non-diatonic and hybrid scales from which one can derive tertian harmonic constructions.

To determine which compound cycles can generate pentatonic and or diatonic pitch content, one must look at the size of the order interval, that is, the interval of the simple interval cycle that is being subdivided. If that interval is able to cyclically generate a pentatonic or diatonic collection, then any of its compound subdivisions that do not contain either semitones or tritones (interval-1 or interval-6) will do so too. A Bb pentatonic scale [Bb–C–D–F–G], for example, can be reordered in terms of the interval-5/7 cycle [D–G–C–F–Bb]. This interval can only be subdivided into two possible compound interval ratios, 1: 4 and 2:3. The latter of the two will generate the Bb pentatonic pitch content [C–D–F–G–Bb], while the former will generate an entirely different pitch content [C–C#–F–F#–A].

The same principle applies to complete diatonic collections. If, from C, we unfold two compound cyclic collections of two different interval ratios [3:4 and 4:3] we will obtain two different diatonic modes. The 3:4 ratio will yield a diatonic pitch content [C–Eb–G–Bb–D–F–A] that, when cast in scalar order, will generate the C Dorian mode [C–D–Eb–F–G–A–Bb]. The 4:3 ratio yields a different diatonic pitch content [C–E–G–B–D–F#–A] that generates the C Lydian mode [C–D–E–F#–G–A–B].

The musical texture of the initial measures (mm. 1–2) of Maurice Ravel's *Jeux D'eau* consists of simple arpeggios in the upper part and arpeggiated dyads in the lower part. Together, they combine to create extended tertian harmonies (E–G#–B–D#–F# or I 9 and A–C#–E–G# or IV 7) that alternate in a traditional functional progression in the stated key of E major. This progression is interrupted when the initial alternating chords are transposed (m. 3). At the new transpositional level, the IV 7 [A–C#–E–G#] chord is made to alternate with a new sonority that cannot be arranged by thirds [D–F#–B#–E–G#]. However, when rearranged in scalar order [B#–D–E–F#–G#], the chord is revealed to be a five-note segment of the interval-2 or whole-tone cycle. It is evident that while the musical context seems tonal, it encompasses harmonic structures that no longer function according to the rules of functional harmonic progression.[5]

The whole-tone harmony cannot be analyzed using the traditional Roman numeral system. If, however, the initial extended chords are reinterpreted in terms of compound interval cycles, the real compositional process behind this passage can be revealed. When the two initial chords [E–G#–B–D#–F# and A–C#–E–G#] are combined, they generate a seven-note compound cyclic collection [A–C#–E–G#–B–D#–F#] of interval ratio 4:3.[6] This cyclic collection can be rearranged in scalar order [E–F#–G#–A–B–C#–D#–(E)] to outline the complete pitch content of the E major scale. Nevertheless, this pitch content is presented in terms of tertian harmonies that could be seen as derived from a scale but could also be abstracted from a compound interval cycle. It is precisely the sudden appearance of the whole-tone that proves the validity of the cyclic interpretation.

When the whole-tone intrusion occurs for the first time (m. 3) the B–D# third of the compound cycle is compressed to B#–D through chromatic alteration. The same process is applied to the A–C# third (m. 4) to obtain Bb–C. In doing this, Ravel transforms the compound (4:3) cycle into a complete whole-tone cycle. This process, a clear instance of chromatic compression,[7] can be represented as follows:

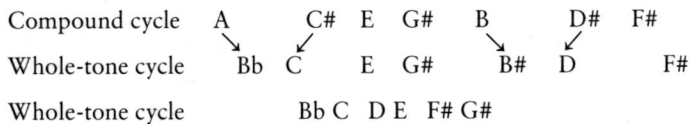

Compound cycle	A		C#	E	G#	B		D#	F#
		↘	↙				↘	↙	
Whole-tone cycle		Bb	C	E	G#		B#	D	F#
Whole-tone cycle			Bb	C	D	E	F#	G#	

In much of the music that is representative of the transition between traditional tonality and the new modern musical language, a traditional harmonic analysis invariably breaks down because it cannot account for structures that operate outside its sphere. An analysis based on the interval cycles and compound cyclic collections tends to be more consistent because it embraces all the pitch relations of the new musical context. The Ravel example is indicative of some of the relational possibilities that exist between the compound cyclic collections themselves and the interval cycles.

PARTITIONING OF COMPOUND CYCLIC COLLECTIONS

Just as two cyclic partitions can be interlocked to generate a compound cyclic collection, so a compound cycle can be partitioned into its single cyclic partitions. In *Psalm XXIV*, already discussed in Chapter 2, Ives not only systematically unfolds expanding single interval cycles but also expanding compound cyclic collections. At the beginning of the second stanza (mm. 12–14) there appears to be an interruption in the systematic unfolding of the expanding interval cycles. Both soprano and bass continue to move in contrary motion, but this time by whole and half steps. The soprano (m. 12) unfolds the segment C–D–D#, while the bass unfolds the segment C–B–A. When combined, these form a five-note octatonic-0 segment [A–B–C–D–D#].[8]

A gapped octatonic-1 segment [A–Bb–C–( )–D#–( )–F#] is generated (mm. 13–14) by the two outer voices. These two octatonic collections are bound by the shared interval-3 cyclic segment, C–D#–F#–A.

$$
\begin{array}{cccccccc}
\text{A} & — & \text{B} & — & \text{C} & — \text{D} — & \text{D\#} & — [\text{F}] — & \text{F\#} \\
\downarrow & & & & \downarrow & & \downarrow & & \downarrow \\
\text{A} & — & \text{Bb} & — & \text{C} — & [\text{C\#}] — & \text{D\#} & — [\text{E}] — & \text{F\#}
\end{array}
$$

While there is no evidence that this "common chord" relationship is exploited or developed in the rest of the work, it demonstrates that such common cyclic segments can be and are used to move from one pitch collection to another in the same way common chords are used to modulate from one key to another.

In the third line of this stanza (mm. 16–21), the two outer voices linearly unfold a series of major and minor thirds: C–E–G–B–D–F#–A–C# in the soprano and C–Ab–F–Db–Bb–Gb–Eb–Cb in the bass. Both sequences have a constant interval ratio of 4:3. Like the octatonic scale, these are also compound cyclic collections. The metric unfolding of these two cycles is significant in cyclic expansion. Every half measure (m. 17f.) partitions the bass cyclic segment [C–Ab–F–Db–Bb–Gb–Eb–Cb] into the two interval-7/5 cycle segments C–F–Bb–Eb and Ab–Db–Gb–Cb (Figure 3.1). These two interval-5 segments are unfolded in the soprano measures of the third stanza. Here, the soprano unfolds a six-note segment of the interval-5/7 cycle [C–F–Bb–Eb–Ab], while the bass generates a second segment of the same cycle [C–G–D–A]. These two segments form the exclusive pitch content of the cadential chord (m. 24). The missing notes are unfolded cyclically in the subsequent phrase, completing the interval-5/7 cycle.

The last portion of the example demonstrates how compound cyclic collections can be partitioned to obtain two interval cycles. This is the converse of the interlocking process. The abstraction of interval cycles from compound cyclic collections is an important compositional technique as it allows composers to either "modulate" from one kind of cycle to another or to bind together two or more compound cyclic collections that share the relevant interval cycle or cyclic segment.

Figure 3.1 Ives, *Psalm XXIV* (mm. 16–19). Psalm XXIV by Charles Ives. Copyright © 1955 by Mercury Music Corp. International copyright secured. All rights reserved. Used with permission of Theodore Presser Company

THE CYCLIC "COMMON CHORD"

Though not developed systematically in the Ives example, the concept of using an interval cycle or cyclic segment as a common pivot chord between different compound cyclic collections is a significant one, for example, the octatonic collection and the interval-3 partitions.

As already stated, a compound cyclic collection can be seen as the interlocking of cyclic segments in various intervallic alignments. This process may be likened to the relative positioning of a mathematical slide rule to obtain different numerical results. The three octatonic collections,[9] for example, can be generated by interlocking paired interval-3/9 cycles. If the interlocking begins with the whole tone, the resulting octatonic cycle will have the interval ratio of 2:1.

C—Eb—F#—A—[C]
$\searrow$ C–D–Eb–F–F#–Ab–A–B–[C] (octatonic-0)
D—F—Ab—B—[D] $\nearrow$

Repeated on C# and D, respectively, the process will generate the octatonic-1 and octatonic-2 collections.

C#—E—G—Bb—[C#]
$\searrow$ C#–Eb–E–F#–G–A–Bb–C–[C#] (octatonic-1)
Eb—F#—A—C—[Eb] $\nearrow$

D—F—Ab—B—[D]
$\searrow$ D–E–F–G–Ab–Bb–B–C#–[D] (octatonic-2)
E—G—Bb—C#—[E] $\nearrow$

When the interval-3/9 cycles are interlocked at the semitone, the octatonic model will be at interval ratio 1:2 for one of the three octatonic collections.

C—Eb—F#—A—[C]
  ⟶ C–C#–Eb–E–F#–G–A–Bb–[C] (octatonic-1)
C#—E—G—Bb—[C#]⟶

From these examples one can see that octatonic-0 and octatonic-1 have an interval-3/9 cycle [C–Eb–F#–A–(C)] in common. Because each octatonic model consists of two interlocked interval-3/9 cycles, each octatonic model will share its component interval-3/9 cycles with two other octatonic collections. The component interval-3/9 cycles can be used to act as common pivots in modulating between octatonic collections or to create simultaneous octatonic combinations.

This concept is applied directly in Toru Takemitsu's piano piece, *Rain Tree Sketch*.[10] In the opening pair of measures, two different octatonic segments unfold in right-hand/left-hand exchanges. A gapped octatonic-0 segment [C–D–( )–F–F#–G#–A] is unfolded linearly by the first chord in the right hand and by the left-hand accompaniment. An octatonic-2 segment [E–F–G–G#–Bb–B–C#] is unfolded linearly by the right-hand part that follows the first chord and by the last two notes of the accompaniment (Figure 3.2).

The two separate octatonic collections are bound together by a common interval-3/9 cycle [D–F–G#–B], each note of the cycle being stressed by accents or held as a longer note value. This interval-3/9 cycle is one of the two component cycles that make up the octatonic-2 collection. The linking of octatonic collections via interval-3 cyclic segments is repeated two more times. In the second repetition, an octatonic-2 segment [G–Ab–Bb–B–C#] is joined to an octatonic-1 segment [C#–Eb–E–G–A–Bb] by an accented cyclic chord [Bb–C#–E–( )]. This cyclic chord represents the second of the two interval-3/9 cycles in the octatonic-2 collection. By using

Figure 3.2 Takemitsu, *Rain Tree Sketch* (mm. 1–6). *Takemitsu*, Rain Tree Sketch. Copyright © 1982 by Schott Music Co. Ltd., Tokyo. All Rights Reserved. Used by permission of European American Music Distributors LLC, sole U.S. and Canadian agent for Schott Music Co. Ltd., Tokyo.

the component interval-3/9 cycles of the octatonic-2 collection, Takemitsu establishes relationships between all three octatonic collections.

To confirm that the texture is composed of separate octatonic collections, the composer isolates them on several occasions. At the first return of Tempo I (m. 14), the entire pitch content of the first half of the measure is octatonic-2 while in the second half, the right hand is in octatonic-0 [Ab–A–B–C–D–( )–F] and the left hand in octatonic-2 [C#–D–E–F–G–Ab]. Although the two different octatonic collections are in different parts, they are nevertheless still bound by the interval-3 cyclic segment, D–F–Ab.[11]

The composer also establishes a connection between the octatonic collection and the whole-tone cycle. At the end of the first phrase (mm. 4, last two notes, to 5), the first four notes of the octatonic-1 segment unfolded by the right hand [Eb–C#–( )–( )–G–A] is also a four-note segment of the whole-tone 1 cycle [C#–Eb–F–G–A–B]. The notes missing to complete the whole-tone cycle [B–F] are supplied by the accompaniment. The B–F tritone also belongs to the octatonic-2 collection that is unfolding in the left hand. It is significant that this dyad is a tritone because it is this interval that is common to the octatonic cyclic collection, the interval-3/9 cycle, and the whole-tone cycle that are all interacting with one another. The reason for this is that all three cyclic collections can be constructed by interlocking tritones at various intervallic differences.

At the minor third, the interlocking tritones [C–F#/Eb–A] generate an interval-3/9 cycle [C–Eb–F#–A], at the major second [C–F#/D–G#/E–A#] the whole-tone cycle [C–D–E–F#–G#–A#] and at the 2:1 ratio [C–F#/D–Ab/Eb–A/F–B] the octatonic collection [C–D–Eb–F–F#–Ab–A–B].

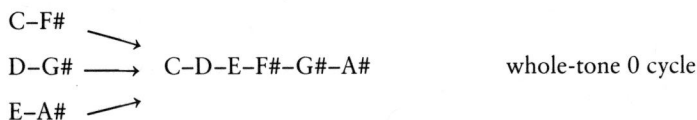

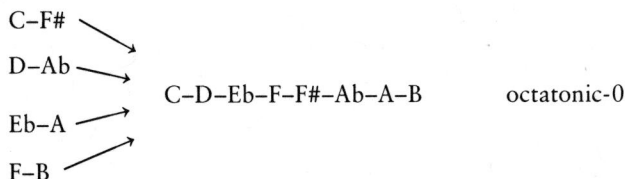

C—F#
          C–Eb–F#–A   interval-3/9 cycle
Eb–A

C–F#
D–G# ⟶ C–D–E–F#–G#–A#   whole-tone 0 cycle
E–A#

C–F#
D–Ab
          C–D–Eb–F–F#–Ab–A–B   octatonic-0
Eb–A
F–B

In Ferrucio Busoni's *Sonatina Seconda* (Figure 3.3), a segment of the 6:5 compound cycle is used as a common pivot between two different octatonic cycles. With the exception of the last pitch, the unmeasured solo theme that

Figure 3.3   Busoni, *Sonatina Seconda* (mm.1–4).

opens the sonatina (m. 1), is based exclusively on the pitch content of the octatonic-2 cycle [D–( )–F–G–Ab–Bb–B–C#–D].

The last note of the theme [C], which is held over as a pedal point, becomes the first note of an ostinato accompaniment that unfolds an arpeggiating six-note segment of the 6:5 compound interval cycle [C–F#–B–F–Bb–E]. The low "A" that punctuates the second arpeggio of these measures extends the 6:5 cycle to [C–F#–B–F–Bb–E–A] but remains isolated form the cyclic arpeggio, leaving it a six-note segment. The only note that seems unaccounted for is the G# that appears at the top of each arpeggio. While this note is common to both the octatonic-2 and the 6:5 cycle, it is not unfolded in cyclic order. In the ensuing measure (m. 4), the continuation of the solo melody is coupled to the unchanging ostinato accompaniment, bringing the two pitch collections together. However, the melody of this measure is based exclusively on the octatonic-1 cycle [C#–D#–E–F#–G–A–Bb–C#] (Figure 3.3). The last note [G] of this measure is projected into a further continuation of the solo melody (m. 5) that now outlines a simple whole-step [G–A] above the still unchanged accompaniment.

While a whole step can belong to various types of pitch collections, we may assume an octatonic-1 significance for the G–A dyad in this case, in view of the preceding two octatonic utterances. In these opening measures, the sudden switches between one octatonic collection and another are rendered seamless because they all occur over the same unchanging accompaniment. Thus, the seemingly effortless changes are due to the shared common chords between each octatonic collection and accompanying 6:5 compound cyclic collection. The common interval class shared by the three compound collections is the tritone. In the 6:5 collection, these unfold by sequential pairings [C–F#/B–F/Bb–E]. In the octatonic-2 collection, they are interlocked at the semitone [E–F–Bb–B] while in the octatonic-1 collection, they are interlocked at the whole-tone [E–F#–Bb–C]. These commonalities are outlined in the diagram below.

Octatonic-2 cycle: D–E̅–F̅–G–Ab–B̅b–B̅–C#
6:5 cyclic segment: C–F#–B–F–Bb–E

Octatonic-1 cycle: C#–D#–E̅–F̅#–G–A–B̅b–C̅

CYCLIC GENERATION OF DIVERSE COMPOUND CYCLIC COLLECTIONS

When two single interval cycles are interlocked at different intervals differences over a period of time, they produce compound cyclic collections of varying interval ratios. Conversely, if the single interval cycles are kept at a fixed intervallic distance, then the resulting compound cyclic collections will have a fixed interval ratio. 20th century composers have used both the fixed and sliding models to achieve different compositional aims.

Robert Muszynski's *Toccata* Op. 15 opens (mm. 1–4) with a melodic *moto perpetuo* based exclusively on alternating perfect fourth (interval-5) dyads. The first and second dyads [F–Bb and B–E] of the first beat are separated by a semitone and generate a compound cyclic segment [B–E–F–Bb] of interval ratio 5:1 (or 1:5). The second pair generates a second segment [A–E–Bb–Eb] of identical interval ratio on the second beat (m. 1). These two compound cyclic segments are interlocked at the semitone in the middle of each of the first three measures to create a new compound cyclic segment of interval ratio 1:4

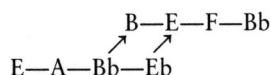

```
        B—E—F—Bb
       ↗   ↗
E—A—Bb—Eb
```

The cyclical representation of this process may be illustrated thus: the odd-numbered dyads outline a three-note segment of the interval-5/7 cycle [F–Bb–Eb], while the even-numbered dyads unfold a second interval-5/7 cyclic segment [B–E–A] that interlocks with the former chromatically.

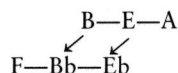

```
     B—E—A
     ↙   ↙
F—Bb—Eb
```

The verification that the process is indeed the interlocking of interval-5 cyclic segments occurs when the newly formed compound cyclic segment

[Bb–B–Eb–E] is not placed between first and second beats, but is encompassed by the second beat alone (m. 3), and is articulated as an entirely independent identity (Figure 3.4).

In the following measure (m. 4), new interval-5 dyads not only extend the simple perfect fourth cycle, but are also interlocked at different intervallic differences, creating new compound cyclic collections. On the downbeat, the two perfect fourths Ab–Db and B–E are interlocked at the minor third to generate a new compound cyclic segment [Ab–B–Db–E] of interval ratio 3:2. The first interval-5/7 cycle is extended to F–Bb–Eb–Ab–Db.

On the second beat, the fourths interlock at the whole tone to generate yet a new compound cyclic segment [Bb–C–Eb–F] that has an interval ratio of 2:3. The perfect fourth has now been compounded in several different ratios, 1:4, 3:2, and 2:3, which confirms the larger system of interlocking of interlocking cycles. These changing intervallic differences interrupt the completion of the second of the two cycles (m. 4), now B–E–A–( )–( )–C–F, as well as the semitonal interlocking of the said cycle-5 segments. The filling in of the missing perfect fourth [D–G] occurs at the sudden change of texture (mm. 5f.) where the single line is replaced by a two-voice texture. In the upper part, the perfect fourth dyads are extended to three-note figures

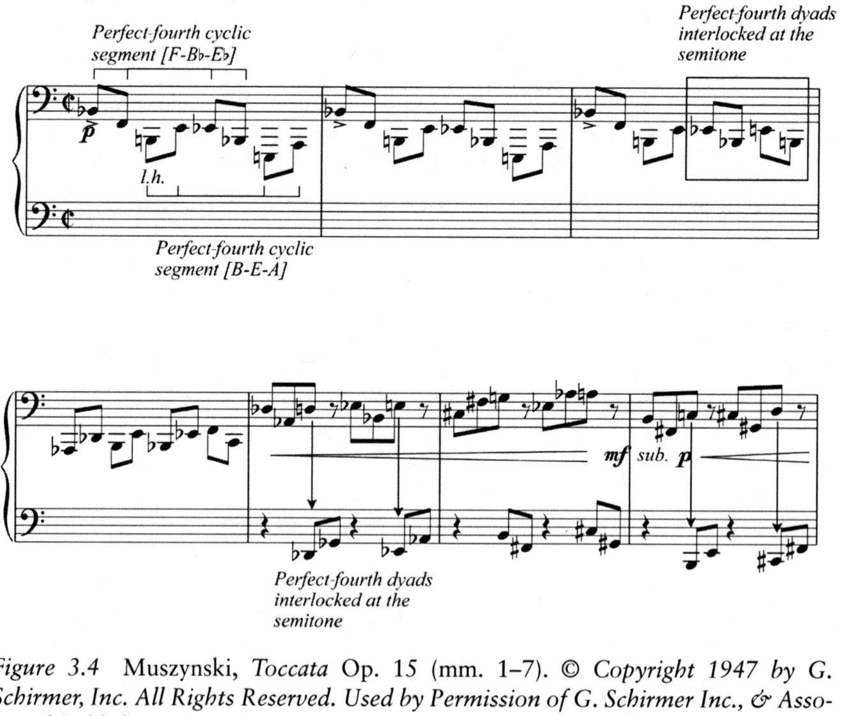

Figure 3.4   Muszynski, *Toccata* Op. 15 (mm. 1–7). © *Copyright 1947 by G. Schirmer, Inc. All Rights Reserved. Used by Permission of G. Schirmer Inc., & Associated Publishers, Inc.*

where the third note of each figure replaces the second of the original alternating perfect fourth dyads. The notes of the missing dyad are unfolded by the three-note figures on the down beats of the new texture (mm. 5–6) and are once again interlocked at the semitone to signal the resumption of the original process (Figure 3.4).

In the course of these measures, the first simple interval-5/7 cycle is extended to F–Bb–Eb–Ab–C#–F# so that the two cycles interlock at the semitone to complete the chromatic continuum.

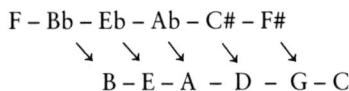

F – Bb – Eb – Ab – C# – F#
    ↘   ↘   ↘   ↘   ↘
     B – E – A – D – G – C

The three-note figures of the upper part signal a return of the original alternating dyads, the second pair of alternating dyads now incomplete. Complete alternating dyads reappear in their original format (mm. 9ff) with the return of the melodic, single-line texture. The derived four-note compound cyclic segments [G–C–C#–F# and E–A–Bb–Eb] interlock to generate the complete octatonic-1 cycle [C#–Eb–E–F#–G–A–Bb–C] as the climax of this passage. This example demonstrates how cyclic segments, combined at various intervallic relations, generate different compound cyclic collections.

CYCLIC TRANSFORMATION

As mentioned earlier, the abstraction of interval cycles from compound cyclic collections can be achieved in different ways. The simplest of these, as was the case in the Ives example, is to partition the compound cycle into its two interlocking simple cycles. When, however, the compound cycle is unfolded in the ordering of its constituent partitions rather than as a complete cycle, any of the intervallic properties of these orderings can be used to abstract different interval cycles to generate new compound cyclic collections.

In the second movement of Alberto Ginastera's first piano sonata, the intervallic proportions of three-note segments of the primary 6:5 compound interval cycle are rotated to "modulate" from one compound cycle to another. The order intervals of the different rotations are used to generate simple interval cycles and modes. These transformations provide a host of musical colors that are fundamental in the articulation of the rondo form of the movement.

The principal theme ritornello of this rondo movement occurs three times. The first and third occurrences are longer than the abbreviated second statement. The referential pitch collection of all three statements is nevertheless c.c. 6:5. All but two of the orders of c.c. 6:5 are presented intermittently in the initial statement of the principal theme (mm. 1–16).[12] The sequence in which these orderings unfold is represented in the diagram below.

C.C. 6:5 C–F#–B–F–Bb–E–A–Eb–Ab–D–G–C#–F#–C–F–B–E–Bb–Eb–A–D–
   G#–Db–G–C
6:5 orders: [F#–B–F][Bb–E–A][Eb–Ab–D][ ][ ][E–Bb–Eb][A–D–G#][Db–G–C]
Sequence: 1   5   6   4   3   2

While the cycle remains incomplete in the second statement of the A theme, one of the missing orders [C–F–B] is unfolded in the third and final statement of the A theme. Since the texture of the movement consists mainly of an unrelenting and unchanging *moto perpetuo*, the unfolding and completion of the 6:5 cycle aids in the individualization and characterization of principal theme statements, separating them from the episodes in terms of referential pitch collections. It also brings unity to the principal theme statements as a set.

The rotations of the original cyclic order of interval ratio 6:5 and the different order intervals they generate also play a fundamental role in the articulation of the formal structure of the movement. The three rotations of the 6:5 cyclic order and their outlining order intervals can be represented as follows:

		Interval Ratio	Order Interval
Original order:	F—B—F#	6:5	interval-11 or -1
First rotation:	B—F#—F	5:1	interval-6 or -6
Second rotation:	F#—F—B	1:6	interval-7 or -5

The 6:5 order [F–B–F#] at the beginning of the principal theme (m. 2). Many times, two consecutive 6:5 orders are presented in cyclic pairs. The order intervals they outline are interval-11 or -1. These order intervals are projected into the ostinato texture of the second episode (mm. 78–116), which now consists of a three-note chromatic segment [Bb–A–B] articulated with various octave displacements.[13]

The 1:5 order rotation [F–F#–B] of the original 6:5 order is introduced shortly after the beginning of the piece (m. 6) but is not developed in any significant way in the movement. It nevertheless represents the first rotational transformation of the original cycle. The order interval of the 5:1 order rotation, that is, the tritone (interval-6), is also not developed as was the case with the 6:5 order interval.

The opposite can be said of the last remaining 1:6 rotation of the original 6:5 order. It is developed both in terms of its order interval and as a new compound cyclic collection. The order interval of the 1:6 rotation of the original order is the perfect fifth (interval-7). It first appears in the middle of the first statement of the principal theme (mm. 17–20) in a texture that disrupts a long sequence of c.c. 6:5 segments and consists exclusively of alternating perfect fifth dyads [Db–Ab and Ab–Eb]. These two dyads generate a three-note segment of the perfect fifth (interval-7/5) cycle [Db–Ab–Eb]. A few measures later (mm. 27–29), the complete perfect fourth (interval-5/7) cycle (complement of the perfect fifth cycle) is unfolded in three-note segments (Figure 3.5). The other ends on a second set of alternating perfect dyads

Figure 3.5 Ginastera, *Piano Sonata* No. 1, Mvt. II (mm. 25–31). *Piano Sonata No. 1, Op. 22 by Alberto Ginastera © Copyright 1954 by Boosey & Hawkes, Inc. Copyright Renewed 1982. Reprinted by Permission.*

[D–A and A–E], highlighting the complementary relationship between the two segments of the perfect fifth cycle.

The first episode commences with the series of chords made up predominantly of perfect fifths and fourths. The pitch content of these chords (mm. 37–39) outlines a five-note segment of the perfect fifth cycle [D–A–E–B–F#]. When expressed linearly, this pitch content unfolds a pentatonic mode [A–B–D–E–F#]. This cyclic/modal transformation is taken one step further in the middle of the episode where cyclic extensions of the five-note segment yields a longer eight-note segment of the perfect fifth cycle [Bb–F–C–G–D–A–E–B–F#]. This new segment can be used to generate a host of diatonic modes. In the climactic *cantando* portion of the episode (mm. 48–55), Ginastera opts to use the Bb–F–C–G–D–A–E segment to generate the D Aeolian mode [D–E–F–G–A–Bb–C] that completes the transformation from cycle to mode.[14]

As a compound cyclic collection, the 1:6 rotation of the original 6:5 order appears at the tail end of the second episode (mm. 105–116) to form part of a bridge passage that links the chromatic material of the second episode to the third and final statement of the principal theme.[15]

The pitch content of a given compound cyclic collection can also be used to move between other compound cyclic collections in much the same way that pivot chords are used to modulate between keys. For instance, where a given set of compound cyclic constructions represent different ratio orderings of the same, exclusively octatonic content, as seen in the diagram below, the pitch content of the complete 2:4 compound cycle [C–D–F#–G#–C] will in this case, be common to both the 5:4 and 2:1 compound cycles.

C.C. 5:4   C—F—A—D—F#—B—Eb—Ab—C
C.C. 2:4   C—D—F#—Ab—C / Eb—F—A—B—Eb
C.C. 2:1   C—D—Eb—F—F#—Ab—A—B—C

The relationships between these cycles can be understood better if we look at how the common cyclic segments are interlocked by the three compound cycles.

If we add the interval ratios of the three cycles (5+4 = 9, 2+4 = 6 and 2+1 =3), we discover that all the results are multiples of three. This means that the minor third (interval-3) cycle is in some way operative in all three compound cyclic collections. Since two minor thirds add up to the tritone, we can deduce that tritones will be generated within each of the three cycles, their formation depending on the required intervallic sequence. In the 2:4 cycle, the first tritone [C–F#] is generated by the first interval order [C–D–F#]. The same tritone in the 2:1 cycle is generated at the completion of the second interval order [C–D–Eb/Eb–F–F#], and in the 5:4 compound cycle, the tritone is formed also at the completion of the second interval order [C–F–A/A–D–F#].

From the analyses presented in this chapter, two fundamental principles emerge. Any compound cyclic collection is the direct result of cyclic-interval interlocking. Strictly speaking, therefore, all textures based on compound cyclic collections can be analyzed in terms of the interval cycles. Nevertheless, the interactions between compound cyclic collections create their own set of pitch relations that generate musical texture different from those generated by the interval cycles.

4 Inversional Symmetry and the Axis Concept

Music: Franz Schubert *Wanderer Fantasy*
Johannes Brahms *Capriccio* Op. 116, No.3
Charles Ives *Psalm XXIV*
Claude Debussy *Prelude "Voiles"*
Anton Webern *Bagatelle for String Quartet* No. 5
Béla Bartók *The Night's Music, Bagatelle* No. 2, *Subject and Reflection*
Krysztof Penderecki *Threnody to the Victims of Hiroshima*

In pitch organization, symmetry is defined by the inversional reflection of a set of intervals, that is, the mapping of the intervals of one half of a given structure into the other half through mirroring. This concept may be mathematically represented by the series of numbers–2,–1, 0, +1, +2, where 0 lies in the center and is said to be the dividing plane or axis of symmetry. We can calculate the axis of this series by adding any two components that lie equidistant from it. This is known as the sum of complementation. For example,–1 + 1 = 0 or–2 + 2 = 0. The axis itself can be represented as the sum of two corresponding components in the symmetry.

In musical constructions, the axis of symmetry is calculated in the exact same manner. Each note of the chromatic scale is assigned numerals from 0 through 12 so that C is 0, C# is 1, D is 2, and so on, and C is 12 (=0). This allows the representation of pitch classes in terms of numerals. In terms of pitches, the axis of symmetry is represented by either a unison [C\C] or a semitone [C\C#]. The reason for this is that all symmetrical musical structures will converge on one of these two intervals. This becomes clear if we calculate the axis of symmetry of different musical constructions.

If we calculate the axis of symmetry of the series C–C#–D–D#–E we see that the axis of symmetry is D/D because in the two equal and opposite sides, C–C#–D and its inversion, E–D#–D converge on this axis. To calculate the axis in terms of the sum, we can use any two points that are equidistant from D—for example, C# and D#, both a semitone away from D, or C and E, both two semitones away from D. If we choose the former set we will get the following equation: 1 + 3 = 4 where C# = 1 and D# = 3. To verify our axial sum we can use the other set of notes. This will yield the following equation 0 + 4 = 4 where C = 0 and E = 4. The final step is to check the interval or sum that represents the axis itself. Where D = 2 its combination with its mirror (D) gives us a D/D axis at sum 4. Thus we can assert that C–C#–D–D#–E is symmetrical around the D/D axis at sum 4.

If we calculate the axis of symmetry of the series C–C#–D–D# we see that the axis of symmetry is C#/D because the two equal and opposite sides C–C# and its inversion D#–D converge on this axis. If we repeat the calculating procedure using equidistant points we obtain the following equations: 0 + 3 = 3 where C = 0 and D# = 3. If we use the axial interval [C#–D], we will get 1 + 2 = 3 where C# = 1 and D = 2. We can now say that the series C–C#–D–D# is symmetrical around the C#/D axis at sum 3.

According to Elliott Antokoletz, "Any symmetrical tetrachord can be analyzed into dyads that have the same sum. These sum dyads will form part of a series of symmetrically related dyads generated by aligning two inversionally complementary semitonal cycles. The axis of symmetry is expressed by the sum of the two pitch class numbers in any dyad."[1] This can be illustrated as follows:

pitch class number	0	1	2	3	4	5	6	7	8	9	10	11	12
	C	C#	D	Eb	E	F	F#	G	Ab	A	Bb	B	C
interval		0	2	4	6	8	10	0	2	4	6	8	10	0

	C	B	Bb	A	Ab	G	F#	F	E	Eb	D	C#	C
pitch class number	12	11	10	9	8	7	6	5	4	3	2	1	0
even sum		0	0	0	0	0	0	0	0	0	0	0	0	0

In this alignment all the intervals have an even sum of 0 and are therefore symmetrical around an axis at sum 0. The two complementary cycles intersect at the two 0/12[2] intervals at C–C and F#–F#. These two points of intersection represent the dual axis of symmetry: they have the same sum (0 + 0 = 6 + 6 = 12 or 0). This means that if two inversionally complementary are projected from any axis, they will intersect at the point of origin and at a second point a tritone away. This phenomenon is made possible by the principle of tritone equivalence that states the tritone remains invariant at its own transposition or in its complementary inversion.

```
                          F#
                      F
                  E
              Eb
          D
      Db
  C
  _____  C/C and F#/F# at sum 0
  C
    B
      Bb
        A
          Ab
            G
              F#
```

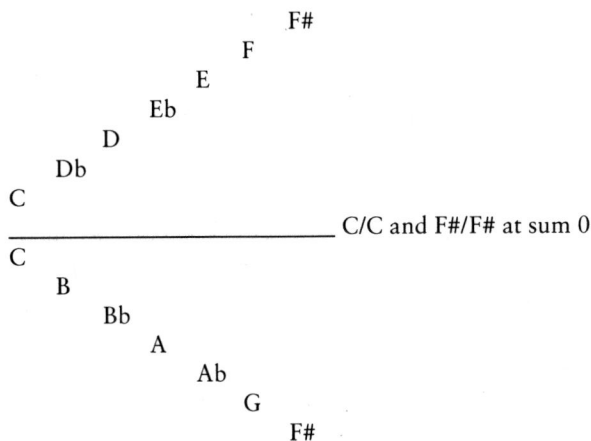

If either cycle is permuted by one semitone relative to the other, the sum will become odd and, as a result, so will the axis of symmetry.

pitch class number	1	2	3	4	5	6	7	8	9	10	11	12	1
	C#	D	Eb	E	F	F#	G	Ab	A	Bb	B	C	C#
interval	1	3	5	7	9	11	1	3	5	7	9	11	1
	C	B	Bb	A	Ab	G	F#	F	E	Eb	D	Db	C
pitch class number	0	11	10	9	8	7	6	5	4	3	2	1	0
odd sum 1	1	1	1	1	1	1	1	1	1	1	1	1	1

In this case, the dual points of intersection are C–C# and F#–G (0 + 1 = 6 + 7 = 1). If either cycle is permuted by an even number of semitones relative to the other, the same collection of interval classes will be generated at a new pitch level.

pitch class number	2	3	4	5	6	7	8	9	10	11	0	1	2
	D	Eb	E	F	F#	G	Ab	A	Bb	B	C	C#	D
interval	2	4	6	8	10	0	2	4	6	8	10	0	2
	C	B	Bb	A	Ab	G	F#	F	E	Eb	D	Db	C
pitch class number	0	11	10	9	8	7	6	5	4	3	2	1	0
even sum 2	2	2	2	2	2	2	2	2	2	2	2	2	2

Antokoletz states further that "through a number of such realignments, a pair of inversionally complementary semitonal cycles that generate even interval numbers will occur at six even sums, and a pair that generates odd interval numbers will occur at six odd sums."[3] The even sums will be 0, 2, 4, 6, 8, 10, 12 (or 0), while the odd sums will be 1, 3, 5, 7, 9, or 11.

SYMMETRIES IN TRADITIONAL TONAL MUSIC

Tonal music gives priority to a single tone, or tonic. In this kind of music all the constituent tones and resulting tonal relationships are heard and identified relative to their tonic. If we accept this definition of tonality, we will realize that the larger portion of the world's folk and art music can be categorized as tonal. Although the principle of tonality applies to a broad range of music, the means by which it is established varies from one culture to another.

The two most widely recognized means of establishing tonality in western music are commonly known as the *modal* and *tonal systems*. The first is based on the church modes and includes monophonic and polyphonic music of the Middle Ages, Renaissance, and early Baroque periods. The characteristics of modal music reflect the character and color of the melodic and harmonic materials derived from the unique structure of the particular modes used in that music.

The second is based on the system of major and minor scales and includes music of the Baroque, Classical, and Romantic eras. Unlike modality, this system is based on a hierarchy of tonal functions ascribed to individual scale degrees. The particular function of each note is determined by its position within the scale. The function of the leading tone, for example, is to resolve to the tonic. As a result of these ascribed functions, the characteristics of music written in the traditional tonal system are determined not only by the character and color of the structures derived from the particular scale being used, but also by the functions that each one must fulfill. It is the component of function that is largely responsible for the difference between modal and tonal music. Although the two systems establish tonality in different ways, both are faithful to the idea of tonic. However, this is not the only important trait they share.

With the exception of the Dorian mode (white keys from D to D), all diatonic modes are asymmetrical structures that subdivide the octave unequally. In the traditional tonal system, based primarily on the Ionian mode (white keys from C to C), the most important derivative harmonic structures are triads built on tertian intervals. Of the triads that can be built on each of the seven modal degrees, all but one are asymmetrical. The only symmetrical one is the diminished triad that is circumscribed by the tritone found within all diatonic modes.

In the modal era, the tritone, the only interval that partitions the octave into two equal halves, was considered to be *diablus in musica* (the devil in music) and avoided at all costs. In the tonal era, the tritone became the cornerstone of tonal function because of its half step proximity to basic elements of the tonic triad: it contains both the leading tone and subdominant scale degree that resolved either inwardly or outwardly to the tonic triad.

The incorporation of symmetrical pitch constructions into the traditional tonal system contributed not only to the dissolution of that system but also to the creation of a new kind musical of language based on symmetrical tonal relationships rather than functional ones. Symmetrical pitch constructions, such as diminished triads and fully diminished seventh chords, have long been used by composers of traditional tonal music to achieve different ends. In Schubert's *Wanderer Fantasy*, for example, the extended diminished seventh chord progressions that exist between functional chords such as the dominant and tonic,[4] create a symmetrical musical space where the "preordained" harmonic sequence is suspended for long periods of time. In these passages there is a building of tonal tension and a frustration of harmonic resolution, both generated by the unrelenting stream of unresolved tritones. Since in the traditional tonal context each chord has a function, a succession of symmetrical chords that have the same function will result in a breakdown of that function.

The use of symmetrical root progressions that suspend or obscure tonal function became ever more pervasive in music of the late romantic period. The chromatic "omnibus" that is found in much of the late romantic repertoire, is a harmonic progression in which the uppermost and lowest voices move chromatically in opposite directions.

This technique, therefore, uses the principle of symmetrical inversion but is still tied to a functional harmonic progression rather than an axis of symmetry. It can nevertheless be seen as a significant forebear of the axial principle when we consider that composers of the late romantic era were using an increasing number of symmetrical musical structures, the omnibus being one of them. In Brahms' Capriccio Op 116, No. 3, the omnibus progression forms the climactic ending of the first formal section.[5] By the end of the 19th and beginning of the 20th centuries, compositions based exclusively on symmetrical relations were realized. These compositions introduced a new kind of musical language that radically altered musical aesthetics and challenged the "common" perception of tonal relationships.

In order to understand how these perceptions were changed, it is important to see how the general principles of symmetry apply to music and how different composers created various types of symmetrical musical spaces.

TOWARD PURE SYMMETRY

The second of Bartók's *"Bagatelles"* opens with an inversionally symmetrical progression around a single axis. Although Bartok assigned a specific tonality to each of the bagatelles, one will often find that many of his pieces are based on a unique set of tonal concepts. A loose sense of tonality is articulated by a perfect fifth [Db–Ab] polarity in the opening and closing sections of the piece. The Db acts as a "tonic" and the Ab acts as a "dominant," but neither functions as such in the traditional sense. More importantly, the notes of the opening and closing sections are arranged symmetrically around an A/A axis suggested by the ostinato Ab–Bb dyad that opens the piece. This dyad (Figure 4.1) establishes an A/A axis at sum

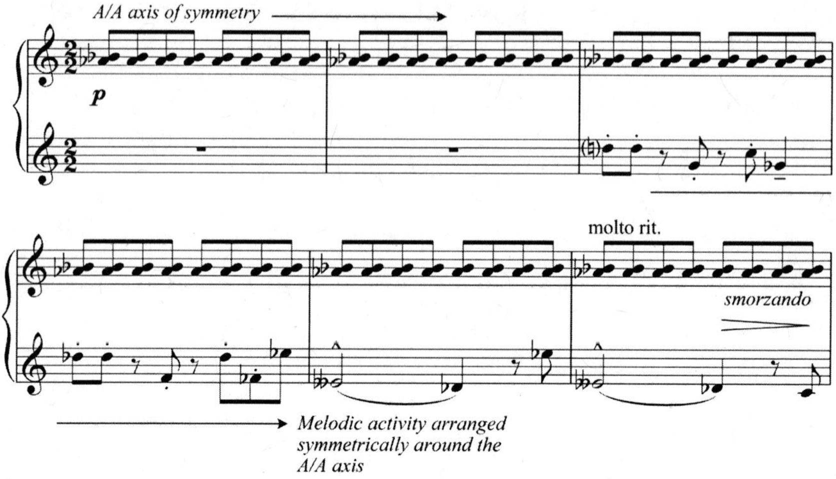

Figure 4.1   Bartók *Bagatelle* No. 2 (mm. 1–6). © *Copyright Editio Musica Budapest. Reprinted by Permission*

6 (9 + 9 = 18—12 modulus = sum 6). The melodic activity surrounding the axis (mm. 3–4) generates two inversionally complementary interval-1 cycles in a set of paired tones, B–G–C–Gb, Db–F, D–Fb and Eb–(Eb).

A symmetrical whole-tone collection [F–G–A–B–Db] opens the central section and reaffirms the A/A axis. At the recapitulation of the opening section (m. 17) the ostinato dyad returns at its tritone transposition, D–E, implying an Eb/Eb (sum 6) axis that represents the dual intersection of the original axis. The chromatically expanding dyads now diverge symmetrically from the Eb/Eb axis. In the final two measures of the recapitulation of the opening phrase (mm. 22–23), the original A/A axis is maintained by the chromatic melodic segment [Bb–Bbb–Ab] which is then taken up by the return of the ostinato Ab–Bb dyad that signals the final return of the first phrase.

While the middle section of the *Bagatelle* does not rely on the axial principle, the two outer sections exemplify a new kind of tonal centricity based on an axis of symmetry. The departure from and return to the axial concept in the arch of a single composition demonstrates the flexibility of choice available to 20th century composers of the unordered (non-serial) twelve-tone system.

SYMMETRY ACHIEVED

Webern's *Fifth Bagatelle for String Quartet* Op. 9 represents a further step in the evolution of axial tonal centricity. Like Bartók's second Bagatelle, it opens with a chord [C–C#–D#–E] that establishes an even D/D axis at sum 4. Toward the end of the first formal section Webern unfolds a new symmetry that chromatically fills in an F#–Bb double stop generating a complete chromatic segment [F#–G–Ab–A–Bb] symmetrical around the dual axis (Ab/Ab) also at sum 4.

Unlike Bartók, Webern continues to adopt the axial concept for the entire piece. The second section (mm. 8–10) "modulates" to a new axis of symmetry by chromatically filling a B–Gb boundary that is symmetrical around an odd dual axis (D–Eb or G#–A) at sum 5.[6] In the third and final section, the original Ab/Ab axis is established (mm. 11–12) by a pair of overlapping dyads (G–Ab/G#–A) at original sum 4. The axial concept is used in a modulatory scheme that lends direction to the tonal progression of the music therefore helping to define the formal structure of the piece. In these respects, the axial concept is much like the system of keys of the traditional tonal system, where the principle of modulation is used to fulfill the same ends. In the Webern and Bartók examples, establishment of axes of symmetry by the symmetrical disposition of single pitches is the core compositional goal of these two pieces.

Claude Debussy was able to unite the concept of tonal centricity based on axes of symmetry to the use of axially generated cyclic and pentatonic pitch collections. In his piano prelude *Voiles* (1910), the change of axes at crucial formal junctures of the piece represents a new and revolutionary means of tonal progression that can be likened to tonal modulation from one tonal center to the next. These shifting axes replace the concept of a single stationary axis. In addition to this, Debussy introduces the concept of using particular symmetrical constructions that characterize the contrasting axes. This not only helps to outline the formal structure of the piece but also fulfills a fundamental prerequisite of impressionistic music, that of color change.

The descending thirds of the opening musical gesture outline a whole-tone scale (G#–F#–E–D–C–Bb–Ab) that is circumscribed by the G#/G# octave (Figure 4.2a).

This collection is symmetrical around the D/D axis (sum 4) that, together with its tritone transposition, G#/G#, forms the dual axis. The C–E dyad at the first cadential point (m. 5) confirms the D/D axis. A repeated bass Bb (Figure 4.2b), which disrupts the symmetry, becomes the new axis (Bb/Bb at sum 8) of the second thematic idea (mm. 7 ff.). The two axes, juxtaposed in the two themes, are sounded simultaneously. The first formal section of the piece ends with the reestablishment of the D/D axis.

The second formal section is based on the pentatonic scale Eb–Gb–Ab–Bb–Db. This particular rotation of the pentatonic scale yields a perfectly symmetrical structure that retains the sum 4 (G#/G#) axis. In the third and final formal section, the original D/D axis is reestablished as the primary one. Thus, the tripartite structure of the prelude is articulated by axial shifts that may be likened to modulations of the traditional tonal system. *Voiles* is yet another example of how inversional symmetry is used both to establish tonal progression and create musical color in an integrated system.

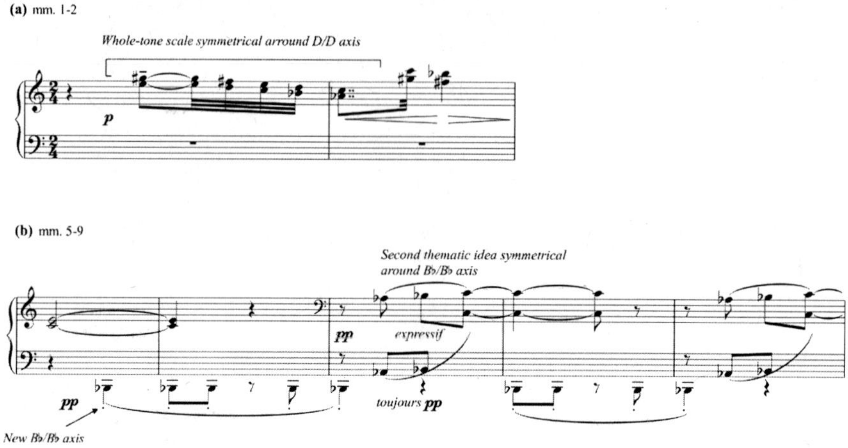

(a) mm. 1-2

(b) mm. 5-9

Figure 4.2a   Debussy, *Voiles* (mm. 1–2).
Figure 4.2b   Debussy, *Voiles* (mm. 5–9).

The examples discussed thus far demonstrate that sonic areas established by the symmetrical organization of a conglomerate of pitches around an axis can take many forms. These sonic areas play the same role as the tonal centers of the traditional tonal system in that both axes and tonal centers establish pitch-class priority. Axes of symmetry may be used as stationary tonal centers against which other symmetries of contrasting sums may sound. Axes can also be used in "modulatory" schemes that vary the tonal color, define the formal structure of the music, and generate a vast array of scalar formations. Thus, the axial principle generates a completely new means of tonal progression.

THE COMPLETE SYSTEM OF AXES OF SYMMETRY

In "The Night's Music" movement from the *Out of Doors Suite*, Bartók achieves a more complex and completely new kind of musical texture using a primary axis of symmetry that acts as a tonal center. Symmetrical structures that create their own axes sound against the main stationary axis. These secondary structures are analogous to the tertian constructions that sound against a tonic key center. This work is comprehensive in its use of axes that comprehends both odd and even sums. They not only establish a new means of tonal progression but also shape the formal structure of the piece by generating both symmetrical and nonsymmetrical pitch collections.

The "night theme" (Figure 4.3) is presented in the opening measures (mm. 1–3) by three chromatic cluster chords that combine to form a chromatic segment [E#–F#–G–G#–A] that is symmetrical around a primary

Figure 4.3 Bartók, *The Night's Music* (m. 1). *The Night's Music from Out of Doors, SZ81 by Béla Bartók © Copyright by Boosey & Hawkes, Inc. Copyright Renewed. Reprinted by Permission.*

G/G axis at sum 2. This basic axis is confirmed by the single notes that appear above the clusters where the Ab and F# form a chromatic segment [F#–G–Ab] based on the G/G axis.

A sequence of characteristic "night motifs" unfolds against the constantly sounding "night theme." These motifs range from single tones to lengthy melismas and they are arranged in a palindrome to portray the intensification and relaxation of nightly activity. The true significance of these motifs, however, is that they are all symmetrical structures that establish new axes at sums different from that of the basic axis thus acting in much the same way as different chords of a tonal piece relative to a tonic. They are, in order of appearance, a repeated F# (F#/F# axis at sum 0), a F#–G dyad (F#/G axis at sum 1), an octatonic-1 tetrachord [C#–D–E–F] (Eb/Eb axis at sum 6), an E–F dyad (E/F axis at sum 9), a C#–D dyad (C#/D axis at sum 3), a D–Eb dyad (D/Eb axis at sum 5), cell X-11 [B–C–C#–D] (C/C# axis at sum 1), a chromatic segment [B–C–C#–D–Eb] (C#/C# axis at sum 2), cell X-1 [C#–D–D#–E] (D/D# axis at sum 5), cycle-5/7 segments A#–D#–G# and E–A–D (F#/F# axis at sum 0).

An isolated F# [F#/F# axis at sum 0] is the first night motif that is repeated increasingly as the piece progresses. It represents the first disruption of the sense of tranquility set up by the chordal "night theme." The second night motif, a simple F#–G dyad placed in an extremely high register (m. 4) introduces the first of the odd axes [F#/G at sum 1]. The third night motif consists of two successive dyads [E–F at sum 9 and C#–D at sum 3] that yield the first pair of complementary axes. These are interchangeable through common chords, much like common pivot chords of closely related keys of the traditional tonal system (this is discussed at length in Chapter 7). The fourth night motif (mm. 6–7) consists of a series of repeated dyads [D–Eb] around the fourth odd axis at sum 5. These repeated dyads are preceded by a grace note figure that unfolds a chromatic segment [B–C–C#–D] with a C/C# axis at sum 1. A transposed version of these two events, with the grace note figure [D–Eb–E–F] at sum 7 and the repeated dyad [F–Gb] now sum 11 yields two more pairs of complementary axes at sums 1 and 7, and 5 and 11. All the odd axes are unfolded in complementary pairs. The fifth night motif [C#–D–D#–E] reestablishes the presence of the odd axes only to be contradicted by the sixth night motif. Contrary to all the preceding motifs, which consist of short chromatic segments, this final motif is made up of two chromatically adjacent segments of the perfect fourth (5/7) cycle [A#–D#–G# and E–A–D] and the chromatic segment B–C–C#–D, which together are symmetrical around the axis at sum 0. The first section of the piece comes to a close (m. 16), on a transposed version of the fourth motif that is now symmetrical at sum 11. While only some of the even axes are unfolded, the complete unfolding of the odd axes in their complementary pairs (1/7, 3/9, and 5/11) defines the tonal progression of the first formal section of the piece.

The tonal progression of the second section (mm. 17–33) is characterized by the unfolding of all the even axes and texturally defined by the only true melody of the entire piece. This unison melody, sounded four octaves apart, is subdivided into four two-measure lengths. The complete set of phrases is anchored to continuously sounding octave Gs that form a G/G axis at sum 2. The octave circumscribes an inner chromatic chord [E#–F#–G–Ab–Bb] that is also symmetrical at sum 2. This highlights the fact that every layer of the texture is bound by the axis of symmetry.[7]

The unisons of the melody unfold all but one of the even axes just as the chromatic segments and dyads of the first section yield the odd axes. By the end of the first phrase sum 0, 2, 8, 4, and 6 are sounded by the F#/F#, G/G, E/E, D/D and D#/D# unisons (spaced some four octaves apart). The only missing unison axis, sum 10, is not yielded by the melody because it does not contain an F/F unison. However, the D#/D# unisons that punctuate each of the first three phrase endings create sum 10 dyads (G–D# or G–Eb) with the repeated Gs of the primary axis. Consistency requires that the other dyads formed by the melody and the Gs of the central axis be interpreted in the same way. The first of these, G/F# (m. 18), creates a sum 1 axis while second and third (G–C# and G–D) create axes at sums 8 and 9, respectively. The sum 8 axis is framed by the C#/C# unison of the melody at sum 2 and yields yet another pair of complementary axes. The third formal section at first reverts to the opening night motives, but soon deviates from pure motif repetition to fulfill a new compositional goal that entails the generation of diatonic and pentatonic modes from the primary (sum 2) axis of symmetry (discussed in detail later in this chapter).

In the first section of "The Night's Music," symmetrical pitch formations constructed with octatonic scale segments also establish axes of symmetry. It must be remembered that any cyclic collection, whether simple or compound, is itself symmetrical and is therefore inexorably linked to the concept of an axis. While the axial generation of purely cyclic collections is natural, it is also possible to generate symmetrical rotations of the pentatonic and diatonic modes along with many nonsymmetrical tertian constructions.

AXIAL GENERATION OF CYCLIC, PENTATONIC, DIATONIC AND NON-DIATONIC COLLECTIONS

Symmetrical tertian constructions can be easily obtained by axial generation of simple cycles such as the interval-3 or interval-4 cycles. For example, if we project two inversionally complementary interval-3 cycles from a C–C unison or even sum axis, we will obtain a pair of mirrored cycles made up of the same pitch classes. In this case, a pair of exact duplicates of the same fully diminished seventh chord is generated [C–Eb–F#–A–C/C–Eb–F#–A–C].

If, however, we project the same kind of cycles from an odd or semitone axis, we will obtain a pair of mirrored cycles identical in every respect but for the pitch-class content. When, for example, two mirrored interval-3 cycles are projected, they generate two different diminished seventh chords [C–Eb–F#–A–C/C#–E–G–Bb–C#].

Familiar harmonic constructions such as major and minor triads and seventh chords can be obtained by axial generation of compound cycles. If, for example, we project two inversionally complementary 3:4 compound cyclic collections [D–F–A–C/C–Eb–G–Bb] from a unison axis we will obtain two minor seventh chords. If we invert the interval ratio to 4:3 and repeat the process, we will obtain two major seventh chords. Each of these major and minor seventh chords contain within them one major and one minor triad. Simple and compound interval cycles can also be used to generate pentatonic and diatonic collections. While simple interval cycles generate pentatonic and diatonic pitch collections in their cyclic forms, compound interval cycles can be made to generate the same collections in their scalar order. The pitch content of the familiar "black note" pentatonic scale [C#–D#–F#–G#–A#] can be axially generated by projecting two inversionally complementary interval-7 cyclic segments [F#–C#–G#/G#–D#–A#]. This pitch content may be easily rearranged into the familiar Chinese model of the pentatonic mode [C#–D#–F#–G#–A#]. A single rotation of the asymmetrical Chinese model yields the less familiar but symmetrical Hungarian model of the same scale [D#–F#–G#–A#–C#]. This particular pentatonic rotation can be axially generated from a G#/G# axis using two inversionally complementary 2:3 compound cyclic segments [D#–F#–G#/G#–A#–C#].

The same two processes can be used to generate pentatonic collections. The pitch content of the nonsymmetrical C major scale or Ionian mode [C–D–E–F–G–A–B–C] can be axially generated by once again using two inversionally complementary interval-7 cyclic segments [F–C–G–D/D–A–E–B].

The symmetrical D Dorian mode [D–E–F–G–A–B–C–D], a rotation of the Ionian mode can, like the symmetrical pentatonic rotation, be generated from a G#/G# axis using two inversionally complementary 2:1 compound cyclic segments. When such collections are used in connection with the axial concept, they lose their tonal characteristics and are no longer recognizable by their tonic.

Charles Ives' *Psalm XXIV* (1898) is perhaps the earliest work that demonstrates the systematic axial generation of simple and compound interval cycles, pentatonic and diatonic pitch collections, as well as several important tertian harmonic structures. In the opening phrase of the work (mm. 1–6) the complete interval 1/11 cycle is axially generated from the initial C unison chord. The soprano and bass move in contrary motion by semitone to complete the entire chromatic cycle (m. 3) Simultaneous to the unfolding of the semitone (interval-1) cycle, the downbeats of these opening measures also generate a complete interval-3/9 cycle [C–D#–F#–A–C and its inversion C–A–Gb–Eb–C].[8]

In the two subsequent phrases that complete the first stanza (mm. 6–11), a new symmetrical space is created by the unfolding of the complete whole-tone 0 cycle from the same C unison chord. The two outer voices again proceed in contrary motion to unfold the complete whole-tone 0 (interval-2) cycle [C–D–E–F#–G#–A#–C]. The downbeats now outline a complete interval-4/8 cycle [D–F#–A#–D]. The end of the stanza concludes with a chord that contains five of the six notes of the whole-tone 0 cycle.[9] In the second stanza, the soprano and bass continue their contrary motion except that this time they each unfold short compound cyclic segments, C–D–D# in the soprano and C–B–A in the bass. When combined, these two segments yield a larger five-note segment of the octatonic-0 cycle [A–B–C–D–D#].[10]

In the third line of the same stanza (mm. 16–21), the voices each generate a sequence of major and minor thirds [C–E–G–B–D–F#–A–C#–E–G#–B–D#–F# in the soprano and C–Ab–F–Db–Bb–Gb–Eb–Cb in the bass]. Both these sequences are of interval ratio 4:3 and each generates a lengthy series of major and minor triads or major and minor seventh chords depending on whether one chooses three-note or four-note segments. Ives generates the pitch content of a rotation of a Gypsy mode [C–Db–E–F–G–Ab–B–C] with the first four notes of the contrary motion (Figure 4.4). Every half measure (m. 17f.) partitions the cyclic bass segment [C–Ab–F–Db–Bb–Gb–Eb–Cb] into the two cyclic-5/7 segments, C–F–Bb–Eb and Ab–Db–Gb–Cb. These two interval-5 segments are unfolded in the soprano measures of the third stanza. Here, the soprano unfolds a six-note segment of the interval-5/7 cycle [C–F–Bb–Eb–Ab], while the bass generates a second segment of the same cycle [C–G–D–A]. These two segments form as the exclusive pitch content of the cadential chord at the end of the phrase.

However, at the beginning of verse three (m. 22), the symmetry is disrupted in two ways. The axial-tone C is preceded by a G that indicates that there are still strong tonal forces at work in this piece, because the perfect fourth relationship gives the strong sensation of a dominant to tonic function. When the C once more asserts itself (mm. 24f.) as the axial tone, the soprano and bass voices no longer create a symmetrical space even though they unfold further symmetrical cyclic collections. Interval-5 and interval-6 cyclic collections unfold in the verse but the verse ends with a complete C major chord. This provides further evidence that the axial concept was not thought of as a systematic means of progression and that tonality still has a powerful influence on the music.

Despite this disruption, strict inversion is briefly reinstated at the opening of the fourth verse (m. 34) that unfolds an incomplete interval 7/5 cycle [Bb–F–C–G–D] from the C axial tone. From this point forward, the axial function of C becomes divergent. The piece ends on a perfect fifth [C–G] that underscores the tonal underpinning of this piece. Although used in a dualistic manner, the axial concept is the primary means of tonal progression in this piece.

As seen in the earlier discussion of *The Night's Music*, the tonal underpinnings extant in *Psalm XXIV* are completely eliminated. In *The Night's Music*, pentatonic and diatonic modes are deliberately generated from an axis of symmetry that has now supplanted the more traditional tonal center.

The third formal section of *The Night's Music* begins with the same motives of the first section, but soon the content of the entire texture is partitioned into "black key" and "white key" collections both of which continue to rotate around the primary axis. The first to be introduced is the black key collection (m. 38), represented by a series of short melodic fragments that unfold a whole-tone segment [F#–G#–A#] at sum 4. This segment is expended upward to yield a four- note octatonic segment [G#–A#–B–C#]. The procedure is repeated (m. 41) in a downward direction to

yield a second octatonic segment [F#–E–D#–C#]. Both these segments are
unfolded in inversion from a common G/G axis at sum 2. Together, they
unfold the complete C# Dorian mode.[11] The same initial fragment [F#–
G#–A#] is used to generate the Hungarian model of the pentatonic scale,
D#–F#–G#–A#–C#. In the symmetrical generation of these two diatonic
collections, they are generated not as traditional tonal constructs, but as a
pitch conglomerates centered on a completely new kind of tonal center, that
is, axis of symmetry.

Bartók's *Mikrokosmos* No. 141, *Subject and Reflection*, is different in
that the sole compositional aim is the axial generation of a special Rumanian
non-diatonic mode[12] at different transpositional levels. It also differs from
the other musical examples because the shifting axes are physically represented by held perfect octaves that frame the symmetrical texture. The piece
opens (m. 1) with a held Bb/Bb axis at sum 8. The pitch content of the right
hand consists of a diatonic tetrachord [Bb–C–D–Eb] that could be described
as either Ionian or Mixolydian. Each note of the right-hand tetrachord is
"reflected" in inversion by the left-hand pitch content that also unfolds an
F Phrygian tetrachord [Bb–Ab–Gb–F]. When cast in scalar order, the two
tetrachords join to form the special Rumanian non-diatonic folk mode Ab–
Bb–C–D–Eb–F–Gb–Ab rotated to F–Gb–Ab–Bb–C–D–Eb (Figure 4.5).
The axial generation of the mode can be represented diagrammatically.

Axially generated Rumanian
nondiatonic mode [F-Gb-Ab-Bb-C-D-Eb]

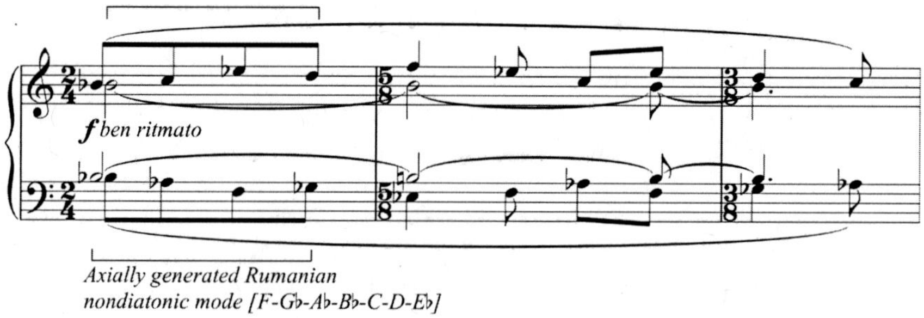

Figure 4.5   Bartók, *Mikrokosmos* No. 141, *Subject and Reflection* (mm. 1–3).
*Subject and Reflection from Mikrokosmos by Béla Bartók © Copyright 1940 by
Hawkes & Son (London) Ltd. [Definitive corrected edition © Copyright 1987 by
Hawkes & Son (London) Ltd.] Reprinted by Permission.*

The combined pitch content remains unaltered in the first four phrases (mm. 1–14) that constitute the initial formal section.

The second formal section (mm. 15 ff.) is marked by a new B/B axis at sum 10. The right hand again unfolds a diatonic tetrachord that is mirrored by a left-hand tetrachord to generate a new transposition of the non-diatonic mode [F#–G–A–B–C#–D#–E].[13] This process is repeated several times during the course of the piece, each new axial shift occurring at the beginning of formal periods that are also characterized by changing tempo indications and contrasting dynamic indications. In this work the axial shifts are truly analogous to traditional modulations because, while the transpositional levels change, the structure of the mode does not.

AXES AND MICROTONES

The axial concept is frequently used in music based on an octave that is subdivided into intervals smaller than the semitone, the smallest interval of the western chromatic. Composers of the "pitch continuum" such as Penderecki, Varèse, and Ligeti have all composed music that relies either in part or wholly on the principle of symmetrical pitch organization. In these works the semitone is further subdivided into smaller microtones that are used in clusters to produce bands of sound.

These bands can be made to expand and contract to create variety or they may be transposed to different sonic areas. Often, the sound bands create microtonal symmetrical structures. The fact that they are constituted by microtones has no effect on their symmetrical disposition around axes of symmetry. The only variable is the scale of intervallic proportions. This is accommodated by newly invented sets of accidentals specially formulated to denote tonal fractions. In Penderecki's *Threnody To the Victims of Hiroshima for 52 strings*, a set of special accidental signs are used to raise or flatten all twelve pitches, whether natural, sharp, or flat, of the chromatic scale by a quarter tone.[14]

The system of numbering is identical to that used for the chromatic scale but now includes fractions of one half (½) to denote the quartertones that exist between the semitones. The numerical representation of Penderecki's quartertone scale is shown in the following table.

Numeric Representation of the Penderecki Quartertone Scale

C	[ ]	C#	[ ]	D	[ ]	Eb	[ ]	E	[ ]	F	[ ]
I	↓	I	↓	I	↓	I	↓	I	↓	I	↓
0	0.5	1	1.5	2	2.5	3	3.5	4	4.5	5	5.5

F#	[ ]	G	[ ]	Ab	[ ]	A	[ ]	Bb	[ ]	B	[ ]
I	↓	I	↓	I	↓	I	↓	I	↓	I	↓
6	6.5	7	7.5	8	8.5	9	9.5	10	10.5	11	11.5

Using this new number scale, it is possible to calculate new sets of axes that can only be represented by fractions. A quartertone collection that is symmetrical around an axis of C (sum 0) and the quartertone above C (sum 0.5) will be symmetrical around a quartertone axis at sum 0.5 (0 + 0.5 = 0.5). The calculation of the new quartertone axes is no different from that used to calculate integer axes (axes represented by zero or any positive whole number).

The different sections of Penderecki's *Threnody to the Victims of Hiroshima*, scored solely for string orchestra, are articulated by two different kinds of musical texture. The first kind consists of indefinite or quasi definite pitch and sound effects created by techniques such as playing between the bridge and the tailpiece, playing on the four strings behind the bridge, or striking the sounding board of the violin with the nut of the bow. The second of the two textures consists of definite pitches generated by traditional bowing techniques. The pitches are organized into either static or expanding and contracting bands[15] of continuous sound. The range of most sound bands is narrow because it is made up of varying numbers of microtones that most often add up to intervals much smaller than an octave. Larger intervals are momentarily generated when the sound bands expand to, or beyond the octave range. The sound bands played by complete sections were specifically assigned to different *divisi* groups. The duration of these bands is calculated in seconds rather than measures because there is no regular meter. While portions of the piece that are based on indeterminate sounds cannot be analyzed in terms of pitch, the tonal progression of the pitched portions is based on both standard axial techniques already used in the pieces analyzed thus far as well as new transformational ones.

The largest of the pitched sections occurs between numbers 10 and 26 for a total time of 3 minutes 42 seconds. The first expanding and contracting band of sound is produced by the celli. It starts on a unison F/F axis (sum 10), expands outward to a D#/G (sum 10.5) and contracts back to the original axis. Just before this sound band ceases it is joined by a new one created by the first *divisi* group of violins that generate an expanding axis that starts on a unison E/E axis (sum 8) and ends at A#/B (sum 9). The sums of these axes duplicated in canonic imitation by the second group of *divisi* violins that sound the tritone transposition of the same axes in an expanding band that starts on a Bb/Bb axis at sum 8 and ends on a E/F axis at sum 9. The remaining viola and contrabasso groups create a new canon based on axes that begin and end at sum 6, the voile axis being Eb/Eb while the contrabassi axis is A/A (Figure 4.6)

While microtonal axes are briefly expressed at different points, all the sound bands of the initial portion of the passage end on integer or whole-number sum axes. An orchestral *tutti* at 15 heralds a sudden and definite shift to microtonal axes that create a sharp contrast with integer axes. At 16, some sound bands remain constant around a single axis while others shift from one microtonal axis to another.[16] This can be represented as follows:

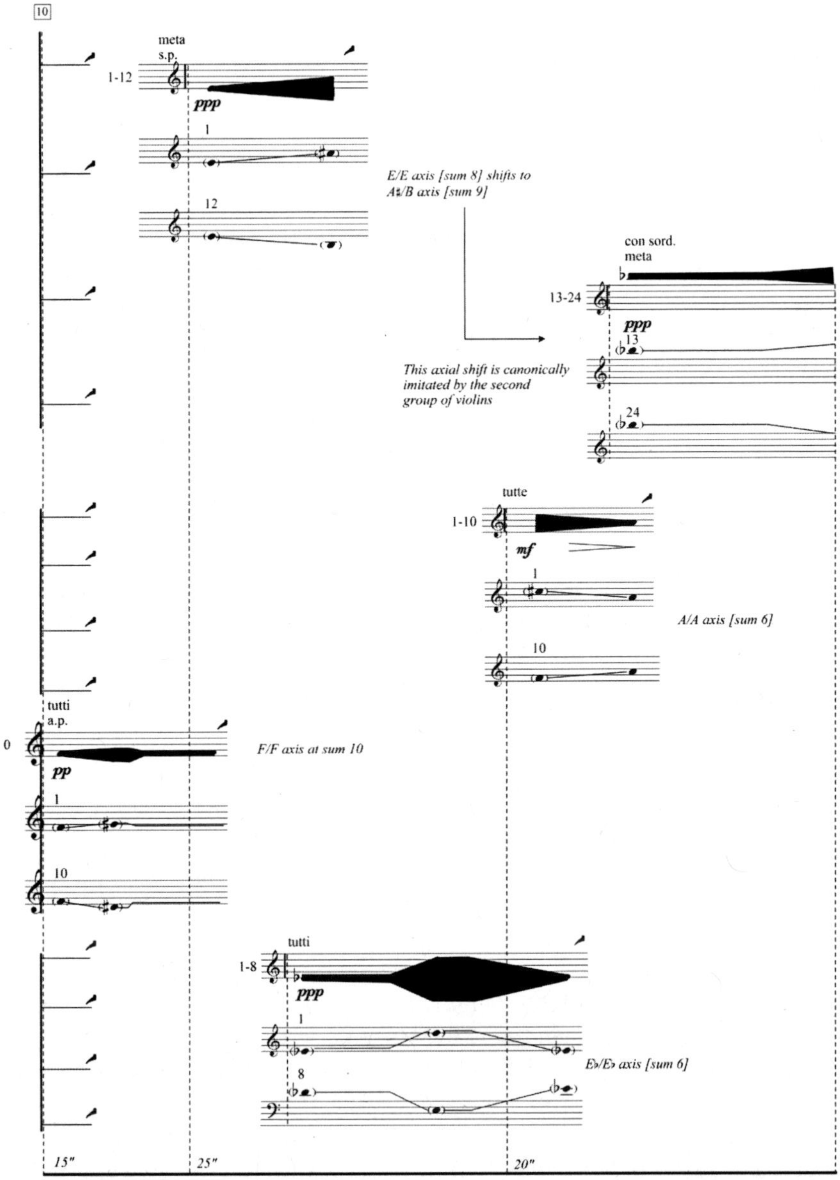

Figure 4.6 Penderecki, *Threnody to the Victims of Hiroshima.* Penderecki Threnos © 1961 Schott Music GmbH & Co, KG. © Renewed. All Rights Reserved. Used by permission of European American Music Distributors agent for Schott Music GmbH & Co, KG in the following countries: Azerbaijan, Georgia, Kazakhstan, Moldova, Russian Federation, Tajikistan, Bulgaria, Hungary, Romania, Albania, Czech Republic, Slovakia, Yugoslavia, Slovenia, Croatia, Latvia, Estonia, Lithuania, Cuba, Vietnam, North Korea, China, Mongolia. Copyright © 1961 (Renewed) EMI DESHON MUSIC, INC. Exclusive Worldwide Print Rights Administered by ALFRED MUSIC PUBLISHING CO., INC. All Rights Reserved. Used by Permission.

Vn I   sum 1.5–9.5
Vn II   sum 7.5
Vl   sum 8.5–11.5
Vc   sum 5.5
Cb   sum 5.5

This is immediately followed by a passage based solely on microtonal axes. The long-range shift from integer axes to fractional axes is compressed into a single durational unit (18) that forms the climax of the section. Every section of the orchestra generates an expanding band of sound that transforms each integer axis into a fractional or microtonal axis in a climactic crescendo from f to ff. Every axis is shifted by 0.5 so that the first violins shift from sum 4 to 4.5, the second violins from sum 0 to sum 11.5, the voile from sum 1 to 1.5, the celli from sum 6 to 5.5 and the contrabassi from sum 8 to sum 8.5.

The final portion of this formal section (19–26) sees a gradual diminuendo created in part by the cessation of sonic activity by the violins, violas, contrabassi and a section of the celli as well as a drop in the actual dynamic levels. The last five seconds of sound are provided by five celli that sound a D–D unison at sum 4. In retrospect, one can see that the long-range switch from unison/semitone–microtonal–unison/semitone axes is foreshadowed by the first band, first expanding and contracting sound band articulated by the celli at the beginning of 10.

Composed in 1894, Ives' *Psalm XXIV* is probably the first work that systematically articulates the interval cycles using axes of symmetry. Despite the fact that some loose tonal references are present in the work, there can be little doubt that this work is based on a specifically designed inversional principle. This principle created a completely new concept of tonal centricity. Compositions that followed the *Psalm* reveal how composers made use of different facets of the concept to create varying types of symmetrical musical space. While the axial principle supplanted the traditional system of "keys" in terms of pitch relations, it fulfilled the same fundamental musical prerequisite of variation through transposition.

Penderecki's *Threnody* of 1960 exemplifies how the axial concept can be extended to encompass compositions that use naturally and synthetically generated microtones. The clear implication is that a good portion of art music composed since that time probably relies on axial principles that may be recalculated to accommodate the intervallic proportions of intervals smaller than the semitone. The principle of tonal centricity based on axial symmetry is therefore the compositional application of cyclic inversional relationship.

5 Modes

Music: Frederick Chopin *Mazurka* Op. 68, No. 3
Béla Bartók *In the Hungarian Style, With pipes and drums*
Aaron Copland *The Cat and the Mouse: Scherzo Humoristique*
Zoltan Kodaly *Valsette*
Carol Szymanowski *Mazurka* Op. 50, No. 1
Igor Stravinski *Sérénade en La*
John Adams *Phrygian Gates*
Isaac Albéniz *El Albaicin*
Witold Lutoslawski *Melodie*

MODAL IDENTITY

Mode, from the Latin word *modus*, can be accurately described by using the three synonyms manner, measure, and form. All three terms are applicable to the different families of modal scales upon which most the world's art and folk music is based. A musical mode is therefore a scalar structure consisting of a specific number of notes arranged according to a specific intervallic order. The C Ionian mode or major scale [C–D–E–F–G–A–B–(C)],[1] for example, consists of seven notes that are arranged according to the familiar intervallic order T–T–S–T–T–T–S. The complete intervallic order of any given mode can be rotated to create a family of modes in which each mode has fixed, but permuted pitch content. For most western musicians, the most familiar are the pentatonic scale and the seven-note diatonic church mode and its rotations. There are, however, a host of modes that originate in the folk and art music of different parts of the world.

There are also many hybrid modes. For the most part, a hybrid mode is created when a tetrachord[2] of one mode is joined with the tetrachord of another mode to create a new hybrid that displays the characteristic of both parent modes. If, for example, we combine Lydian tetrachords [C–D–E–F# and G–A–B–C] with the Aeolian modal tetrachords [C–D–Eb–F and G–Ab–Bb–C], we can obtain different hybrid modes that can either be diatonic or non-diatonic, depending on the tetrachords chosen for the hybrid derivative. The Aeolian lower tetrachord combined to the Lydian upper tetrachord[3] will yield an Aeolian/Lydian hybrid [C–D–Eb–F–G–A–B–(C)], while the combination of the lower Lydian tetrachord with an Aeolian upper tetrachord will result in a Lydian/Aeolian hybrid mode [C–D–E–F#–G–Ab–Bb–(C)]. Both of these hybrid modes are non-diatonic.

In the mid to late 19th century, many composers outside of Germany and Italy began to look to the music of their native homelands in order to express aspects of their national identity. This nationalistic movement, championed by such composers as Chopin, Grieg, Smetana, and Mussorgsky, generated a slue of compositions colored by many different elements of these composers' native folk music. A good portion of this folk music is based on diatonic modes other than the Ionian. Often the incorporation of these modes created textures in which normal harmonic function was either altered or suspended altogether because the modes could not generate functional harmonic structures.

The middle section of Chopin's *Mazurka* Op. 68, No. 3 (mm. 33–44) contrasts starkly with the outer two sections (mm. 1–32 and mm. 45–60). While in the outer sections the melody and all its accompanying chords function normally, within the F major tonal context, the use of the Bb Lydian mode in the central portion suspends all the harmonic activity. The functional chords are substituted by a single perfect fifth [Bb–F] that forms a drone accompaniment to the Lydian melody.[4] The reason that normal harmonic function is impaired by the use of the Lydian mode is that the tritone [Eb–A] that generates much of the harmonic function within the Bb major context is altered by the Lydian E natural. It is only when the composer incorporates the Lydian fourth into a dominant seventh chord [C–E–G–Bb] to modulate back to the key of F major that normal harmonic function resumes.

At the beginning of the 20th century, many European composers increased their use of the diatonic church modes other than the Ionian, pentatonic, and non-diatonic folk modes of eastern Europe, the Middle East, Asia, and South America. While tertian harmonic structures derived from these modes can sound *quasi* tonal in the traditional or common practice sense of the word, they are incapable of generating harmonic function. As a result, the adoption of these modes and their harmonic derivatives helped to further weaken an already fragile tonal system. When composers began to derive harmonic structures based on intervals other than major and minor thirds a new and completely non functional harmonic vocabulary came into existence.

In the context of the unordered twelve-tone system, all the modes and most partitions of the interval cycles are but subsets of the chromatic continuum. As such, their constituent pitches have no functional roles. Since it is the chromatic scale and not the single modes or interval cycles that constitute the referential pitch collection of the system, the establishment of a tonal center is not necessarily based on the concept of a modal tonic but can also be based on diverse principles such as axes of symmetry or established by rhythmic assertion. Modal identity is no longer a direct consequence of sequential order.

As subsets of the chromatic continuum, modes can be manipulated in ways not allowed when they are basic in establishing the modal tonality of a work. The manipulations to which modes are subjected may alter their structure without breaching the integrity of the unordered twelve-tone system. In this system, the identity of a subcollection such as a mode or interval cycle is consequential to the musical context in which it exists.

Since all the modes and interval cycles derived from the chromatic continuum are but different manifestations of the same chromatic source, they are all potentially related to one another.[5] It is because of this that any derivative subcollection, modal or cyclic, can be transformed into a different modal or cyclic subcollection. The only proviso is that the two subcollections share a minimum number of common elements. These can be represented by common pitches, shared interval ratios, and relationships based on inversion or complementation.

THE PENTATONIC SCALE

We arbitrarily assume that the C–D–F–G–A–(C) referential order is a five-note scale characterized by a 2–3–2–2–3 intervallic structure. Any one of its five constituent notes can serve as tonic, thus implying the presence of a complete family that consists of five different modal rotations.[6]

Tonal Pentatonic Rotations
Rotation 1   C–D–F–G–A–(C)
Rotation 2   D–F–G–A–C–(D)
Rotation 3   F–G–A–C–D–(F)
Rotation 4   G–A–C–D–F–(G)
Rotation 5   A–C–D–F–G–(A)

Tonal Pentatonic Rotations Transposed to a Common Tonic
Rotation 1   C–D–F–G–A–(C)
Rotation 2   C–Eb–F–G–Bb–(C)
Rotation 3   C–D–E–G–A–(C)
Rotation 4   C–D–F–G–Bb–(C)
Rotation 5   C–Eb–F–Ab–Bb–(C)

In its first mode or rotation, the scale forms the nucleus of the music of many ancient cultures, for example, China, Africa, Polynesia, and Scotland. It also forms the core scalar collection of much of western and eastern European folk music. It has been used throughout the history of European art music, from Gregorian chant melodies to Mendelssohn's *Scotch Symphony* to a host of works by different 20th century composers. Debussy and Bartók, influenced by pentatonic-based folk music of Russia and Hungary, respectively, began to use it in their own works and eventually synthesized it into their personal musical language. They, like many of their contemporaries, not only appreciated the distinctive sound provided by the scale but also understood the compositional possibilities afforded by its unique intervallic structure.

Relative to the seven-note diatonic and non-diatonic modes, its "gapped" five-note structure renders the pentatonic scale a more flexible construction. While the sequence of whole and half steps of a diatonic mode may suggest a tonal center (tonic) as well as its modal color, the lack of semitones in the pentatonic scale make the identification of a modal tonic ambiguous. Since there are no semitones that serve as tendency tones, any of the five tones of the scale can be asserted.

While the pentatonic scale can be used as the referential pitch collection of a work, in many 20th century compositions, it often serves as the nucleus of larger diatonic and non-diatonic modes. A single diatonic mode, for example, contains three different rotations of the pentatonic scale. The transformation of a pentatonic nucleus into a seven-note mode requires the addition of only two notes that can be placed at different intervallic differences within the minor third gaps and or at the end of the pentatonic scale. Six of the seven diatonic modes can be generated by using three different rotations of the pentatonic scale that exist within the "white note" diatonic pitch collection. The only diatonic mode that cannot be generated from any rotation of the pentatonic scale is the Locrian mode. This is due to the fixed perfect fifth above the initial note of any pentatonic rotation. The tritone replaces the fifth in the corresponding degrees of the Locrian mode.

Completion of Diatonic Modes from a Pentatonic Nucleus

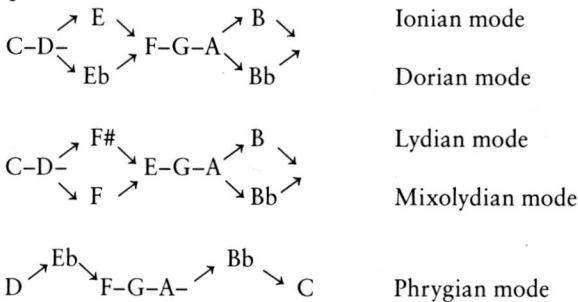

```
         ↗ E ↘           ↗ B ↘          Ionian mode
   C–D⟨        ⟩F–G–A⟨       ⟩
         ↘ Eb ↗           ↘ Bb ↗        Dorian mode


         ↗ F# ↘           ↗ B ↘         Lydian mode
   C–D⟨        ⟩E–G–A⟨       ⟩
         ↘ F ↗            ↘ Bb ↗        Mixolydian mode


        ↗ Eb ↘            ↗ Bb ↘
   D⟨        ⟩F–G–A–⟨        ⟩ C        Phrygian mode
```

The completion of a diatonic, non-diatonic, or hybrid mode from a pentatonic nucleus is a compositional technique favored by many 20th century composers. It identical to that used for the completion of specific interval cycles or the chromatic continuum except that it takes place within a modal context. If a piece is based on definite diatonic or non-diatonic modes, the pentatonic scale can be viewed as an incomplete pitch collection thereof.

This principle is articulated in the opening section (mm. 1–12) of Kodaly's *Valsette*. After a brief introduction (mm. 1–4), in which the left hand establishes the Bb tonality, the first melodic flourish (mm. 4–7) outlines a complete pentatonic rotation [D–F–G–Bb–C]. At the termination of this melodic statement (m. 8), the change of harmony in the accompaniment supplies an Eb which begins to complete the diatonic scale

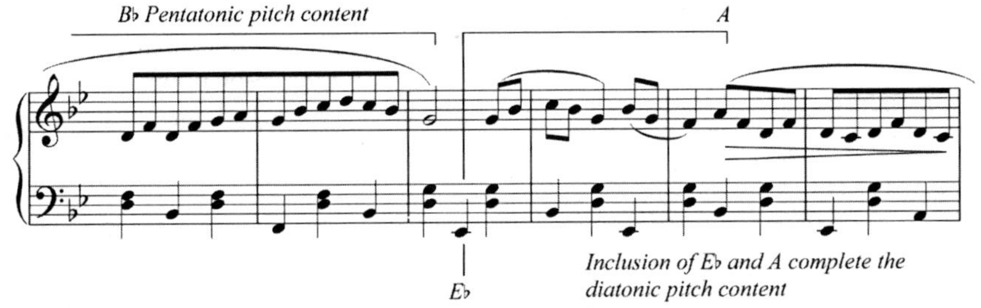

Figure 5.1 Kodaly, *Valsette* (mm. 6–11). Copyright © Editio Musica Budapest. Used by Permission.

[Bb–C–D–Eb–F–G–( )]. Immediately preceding this (m. 6), a new melodic gesture supplies the missing A to complete the Bb Ionian mode [Bb–C–D–Eb–F–G–A] (Figure 5.1).

In this tonal context, the occurrence would seem ordinary were it not for the fact that a second pentatonic collection [C–D–F–G–A] emerges from the larger diatonic mode in the second half of the eight-measure melody. The extraction of the new pentatonic collection from the larger diatonic one reverses the process of diatonic completion used in the first half of the melody. This demonstrates the primacy of the pentatonic collection. The entire completion and extraction process of the pentatonic collection may be graphically represented as follows:

Original Pentatonic mode: Bb—C—D — F—G
Completed Diatonic mode: Bb—C—D—Eb—F—G—A
Extracted Pentatonic mode: C—D — F—G—A

Hybrid modes, such as the Lydian/Mixolydian hybrid mode can also be constructed around a pentatonic nucleus.

C–D–E– F# G–A Bb   Lydian mode → Lydian/Mixolydian Hybrid mode   Mixolydian mode

The introduction (mm. 1–4) to Copland's *The Cat and the Mouse: Scherzo Humoristique* starts with a single melodic statement that unfolds an ascending pentatonic scale [A–B–D–E–F#]. The chord that follows [B–C#–F–A] supplies a new note to the already-existing pentatonic collection but alters the pentatonic structure by lowering the F# a semitone. This alteration foreshadows the polymodal interplay that starts to occur later in the piece. The original ascending pentatonic collection is immediately reinstated (m.

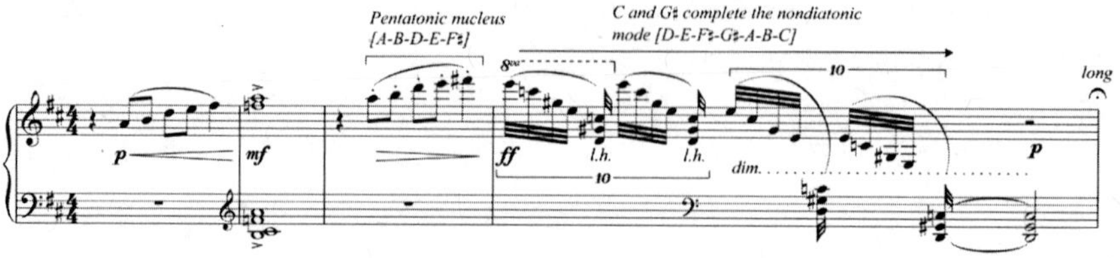

Figure 5.2   Copland, *The Cat and the Mouse: Scherzo Humoristique* (mm. 1–4). *The Cat and the Mouse by Aaron Copland © Copyright 1921 The Aaron Copland Fund for Music, Inc. Copyright Renewed. Boosey & Hawkes, Inc. Sole Licensee, for the USA. Reprinted by Permission.*

3) an octave higher and is followed by a rapidly descending arpeggio punctuated regularly by chords. The pitch content of this descent [D–E–G#–C] supplies two new notes that complete the pentatonic collection to unfold a complete Lydian/Mixolydian hybrid mode [D–E–F#–G#–A–B–C] secured to a D modal tonic (Figure 5.2). This is confirmed by the continued assertion of this tonic in the following measures (mm. 5–6).

THE SEVEN DIATONIC MODES

The seven rotations of the diatonic model make up the complete diatonic modal family that consists of the Ionian (rotation 1), Dorian (rotation 2), Phrygian (rotation 3), Lydian (rotation 4), Mixolydian (rotation 5), Aeolian (rotation 6), and Locrian (rotation 7) modes.

The Seven Diatonic Rotations

	Mode	Intervallic order
C Ionian	C–D–E–F–G–A–B–C	W–W–H–W–W–W–H
D Dorian	D–E–F–G–A–B–C–D	W–H–W–W–W–H–W
E Phrygian	E–F–G–A–B–C–D–E	H–W–W–W–H–W–W
F Lydian	F–G–A–B–C–D–E–F	W–W–W–H–W–W–H
G Mixolydian	G–A–B–C–D–E–F–G	W–W–H–W–W–H–W
A Aeolian	A–B–C–D–E–F–G–A	W–H–W–W–H–W–W
B Locrian	B–C–D–E–F–G–A–B	H–W–W–H–W–W–W

All the diatonic intervallic orders can be rotated to a common tonic to yield all seven diatonic modal rotations at the same transpositional level.[7]

C Ionian	C–D–E–F–G–A–B–C
C Dorian	C–D–Eb–F–G–A–Bb–C
C Phrygian	C–Db–Eb–F–G–Ab–Bb–C
C Lydian	C–D–E–F#–G–A–B–C
C Mixolydian	C–D–E–F–G–A–Bb–C
C Aeolian	C–D–Eb–F–G–Ab–Bb–C
C Locrian	C–Db–Eb–F–Gb–Ab–Bb–C

While all the modes in the diatonic family contain the same number of whole tones (5) and semitones (2), the scalar distribution of these tones and semitones changes with each rotation. Each diatonic mode exhibits its own unique characteristic that hinges primarily on the tetrachordal structure and or the harmonic intervals formed above the modal tonic. The expanding intervals created above the tonic of each diatonic mode can be mapped as follows:

Mode	Intervals Created Above the Tonic
Ionian	M2, M3, P4, P5, M6, M7, P8
Dorian	M2, m3, P4, P5, M6, m7, P8
Phrygian	m2, m3, P4, P5, m6, m7, P8
Lydian	M2, M3, A4, P5, M6, M7, P8
Mixolydian	M2, M3, P4, P5, M6, m7, P8
Aeolian	M2, m3, P4, P5, m6, m7, P8
Locrian	m2, m3, P4, D5, m6, m7, P8

This table is of great significance when comparing the intervallic structure of incomplete harmonic structures or intervallic pitch cells derived from different modal families. A simple C–D–F–G tetrachord, for example, can be derived from various rotations of four different modes that all share a common "C" tonic, the pentatonic rotation [C–D–F–G–A], the Mixolydian modal rotation [C–D–E–F–G–A–Bb–(C)], rotation 2 of the Acoustic scale [C–D–E–F–G–Ab–Bb–(C)], and rotation 4 of the Phrygian dominant mode [C–D–Eb–F–G–Ab–B–(C)].[8]

Strictly speaking, while all modal intervals are structural, some have come to be more closely associated with modal "color" rather than structure. The reason is that in terms of structure, modes are generally evaluated for their capacity to generate tonal or tonal-like function and are therefore compared to the Ionian mode better known as the major scale. While all the diatonic modes contain a tritone, the Ionian mode is the only one that generates tonal function because of the half-step adjacency of its tritone (key-defining interval to two basic components of the tonic triad) formed as the fourth and seventh modal degrees. In this contextual position it is perceived as being able to generate a special kind of tonal tension that requires resolution and is the cornerstone of traditional tonal progression. This is why in describing modes such as the Lydian, we say that it is like a major scale with a raised fourth. In the case of the Dorian mode we say that it is like a minor scale with a flattened seventh. Neither mode is capable of generating traditional harmonic function.

From this perspective, both fourth and seventh modal degrees in question (the tritone) are fundamental to the structure rather than color of the mode. One can alter the third and sixth degree of the Ionian mode without compromising its functional structure, whereas changing either fourth or seventh modal degrees results in the weakening of tonal function. Accordingly, the intervals created above the modal tonic may be divided into two categories. The first category that consists of the second, fourth, fifth, and seventh can be used to describe the structural "skeleton" of the mode. The second category, consisting of the third and sixth describe the "color" of the mode.

The traditional criteria used to describe the color of each mode details how the remaining five modes of the diatonic family compare to the major (Ionian) or minor (Aeolian) modes. The generally accepted view is that the Dorian, Phrygian, and Locrian are "minor-like" whereas the Lydian and Mixolydian are "major-like." This interpretation of modal color relies mostly on the minor or major third and sixth modal degrees found in these modes. While such comparisons are valid when dealing with individual modes in a closed modal system, they become ineffective when used to describe modal color in a 20th century musical context.

POLYMODAL CHROMATICISM

There are many instances in 20th century music where bimodal or poly-modal combinations are used. The use of multiple modes gives rise to a phenomenon called polymodal chromaticism. There are two ways in which polymodal chromaticism can be generated. It will arise when two or more modes, whether like or unlike, are simultaneously sounded at different transpositional levels. It will also occur when two different modes that share a common tonic are sounded simultaneously. Two different modes on C, C Ionian and C Aeolian, for example, will produce a bimodal pitch content because even if they are both C modes, they each supply different pitches. The bimodal pitch content will simultaneously contain both major and minor thirds and sixths (C–E + C–Eb and C–A + C–Ab). The modal degrees of both modes are at the same time structural and coloristic because they all serve to create a polymodal chromatic context. In such a context, the structure of a mode may or may not be of any consequence. In terms of color, the two modes of the previously mentioned modal combination will mutually cancel each others modal color and give rise to a new bimodal color that is neither "major" nor "minor."

Lutoslawski *Melodie*, a piano miniature, opens with a bimodal accompaniment figure [D–F–F#–A] that indicates the presence of at least two different modes on the same tonic. The first two melodic fragments (mm. 2–4) also indicate the presence of more than one mode because they also unfold a bimodal pitch content [A–C/C#]. Since the opening is solidly anchored to a D modal tonic, the total pitch content of the first measures [D–( )–F/F#–( )–A–( )–C/C#–D] could be interpreted as the combination of a number of modal pairs. The chromatic ending of the first phrase of the melodic statement fills the gap [A–( )–C/C#] with a Bb.[9]

This note indicates that both diatonic and non-diatonic modes are implicated because the bimodal pitch content generated by the upper

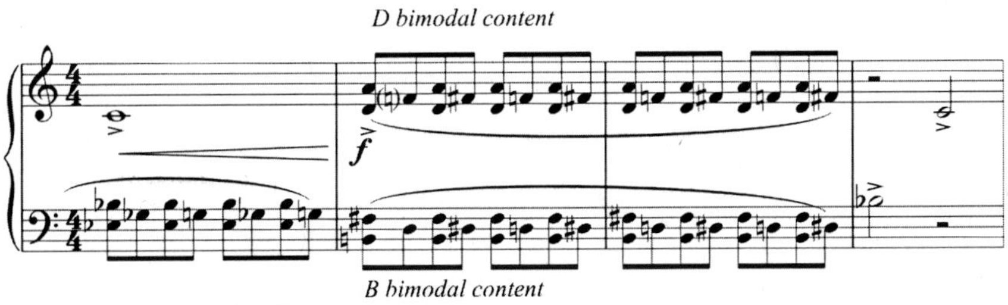

D bimodal content

B bimodal content

Figure 5.3 Lutoslawski, *Melodie* (mm. 25–28). Copyright © 1946 by PWM Edition. Used by kind permission of Chester Music Ltd., London and Polskie Wydawnictwo Muzyczne S.A., Kraków.

tetrachord. This consists of a diatonic component [A–Bb–C–D] and a non-diatonic component [A–Bb–C#–D]. The bimodal pair is never fully clarified because the pitches required to complete it are not given. Nevertheless, they are all rotated to a common tonic. A new accompaniment that establishes a new G modal center (m. 7) is unfolded after a brief chromatic descent. A complete melody (mm. 8–14), also rooted in G, generates a second set of bimodal possibilities. However, while the melody remains in G, the accompaniment transposes chromatically so that its implied bimodal combinations occur at diverging transpositional levels. The process ends (mm. 26f) when the upper part comes to rest on the opening bimodal combination [D–F–F#–A] while the lower part suggests a similar bimodal combination on B [B–D/D#–F#] (Figure 5.3). The polymodal chromaticism of the work is therefore generated in two different ways according to two different principles.

Though most musicians are accustomed to doing so, the comparison of modes to the major scale is severely limited because it can only describe modal aspects relative to it. In the realm of 20th century music, it is of little or no consequence because the major scale is no longer the referential pitch collection. It is but one of the many subcollections of the chromatic scale within which all twelve tones are of equal value. In order to evaluate the structural properties of different modes in a polymodal context, it is beneficial to compare modes not only to the modal families to which they belong, but also to different modal families as well as the interval cycles and compound cyclic collections. The reason is that a diatonic mode can exist alongside another diatonic mode as well as many other modal and cyclic constructions. It is only when this occurs that one can ascertain whether the structure of the mode plays a role in the tonal progression of the music.

The easiest way to see some of the relationships that give rise to polymodal chromaticism is to subdivide the modes into their lower and upper tetrachords. In doing so, we discover that different modal tetrachords relate not only to one another but also to different non-diatonic and cyclic collections.

Mode	Lower Tetrachord		Upper Tetrachord	
C Ionian	[C–D–E–F]	(diatonic)	[G–A–B–C]	(diatonic)
C Dorian	[C–D–Eb–F]	(octatonic, acoustic)	[G–A–Bb–C]	(octatonic, acoustic)
C Phrygian	[C–Db–Eb–F]	(diatonic)	[G–Ab–Bb–C]	(diatonic)
C Lydian	[C–D–E–F#]	(whole tone, acoustic)	[G–A–B–C]	(diatonic)
C Mixolydian	[C–D–E–F]	(diatonic)	[G–A–Bb–C]	(octatonic, acoustic)
C Aeolian	[C–D–Eb–F]	(octatonic, acoustic)	[G–Ab–Bb–C]	(diatonic)
C Locrian	[C–Db–Eb–F]	(diatonic)	[Gb–Ab–Bb–C]	(whole tone, acoustic)

If we compare lower and upper diatonic tetrachords of interval ratio 2:2:1 [e.g., C–D–E–F], we discover that the lower tetrachord of the Ionian mode is identical to that of the lower tetrachord of the Mixolydian. In terms of interval ratio, this tetrachord is identical to its own upper tetrachord [G–A–B–C][10] as well as the upper tetrachord of the C Lydian mode. This last tetrachord could also be the lower tetrachord of the G Ionian and G Mixolydian modes. The same kinds of relationships exist for the diatonic tetrachords of interval ratio 1:2:2 as well as the octatonic (2:1:2) and whole-tone (2:2) tetrachords.

The octatonic lower tetrachord of the Dorian mode is identical to its own upper tetrachord as well as the lower tetrachord of the Aeolian mode and the upper tetrachord of the Mixolydian mode. The lower whole-tone tetrachord of the Lydian mode [C–D–E–F#] is identical to that of the upper tetrachord of the Locrian mode. From the comparisons of the diatonic tetrachords, we can see that their similarities and differences can be used to generate the discrepancies that make up polymodal chromaticism.[11] Since this concept serves as the compositional basis for an enormous number of 20th century works, "In the Hungarian Style," from Bartók's *Mikrokosmos*, will serve to demonstrate this principle. In this short two-piano work, various modes that all share a common D tonic are unfolded both linearly and vertically.

Piano I (mm. 1–2) unfolds the lower pentachord of a D mode that cannot be fully identified because it is incomplete [D–E–F–G–A]. Below this, Piano II unfolds the upper pentachord of two possible modes that cannot be certified [G–A–B–C/C#–D] exclusively as one or the other.[12] Nevertheless, the combined pitch content of both pianos implies the simultaneous presence of a non-diatonic hybrid mode, that is, a rotation of the acoustic scale [D–E–F–G–A–B–C#] as well as the D Dorian mode [D–E–F–G–A–B–C–D]. In the following measures, however (mm. 3–4), Piano I confirms the D Dorian mode [D–E–F–G–A–B–C–D] by unfolding it linearly, while Piano II suggests the linear completion of the D Lydian mode [D–E–F#–G#–A–B–C#–D] (Figure 5.4). The combined pitch content of these two measures (mm. 3–4) yields a different model of the hybrid mode rotated to the common tonic of D [D–E–F#–G#–A–B–C–D].

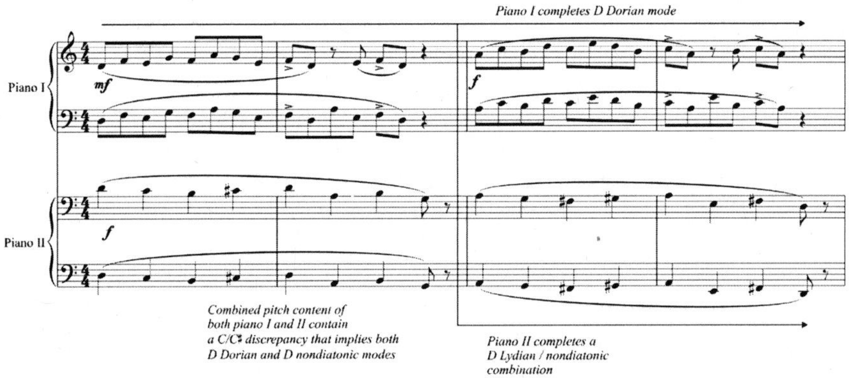

Figure 5.4 Bartók, *In the Hungarian Style* (mm. 1–4). *In the Hungarian Style from Mikrokosmos by Béla Bartók © Copyright 1940 by Hawkes & Son (London) Ltd. [Definitive corrected edition © Copyright 1987 by Hawkes & Son (London) Ltd.] Reprinted by Permission.*

In a single four-measure phrase, the composer thus unfolds four different modes (two diatonic and two hybrid rotations) that all share the same modal tonic. Even though the modes of this particular combination differ from one another, the piece is unambiguously rooted to a D modal center. In many 20th century works, the discrepancies that result from polymodal chromaticism are often used to create symmetrical structures that are capable of generating cyclic and compound cyclic pitch collections.[13]

MODAL ROTATION

As shown by the Bartók example, the concept of polymodal chromaticism is directly related to the concept of modal rotation. The idea of rotating or revolving the pitch order of a musical structure is not new. Any musician who has had to practice arpeggios in all their inversions is familiar with this concept. There are two kinds of modal rotation.

The first consists of literally rotating the order of a given pitch content. When this is done, the pitch content stays the same but the intervallic structure changes. In effect what one is doing is rotating the intervallic structure of a single modal model. As can be seen from any of the modal tables, when the process is applied to a modal model, the number of modal rotations is the same as the number of the model's constituent pitches. While each new mode has the identical pitch content, each has a new intervallic structure and is at a different transpositional level. This kind of rotation will not produce polymodal chromaticism.

The second kind of modal rotation consists of rotating the intervallic structure of all the constituent modes of a modal family to a single modal tonic. The result is that one will obtain all the modes of a particular modal family at one transpositional level. In this case, both the pitch content and the intervallic structure of each mode will be different. Polymodal chromaticism will result from this kind of rotation.

The *Hymne* from Stravinsky's *Sérénade en La* is based on the systematic rotation of four diatonic bimodal combinations to a single tonic. The bimodal pitch content of the principal motive [A–Bb/B–C–D–E–F–G] is generated (mm. 1–2) by the combination of the A Aeolian and A Phrygian modes (Figure 5.5a).

This combination remains unchanged for almost all of the first double period (mm. 1–14). It is only toward the end of this formal structure (second half of m. 12) that two new bimodal combinations occur. The A Aeolian is maintained and paired to the A Dorian to yield the pitch content of the new combination [A–B–C–D–E–F/F#–G]. This is immediately followed by an A Dorian/A Mixolydian combination [A–B–C/C#–D–E–F#–G] that concludes the double period (Figure 5.5b).

(a) mm. 1-2

(b) mm. 12-14

Figure 5.5a   Stravinsky, *Hymne* (mm. 1–2).
Figure 5.5b   Stravinsky, *Hymne* (mm. 12–14). *Serenade in A by Igor Stravinsky ©️ Copyright 1926 by Hawkes & Son (London), Ltd. Reprinted by Permission.*

The return of the principal motive (m. 15) sees the reinstatement of the original bimodal combination. This, however, is short-lived because at the beginning of the very next four-measure phrase (mm. 20f.) the A Ionian and the A Lydian combine to generate the pitch content of the fourth bimodal combination [A–B–C#–D/D#–E–F#–G#].

It is almost unavoidable to notice that the sequence of chromatic discrepancies [Bb/B–F/F#–C/C#] of bimodal combinations in the first double period is cyclic. The G/G# discrepancy that would form a cyclic link between those of the opening and the D/D# discrepancy of the final A Ionian/Lydian seems to be the only missing one. It disclosed (m. 22) by the unfolding of an incomplete Ab Ionian mode [Ab–Bb–C–Db–Eb–( )–G] and confirmed by a second modulation to G Mixolydian within the same measure. The cyclic segment is therefore completed [Bb/B–F/F#–C/C#–G/Ab–D/D#] and itself bound by the perfect fifth [A–E] completes the entire chromatic cycle. This clearly demonstrates that the modal pitch relations are not conceived in a traditional way but from a greater perspective that involves symmetrical pitch relations. Common-tonic modal rotation is especially significant in demonstrating that each mode is but an individual part of the referential chromatic scale that comprehends the unordered twelve-tone system.

The extraction of diatonic modes as subsets of the chromatic scale need not involve so many different modal pairs. The reason for this is that certain bimodal combinations complement one another to complete the chromatic scale. In the diatonic modal family the Locrian/Ionian, the Locrian/ Lydian and the Phrygian/Lydian combinations will all fulfill this goal. The latter of the three combinations forms the compositional basis for Adam's *Phrygian Gates*. Except for its middle section, this continuous four-movement work is entirely dedicated to the systematic presentation of the Lydian and Phrygian modes, nearly all of its pitch relations being governed by the perfect fifth cycle.[14]

The process of presentation is achieved by individually rotating each of the two successive modes to the same tonic. Since this process is repeated several times, the rotation of the two modes to the E tonic can serve as a representative example. After a long additive process (mm. 137–263) that slowly unfold the complete pitch content of the E Lydian mode [E–F#–G#–A#–B–C#–D#], a relatively short but dramatic *cresc* leads to a sudden key change in which all the sharps of the Lydian key signature [F#–C#–G#–D#–A#] are replaced by the naturals of the Phrygian one (Figure 5.6). To highlight the arrival of the "Phrygian gate," the continuous ostinato texture moves from a high to an extremely low register.

In the switch from Lydian to Phrygian mode all the sharps of the former mode are chromatically lowered by the naturals of the latter mode that highlight all the semitones of the chromatic cycle. The relationship of these two modes to the chromatic cycle is not the only modal/cyclic

Figure 5.6 Adams, *Phrygian Gates* (mm. 234–238). Copyright © 1983 by Associated Music Publishers, Inc., NY. All rights Reserved. Used by permission of G. Schirmer, Inc. & Associated Music Publishers, Inc.

relationship. The sequence of tonal areas [A–E–B–F#–C#–Ab–Eb], for example, follows the perfect fifth cycle. Even the gradual additive process that is used for formation of a mode within a single tonal area is governed by this cycle. The first three pitches [E–B–F#] generate a three-note segment (mm. 1–8) of the perfect fifth cycle.[15] An added D# (m. 21) extends the cycle to an incomplete cyclic segment [E–B–F#–( )–( )–D#]. The missing notes are filled in cyclical order to complete the segment [E–B–F#–C#–G#–D#] that is cyclically extended to complete the modal pitch content of the mode [A–E–B–F#–C#–G#–D#]. It is therefore clear that even though the texture of this piece is modal, both the choice of chromatically complementary modes and modal pitch relations are cyclical. Again the modes have been shown to be reflections of the unordered twelve-tone system.

MODAL COMPLEMENTATION

As was previously shown, modes can be generated from an axis of symmetry.[16] This concept can also be demonstrated using a specific kind of bimodal combination based on the principle of inversion. If the intervallic structure of a given mode is applied to an inversionally related form of the original, then a new mode will be generated. Both the original and inverted form will belong to the same modal family because both will have an identical intervallic structure. The principle of complementary inversion can be applied to the entire diatonic modal family. This will result in three complementary pairs where one mode is the inversion of the other. This is can be more clearly represented in a more visual form.

Pair 1

```
                                        C
                                   B
                              A
                         G                    C Ionian mode
                    F
               E
          D
C_ 2____ 2 ____ 1___ 2___ 2___ 2___ 1___      number of semitones
C   2     2     1     2     2     2     1      between modal pitches
     Bb
          Ab
               G                              C Phrygian mode
                    F
                         Eb
                              Db
                                   C
```

Pair 2

```
                                   C
                              B
                         A
                    G                         C Lydian mode
               F#
          E
     D
C_ 2___ 2 ____ 2___ 1___ 2___ 2___ 1___       number of semitones
C   2    2     2     1     2     2     1       between modal pitches
     Bb
          Ab
               Gb                             C Locrian mode
                    F
                         Eb
                              Db
                                   C
```

Pair 3

```
                                   C
                              Bb
                         Ab
                    G                         C Aeolian mode
               F
          Eb
     D
C_ 2___ 1 ____ 2___ 2___ 1___ 2___ 2____      number of semitones
C   2    1     2     2     1     2     2       between modal pitches
     Bb
          Ab
               G                              C Mixolydian mode
                    F
                         Eb
                              Db
                                   C
```

The Dorian mode is the only one that generates such a pair because it is a symmetrical structure that will generate a duplicate of itself when inverted.

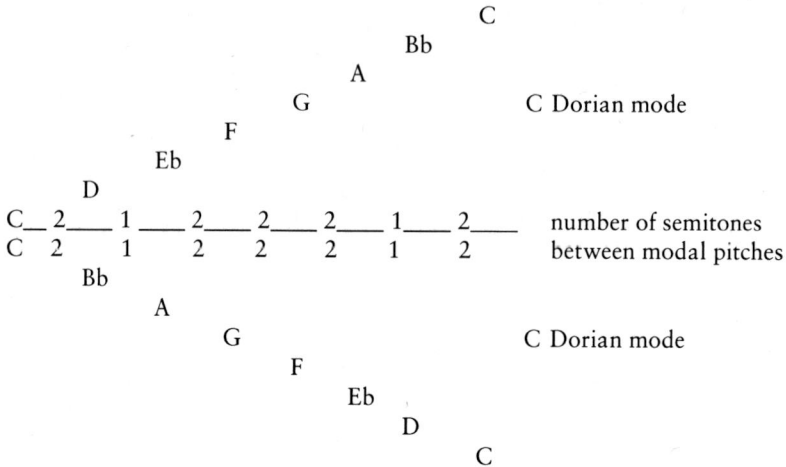

```
                                        C
                                  Bb
                            A
                      G                       C Dorian mode
                F
          Eb
      D
C_ 2___ 1 ___ 2___ 2___ 2___ 1___ 2____   number of semitones
C   2    1     2     2     2    1    2      between modal pitches
  Bb
    A
      G                                   C Dorian mode
        F
          Eb
            D
              C
```

These complementary pairs demonstrate how nonsymmetrical modal pairs, Dorian excluded, can generate symmetrical modal and cyclic collections. If we take the Aeolian/Mixolydian pair, for example, we can see that the first four notes of the original and complementary inversion result in the complete, symmetrical Dorian mode (G–A–Bb–C/C–D–Eb–F = C–D–Eb–F–G–A–Bb–C). Using the same principle, the Locrian/Lydian pair will generate the complete whole-tone cycle [Gb–Ab–Bb–C/C–D–E–F# = Gb–Ab–Bb–C–D–E–F#]. The pairs integrate nonsymmetrical structures into a system based primarily on symmetry.

Bartók's *Mikrokosmos* No. 12, "Reflection," is based on the principle of modal inversion. As its name suggests the entire miniature consists of two gradually unfolding pentachords [D–E–F–G–A and G–A–B–C–D] that mirror one another to generate the complete Dorian mode [D–E–F–G–A–B–C–D].[17] Again this shows that even in a strictly modal context, a mode has the propensity of being able to exist in another, broader, musical context.

NON-DIATONIC MODES

It is also the same as the lower tetrachord of the Lydian/Mixolydian mode that can be rotated to generate a family of hybrid modes that are found in a large number of 20th century works. The Lydian/Mixolydian mode or Acoustic scale exists as a seven-note non-diatonic mode (C–D–E–F#–G–A–Bb) in authentic Romanian folk music. In this context it is known as the Romanian non-diatonic folk mode. The intervals formed above the tonic of each of its rotations appear in the table below.

Acoustic Scale/Rumanian Non-Diatonic/Lydian/Mixolydian Hybrid Mode

Rotation 1	C–D–E–F#–G–A–Bb–(C)	M2, M3, A4, P5, M6, m7, P8
Rotation 2	C–D–E–F–G–Ab–Bb–(C)	M2, M3, P4, P5, m6, m7, P8
Rotation 3	C–D–Eb–F–Gb–Ab–Bb–(C)	M2, m3, P4, d5, m6, m7, P8
Rotation 4	C–Db–Eb–Fb–Gb–Ab–Bb–(C)	m2, m3, d4, d5, m6, m7, P8
Rotation 5	C–D–Eb–F–G–A–B–(C)	M2, m3, P4, P5, M6, M7, P8
Rotation 6	C–Db–Eb–F–G–A–Bb–(C)	m2, m3, P4, P5, M6, m7, P8
Rotation 7	C–D–E–F#–G#–A–B–(C)	M2, M3, A4, A5, M6, M7, P8

The lower and upper tetrachords of this mode, listed in the following table, reveal significant differences between it and the diatonic modes especially with regards to the number of relationships the two modal families share with the interval cycles.

Rotation 1	C–D–E–F#	(whole tone)	G–A–Bb–(C)	(octatonic)
Rotation 2	C–D–E–F	(diatonic)	G–Ab–Bb–(C)	(diatonic)
Rotation 3	C–D–Eb–F	(octatonic)	Gb–Ab–Bb–(C)	(whole tone)
Rotation 4	C–Db–Eb–Fb	(octatonic)	Gb–Ab–Bb–(C)	(whole tone)
Rotation 5	C–D–Eb–F	(octatonic)	G–A–B–(C)	(diatonic)
Rotation 6	C–Db–Eb–F	(diatonic)	G–A–Bb–(C)	(octatonic)
Rotation 7	C–D–E–F#	(whole tone)	G#–A–B–(C)	(octatonic)

The lower tetrachord of rotation 2 is the same as the lower tetrachords of both the Ionian and Mixolydian modes. Its upper tetrachord is equal to the upper tetrachords of the Phrygian and Aeolian modes. The upper tetrachord of rotation 5 is the same as the upper tetrachord of the Ionian and Lydian modes while the lower tetrachord of rotation 6 is identical to that of the Phrygian and Locrian modes. While this hybrid mode shares some common tetrachords with various diatonic modes, the table clearly demonstrates that both lower and upper tetrachords of the Lydian/Mixolydian modal rotations have far more in common with cyclic collections than the diatonic modes. Of the fourteen tetrachords yielded by all the rotations of the hybrid mode, ten are cyclic or compound cyclic (six octatonic and four whole tone).

The breakdown of the modes into component tetrachords is customary when dealing with modes that have similar modal structure, particularly with regards to constituent note numbers, it does not satisfy comparisons with scalar and cyclic collections that cannot be broken down into two equal-number tetrachords. The Lydian/Mixolydian mode serves to demonstrate this point. If we look at rotation 7 [C–D–E–F#–G#–A–B–(C)] of the mode, we discover that the first five modal tones generate a five-note segment of the whole-tone 0 cycle [C–D–E–F#–G#–( )], one note shy of cyclic completion. The first six modal tones of rotation 3 [C–D–Eb–F–Gb–Ab–Bb–(C)] generate a complete octatonic-0 hexachord [C–D–Eb–F–Gb–Ab]. This is the reason why this particular mode appears so often in 20th century music where modal/cyclic transformations play a significant role in the generation of tonal progression.[18] Since this mode is so closely related to so many modal and cyclic collections, it stands to reason that it would be used in textures where its versatile structure can be used to generate polymodal chromaticism and cyclic transformations.

In *Pipes and Drums*, for example, Bartók uses different rotations of the hybrid mode to start its new cyclic transformations and help outline the formal structure of the work by presenting it as the referential pitch collection at significant formal junctures. The opening of the work (mm. 1–10), a succession of "drum" dyads assert an E tonic. The first ritornello and episode are dedicated to the gradual unfolding of the third rotation of the special non-diatonic mode [E–F#–G–A–Bb ( )–D] in an incomplete form. After a brief restatement of the drum *ritornello* (mm. 12–14), a new rotation of the mode (rotation 7), also in incomplete form, is unfolded separately (mm. 19–20) by the upper register [D–E–F#–G#–A#] and lower [C#–D–E] registers. The fourth *ritornello* unfolds (mm. 41–43) the complete original transposition of the non-diatonic mode [E–F#–G–A–Bb–C–D]. After octatonic and whole-tone transformations, a newly rotated transposition of the mode is used to conclude the fourth episode. After the final ritornello (mm. 89–104), the coda of the work (mm. 105–114), the lower tetrachord [E–F–G–A] of rotation 6 of the basic mode is introduced and followed by an octatonic segment [F#–G–A–Bb] that alludes to the original rotation (rotation 3). As a referential collection in a polymodal chromatic context, the structure of the Lydian/Mixolydian lends itself to the generation of a variety of both diatonic and non-diatonic modal combinations.[19]

In Szymanowski's *Mazurka* Op. 50, No. 1, the Lydian/Mixolydian hybrid mode is used as the source pitch collection for a number of polymodal combinations and transformations.[20] The descending hybrid mode [E–F#–G#–A#–B–C#–D] is unfolded in its complete form (mm. 1–2, second beat) as the basic melodic idea of the piece.[21] Immediately following this (m. 2, third beat), the first polymodal combination is introduced [E–F#–G#–A#–B–C/C#–D#–E] by both melody and harmony. This suggests the presence of the E Lydian mode [E–F#–G#–A#–B–C#–D#–E] as well one of its non-diatonic variants [E–F#–G#–A#–B–C–D#–E]. At the end of the first phrase (m. 4), all but one of the Lydian sharps are lowered so that the combined pitch content of the melody and accompaniment unfolds the E Aeolian mode [E–F#–G–A–B–C–D–E].

A new polymodal combination is introduced in the second half of the first formal section (mm. 1–16), where two bimodal discrepancies [G/G# and C/C#] combine to once more suggest the Lydian mode as well as an non-diatonic E Phrygian Dominant rotation [E–F#–G–A–B–C–D#–E], that is, the fourth rotation of B–C–D#–E–F#–G–A–B.[22] After an intensely chromatic passage at the beginning of the second section (mm. 17–53) a new non-diatonic mode [E–F#–G–A–Bb–C#–D–E]. The principle Lydian/Mixolydian melodic statement is brought back in the final measures to confirm the primacy of the mode as the referential pitch collection of the work. The Gypsy and Phrygian Dominant Modes are also non-diatonic modes. Perhaps the easiest way to describe the non-diatonic Gypsy mode is to say that it is a natural minor scale with a raised fourth degree. Its most striking structural feature is that it contains the interval of the augmented second.

Gypsy Modal Rotations

Rotation 1	C–D–Eb–F#–G–Ab–Bb–(C)
Rotation 2	C–Db–E–F–Gb–Ab–Bb–(C)
Rotation 3	C–D#–E–F–G–A–B–(C)
Rotation 4	C–C#–D–E–F#–G#–A–(C)
Rotation 5	C–Db–Eb–F–G–Ab–B–(C)
Rotation 6	C–D–E–F#–G–A#–B–(C)
Rotation 7	C–D–E–F–G#–A–Bb–(C)

The non-diatonic Phrygian Dominant is also frequently found in 20th century works. Like the Gypsy mode it contains the interval of the augmented second. When this interval is rotated so that it lies between the sixth and seventh modal degrees it forms what is more commonly known as the *harmonic minor scale*.[23]

Phrygian Dominant Modal Rotations

Rotation 1	C–Db–E–F–G–Ab–Bb–(C)
Rotation 2	C–D#–E–F#–G–A–B–(C)
Rotation 3	C–Db–Eb–Fb–Gb–Ab–Bbb–(C)
Rotation 4	C–D–Eb–F–G–Ab–B–(C)
Rotation 5	C–Db–Eb–F–Gb–A–Bb–(C)
Rotation 6	C–D–E–F–G#–A–B–(C)
Rotation 7	C–D–Eb–F#–G–A–Bb–(C)

With the exception of the Mixolydian mode, every other diatonic family member has a complementary rotation of the Phrygian Dominant mode that will be identical to it but for one note. The same thing can be said about the relationship between the diatonic modes and Gypsy modal rotations except that in this case, all but the Dorian mode share this relationship with complementary Gypsy modal rotations.

	Diatonic Mode		Gypsy Modal Rotations
C Ionian	C–D–E–F–G–A–B–C	Rotation 3	C–D#–E–F–G–A–B–(C)
C Dorian	C–D–Eb–F–G–A–Bb–C		
C Phrygian	C–Db–Eb–F–G–Ab–Bb–C	Rotation 5	C–Db–Eb–F–G–Ab–B–(C)
C Lydian	C–D–E–F#–G–A–B–C	Rotation 6	C–D–E–F#–G–A#–B–(C)
C Mixolydian	C–D–E–F–G–A–Bb–C	Rotation 7	C–D–E–F–G#–A–Bb–(C)
C Aeolian	C–D–Eb–F–G–Ab–Bb–C	Rotation 1	C–D–Eb–F#–G–Ab–Bb–(C)
C Locrian	C–Db–Eb–F–Gb–Ab–Bb–C	Rotation 2	C–Db–E–F–Gb–Ab–Bb–(C)

	Diatonic Mode		Phrygian Dominant Modal Rotations
C Ionian	C–D–E–F–G–A–B–C	Rotation 6	C–D–E–F–G#–A–B–C
C Dorian	C–D–Eb–F–G–A–Bb–C	Rotation 7	C–D–Eb–F#–G–A–Bb–C
C Phrygian	C–Db–Eb–F–G–Ab–Bb–C	Rotation 1	C–Db–E–F–G–Ab–Bb–C
C Lydian	C–D–E–F#–G–A–B–C	Rotation 2	C–D#–E–F#–G–A–B–C
C Mixolydian	C–D–E–F–G–A–Bb–C		
C Aeolian	C–D–Eb–F–G–Ab–Bb–C	Rotation 4	C–D–Eb–F–G–Ab–B–C
C Locrian	C–Db–Eb–F–Gb–Ab–Bb–C	Rotation 5	C–Db–Eb–F–Gb–A–Bb–C

Both Gypsy and Phrygian Dominant modes share an even more complete relationship with the Lydian/Mixolydian mode because, for every rotation of either Gypsy or Phrygian dominant modes, there is a complementary rotation of the Lydian/Mixolydian mode that is identical but for one note. It is therefore clear that all diatonic and non-diatonic modes share a high degree of pitch content, their mutual transformations being a question of single pitches. The augmented second of both the Gypsy and Phrygian Dominant modes is of special interest when it comes to the question of how polymodal chromaticism can play a significant role in generating a new means of tonal progression. In the realm of diatonic harmony, the augmented second creates a tendency tone that in both modes alludes to a tonic other than that of the mode itself. The modal tonic of the first rotation of the Gypsy mode is a C. Nevertheless, the augmented second between Eb and F# implies a G tonic as well. At the same time, the augmented second of both these two modes can be filled in different way to create different polymodal combinations. In the polymodal context, both these factors can play a role in tonal progression.

This concept is articulated in Albéniz's *El Albaicin*.[24] The ostinato pattern that opens the work generates a Bb Aeolian/harmonic minor polymodal pitch content [Bb–C–Db–Eb–F–Gb–Ab/A–Bb] that establishes Bb (mm. 1–32) as the primary tonal center. Midway through this section (mm. 15–17), the upper harmonic tetrachord [F–Gb–A–Bb] of the Bb harmonic minor bimodal component is accompanied by a continuously asserted F.[25] While the augmented second occurs in the upper tetrachord of the Bb harmonic minor scale, it also forms the lower tetrachord of the now suggested F Phrygian Dominant mode [F–Gb–A–Bb–C–Db–Eb–F].[26] This mode foreshadows the eventual modulation to an F Phrygian mode (m.69) that is extracted from an F bimodal combination that unfolds prior to the modulation (m. 68). In the transition that precedes this modulation (mm. 33ff.), the pitch content is altered to unfold a Bb Gypsy mode [Bb–C–Db–E–F–Gb–Ab–Bb],[27] which contains in its lower tetrachord the augmented second [Db–E], which transforms the E into a "leading tone."

The same augmented second is contained in the F Phrygian/harmonic minor combination [F–Gb–Ab–Bb–C–Db–E–F] used to modulate (m. 69) to the final F Phrygian mode.[28] While the modulation from a Bb to an F tonal area is a traditional one, the means employed to do so are not. Rather than using traditional modulatory means, Albéniz uses the polymodal combination of the Bb harmonic minor and Bb Gypsy modes that supply both the "leading tones" to the starting Bb and final F modal areas.

Bb Harmonic minor:	Bb C Db Eb F Gb A Bb
Bb Gypsy:	Bb C Db E F Gb Ab Bb
Bb polymodal combination:	Bb C Db Eb E F Gb Ab A Bb

It shows how the use of both diatonic and non-diatonic modes are a viable alternative to the traditional forms of modulation in that modal combinations such as this one also supply the complete pitch content from which all preparatory and final modes can be extracted.

While most of the pitch relations discussed in this chapter are purely modal, the latter studies indicate that the 20th century use of modes occurs within a larger system in which their identity is no longer strictly modal. In the next chapter, the cyclic transformation of these modal constructs will show their existence both as asymmetrical modes and nonsymmetrical cyclic constructions.

6 Modal/Cyclic Relationships

Music : W. A. Mozart *Sonata in C major*
Maurice Ravel *Laideronnette, Imperatrice des pagodes*
Vladimir Rebikov *In the Forest*
George Ligeti *Désordre*
Claude Debussy *L'isle Joyeuse*
Igor Stravinsky *Petrushka*
Béla Bartók *Sonata for Piano, Out of Doors Suite*
Alexander Scriabin *Prelude* Op. 74, No. 3
Manuel De Falla *Noches en los jardines de España*

MODALITY AND THE TWELVE-TONE SCALE

Throughout the evolution of western musical language, changes have occurred in the conception of the structure and identity of scales and their interactions. Western music from the early Christian era to the early Baroque was based on the system of diatonic church modes. Each of these modes is unequally constructed according to a specific, fixed succession of whole and half steps in relation to a fundamental modal tonic. If notes foreign to the mode are temporarily introduced into the musical texture, they will be heard as chromatic intrusions. These intrusions do not threaten modal integrity but rather serve to embellish the diatonic modal degrees. If a modal element is altered, then a change of mode or true modulation takes place. Modulation produces a change of modal identity. In the modal system, modulation can only occur between modes that belong to that system. In early modal music, modulation can only occur linearly because the music can only be based on one mode at a time.

In tonal music of the common practice era, the major scale is primary since two of the minor modes are not diatonic. Like the modes, the structure of the major scale is a fixed succession of whole and half steps in relation to the tonic degree. It cannot be altered without compromising the tonal integrity of that scale. Unlike the modes of the early modal system, each degree of a major or minor scale fulfills a specific functional role. Each role has its place within a larger system that is based on a tonal hierarchy. Temporary alterations of the scalar structure of major and minor scales are also perceived as chromatic intrusions. The only real modulation that can occur within the tonal system is that of a switch from the major to minor mode, or vice versa. What we commonly call *modulation* is for the most part actually *transposition* (e.g., from C major to G major). Modulation from major to minor and vice versa entails the alteration of the third and sixth scale degrees and has no effect on tonal function. However, the permanent alteration of other scale degrees, such as the leading tone, would result in the complete collapse of the tonal hierarchy because functions such as that of the leading tone generate progression in tonal music.

As in the modal system, modulations can be said to occur between major and minor modes because the music can only be based on one or the other mode at any given time, though major/minor mixture was increasingly prevalent in the 19th century in the move toward a more chromatic tonal system. Toward the end of the common practice era an ever-increasing number of chromatic alterations began to weaken tonal function so essential to traditional tonal progression. This was compounded by the incorporation of modes and scales that could not generate functional pitch relationships but instead served to weaken and eventually obliterate tonal function. As a result, the twelve chromatic tones were made equal and a new conception of the identity of the chromatic scale was achieved.

The chromatic scale was no longer viewed as the set of pitches that lie outside modes and major/minor scales. It therefore ceased to be the source of chromatic color for modal and tonal music. It supplanted the major and minor scales of the crumbling tonal system as the prime or basic pitch collection of the modern era. This change of conception had far-reaching implications. A limitless realm of new tonal relationships was unveiled. These relationships could now be based on newly established sets of rules. The new tonal relations would generate new means of harmonic progression and tonal centricity. It also meant that all existing scalar formations, now viewed as subsets of the chromatic continuum, could be used in new ways.

THE TWO TWELVE-TONE SYSTEMS

Compositions based on the system of twelve equal tones first fell into two broad categories: serial or ordered twelve-tone idea used by composers of the Second Viennese School, and non-serial, unordered twelve-tone idea used by composers as wide-ranging as Bartók, Stravinsky, Ligeti, and Tower.

In serial twelve-tone composition, the chromatic scale is completed by an ordered (thematic) succession of all twelve tones. The order in which the twelve tones are cast is chosen by the composer. The "ordered" chromatic scale is the fixed pre-compositional referent. It is from this that other set forms of the original order—transformations and transpositions—are derived. No matter how the derived forms of the row are used in the music, chromatic completion will always occur because it is preordained by the system. Every note within the system has equal value, which eliminates any form of pitch-class priority.

In unordered twelve-tone composition, the complete chromatic scale is the pre-compositional premise based on the content but not order of its subcollections. However, since it is not made to follow any prearranged order, it may be used in any number of ways. In a large portion of 20th century music, the chromatic spectrum is partitioned into subset pitch collections. These can include segments of the chromatic scale itself, complete or incomplete diatonic and non-diatonic modes, and complete or incomplete simple and compound interval cycles. These may be used either singly or in simultaneous combinations. In unordered twelve-tone composition, chromatic completion is not a prerequisite but often occurs as a matter of course at important structural junctures. The system accommodates various forms of tonal centricity based on the use of diatonic collections that establish tonal centers as a matter of course or the symmetrical arrangement of tones around axes of symmetry that act as tonal centers. It also accommodates textures that have no tonal center. In twelve-tone serialism, the "ordered" chromatic scale is always in the foreground, as a surface phenomenon, while in the non-serial conception, the chromatic scale is usually reserved as background material from which one can draw chosen elements to the fore. It is precisely this peculiarity of the unordered twelve-tone idiom that allows for an array of modal techniques not permitted by the early modal, traditional tonal, and serial twelve-tone systems, each of which is based on a single source pitch collection that ensures the integrity of the system it represents.

In order to understand the array of modal techniques used in a large body of 20th century music, it is necessary to study the structural properties of elements common to both the modes and the interval cycles. On the surface, it would seem that modes and interval cycles have little in common because the interval cycles are symmetrical while the modes are not. It is only when the modes are reordered and or reinterpreted, that we are able to reveal their cyclic properties/elements and therefore explain how these are utilized to transform modes into cyclic sets and vice versa. It must be remembered that modal reinterpretation is possible because of the 20th century view of the modes themselves. In a large portion of 20th century music, the modes of the old modal era no longer generate a closed and unified modal system, but become component substructures of a much larger system based on the unordered twelve tones of the chromatic scale.[1]

MODAL/CYCLIC TRANSFORMATIONS

The seven diatonic modes are obtained by rotating the tone/semitone sequence of the Ionian mode [major scale] six times so as to obtain the Dorian, Phrygian, Lydian, Mixolydian, Aeolian and Locrian modes.

Diatonic Modal Rotations

C Ionian	C–D–E–F–G–A–B–C
D Dorian	D–E–F–G–A–B–C–D
E Phrygian	E–F–G–A–B–C–D–E
F Lydian	F–G–A–B–C–D–E–F
G Mixolydian	G–A–B–C–D–E–F–G
A Aeolian	A–B–C–D–E–F–G–A
B Locrian	B–C–D–E–F–G–A–B

All the modes have the same number of whole tones and semitones, but the sequence of these is systematically permuted in each mode.

Most often, the diatonic modes are studied relative to the major and minor scales of the traditional tonal system. From this tonal perspective, they are likened to the major or minor scales by the intervallic qualities they display. These qualities are determined by the third and sixth degrees of each mode. They are also identified by comparing the differences of respective structural tones that render the modes "odd" relative to the major and minor scales. The structural tones of the major minor scales are those that cannot be changed without compromising the fundamental tonal integrity of the scale. One can alter the third and sixth degrees freely without any structural consequences. If, however, an alteration is made to the second, fourth, fifth, and seventh degrees, the tonal integrity of the scale is compromised because the functional hierarchy that exists within the major or minor scale is either weakened or destroyed.

Identifying the modes by their "major" or "minor" qualities works well within a tonal framework but is of little relevance to the interval cycles because of their neutrality in terms of modal or tonal structure. The incorporation of modes into the traditional tonal system served to first weaken and then destroy tonal function in the major/minor system. This development played a significant part in the equalization of the twelve tones.

The most familiar of the modes is the Ionian, also known as the major scale. The Ionian mode is unique because it is the only one that places the tritone as the fourth and seventh modal degrees. The position of the tritone creates tonal hierarchy within the mode and thus functional tonal harmony. When the order is rotated, the tritone is shifted and the leading-tone function that would exist in the major and minor scales is eliminated because rotation causes the half-step adjacencies to the tonic to be replaced by the whole step. The loss of the half-step relation neutralizes the leading-tone tendency. The following table shows how this holds true for the Dorian, Phrygian, Mixolydian, Aeolian, and Locrian modes.

Complete Family of Diatonic Modes Rotated to Common Tonic

C Ionian	C–D–E–F–G A–B–C	
C Dorian	C–D–Eb–F–G–A–Bb–C	[flattened 7th]
C Phrygian	C–Db–Eb–F–G–Ab–Bb–C	[flattened 2nd and 7th]
C Lydian	C–D–E–F#–G–A–B–C	[raised 4th]

C Mixolydian	C–D–E–F–G–A–Bb–C	[flattened 7th]
C Aeolian	C–D–Eb–F–G–Ab–Bb–C	[flattened 7th]
C Locrian	C–Db–Eb–F–Gb–Ab–Bb–C	[flattened 2nd, 5th, and 7th]

The loss of leading tonal function can be easily illustrated using Mozart's *Piano Sonata in C major.* [2]

In the Ionian mode the resolution of the tritone (mm. 1–2) is as it should be, the leading tone resolving directly to the tonic. If the same excerpt were to be in the C. Mixolydian mode, the lowered Bb would destroy the leading tone function. In the Lydian mode the leading tone function like that of major and minor scales is retained, but the fourth (subdominant) modal degree is raised, thus weakening its tendency to resolve to the third modal degree. In this case, the neutralizing effect is brought to bear on the fourth degree.

The semitones between the third and fourth, and seventh and eighth scale degrees render major and minor scales nonsymmetrical. Nonsymmetry creates a tonal tension that requires resolution of the fourth to third, and seventh to eighth scale degrees. Flattening the second degree of a major or minor scale creates a semitone directly above the tonic, bestowing upon the tonic a false leading-tone function that completely destabilizes tonal centricity of the scale. This is perhaps why the Phrygian and Locrian are perceived as the most unusual modes.

Many late 19th and early 20th century composers began to extract harmonies based on the structural rather than coloristic modal tones. Tertian harmonies (harmonic structures based on thirds) were replaced by harmonies based on seconds, fourths, fifths, and sevenths. Chords built on such intervals needed no preparation or resolution because of their self-evident stable structure.

At the same time that the modes were being incorporated and exploited for the "new" sonorities they offered, composers were also making extensive use of abstract pitch sets such as the whole-tone and octatonic scales. These too yielded a plethora of new musical sounds. Several composers began to use these abstract pitch sets alongside the modes and soon came to the realization that the two categories of scalar formations had so many elements in common that they could easily be transformed into one another. The fundamental principle composers discovered was that all pentatonic, diatonic, non-diatonic, and hybrid modes can be shown to be scalar expressions of various interval cycles.

If we subdivide each of the seven diatonic modes into their upper and lower tetrachords, we will discover that many of these tetrachords are symmetrical.

Modal Tetrachords

C Ionian	C–D–E–F = Diatonic	G–A–B–C = Diatonic
C Dorian	C–D–Eb–F = Octatonic	G–A–Bb–C = Octatonic
C Phrygian	C–Db–Eb–F = Diatonic	G–Ab–Bb–C = Diatonic

C Lydian	C–D–E–F# = Whole tone	G–A–B–C = Diatonic
C Mixolydian	C–D–E–F =Diatonic	G–A–Bb–C = Octatonic
C Aeolian	C–D–Eb–F = Octatonic	G–Ab–Bb–C = Diatonic
C Locrian	C–Db–Eb–F = Diatonic	G–Ab–Bb–C =Diatonic

The octatonic tetrachords of the Dorian, Mixolydian, and Aeolian modes, and the whole-tone tetrachord of the Lydian mode, are all segments of simple or compound interval cycles. This indicates that the diatonic mode contains inherent cyclic properties that remain implicit or become explicit depending on the modal rotation. The Dorian rotation, for example, is a perfectly symmetrical structure made up of two octatonic tetrachords, while the Locrian rotation is made up of two diatonic tetrachords that render it completely nonsymmetrical.

We consider the division of the modes into upper and lower tetrachords customary, but because the modes are related to different interval cycles of varying lengths, strict tetrachordal subdivision of the modes must be modified to accommodate the new relationships. While the C Ionian mode can be subdivided into its two traditional diatonic tetrachords, C–D–E–F and G–A–B–C, a cyclic whole-tone interpretation of the same mode reveals that it can be subdivided into two mutually exclusive whole-tone segments from each of the whole-tone cycles, C–D–E from whole-tone 0 and F–G–A–B from whole-tone 1. Since the two whole-tone cycles have been shown to be systematically related to both interval-1/11 and interval-7/5 cycles,[3] it follows that the mode itself must also be related to these. Just as the interval-7/5 cycle is a systematic reordering of the interval-1/11 cycle, so the diatonic mode is a systematic reordering of the interval-7/5 cycle.

C Ionian mode in scalar order C–D–E–F–G–A–B
C Ionian mode in cyclic order F–C–G–D–A–E–B

Direct relationships also exist between the five modal pentatonic rotations and the interval cycles. Regardless of which of the five notes is selected to be the tonic or which of the five rotations is prevalent in a piece of music, the relationship between the pentatonic modes and the interval cycles does not change.

Pentatonic Rotations
Mode 1   C–D–F–G–A
Mode 2   D–F–G–A–C
Mode 3   F–G–A–C–D
Mode 4   G–A–C–D–F
Mode 5   A–C–D–F–G

As was done for the diatonic modes, rotation to a common tonic can be applied to the pentatonic modes.

Mode 1	C–D–F–G–A	C–D (whole-tone 0)	F–G–A (whole-tone 1)
Mode 2	C–Eb–F–G–Bb	Bb–C (whole-tone 0)	Eb–F–G (whole-tone 1)
Mode 3	C–D–E–G–A	C–D–E (whole-tone 0)	G–A (whole-tone 1)
Mode 4	C–D–F–G–Bb	Bb–C–D (whole-tone 0)	F–G (whole-tone 1)
Mode 5	C–Eb–F–Ab–Bb	Ab–Bb–C (whole-tone 0)	Eb–F (whole-tone 1)

Like the diatonic modes, the pentatonic scale can be subdivided into two whole-tone segments. The only difference is that the whole-tone segments that make up the pentatonic scale are shorter. The transposition of a particular rotation of the pentatonic mode will determine whence the whole-tone segments come. The procedure used to demonstrate the relationship between the diatonic modes and the interval-7/5 cycle can be repeated to show the relationship between the pentatonic modes and that same cycle.

C Pentatonic in scalar order   C–D–F–G–A
C Pentatonic in cyclic order   F–C–G–D–A

It is interesting to note that the ancient Chinese constructed the pentatonic scale as a series of descending fourths or ascending fifths. The cyclic interpretation of the modes can be seen as an extension of the same process that gave the chromatic scale its new identity. While the scalar order of the mode is based on a tonal center, the cyclic order of the same mode is not. In the new musical language that was emerging at the beginning of the 20th century, tonality and progression were no longer dictated by the rules of harmonic function but established by compositional and aesthetic ideals of the composers themselves. In this new language pitch, content often superseded pitch order, and as a result, modes and cycles were seen as two different expressions of the same pitch content. This allowed for a revolutionary process in which mutual transformation between mode and cycle could take place. Transformation can be broadly defined as the act or operation of changing the form or external appearance of something. The term has been adopted in many different fields of study. In physics, for example, the potential energy of a stationary object is transformed into kinetic energy when that object is in motion. In geometry, transformation occurs when a geometrical figure is changed into another that has an equal area but a different number of sides. Metamorphosis describes the biological transformation of a caterpillar into a butterfly. These examples clearly demonstrate that transformation is that process which lies between an initial and terminal state that must share a number of common elements. Modal/cyclic and cyclic/modal transformations are no exception. All rely on common elements shared by both cycle and mode, be it an equal interval ratio, an identical number of pitches or any other structural feature can be used in the transformational process.

Perhaps the most significant of transformational processes is the cyclic generation of the modes. In this type of transformation, a specific modal pitch content is cyclically generated to outline a segment of a particular interval cycle. In this initial cyclic state, the pitch content cannot be recognized as a mode because the symmetrical cyclic segment has no tonic. It is precisely at this point that the composer can choose to transform the cyclic segment by bestowing the role of modal tonic to any of the constituent pitches. This can be achieved by presenting the mode in its scalar order or by asserting a modal center through continuous repetition of a single tonic that establishes new contextual pitch relations with remaining modal pitches.

In the opening measures (mm. 1–3) of Ravel's *Laideronnette, Imperatrice des pagodes* ("Little Homely, Empress of the Toy Mandarins"), a series of whole-tone dyads C#–D#, G#–A#, and F#–G#, interlocked at the perfect fifth on every downbeat, unfolds two interval-7 cyclic segments [C#–G#–D#–A# and F#–C#–G#–D#] that when joined generate a five-note segment of the interval-7/5 cycle [F#–C#–G#–D#–A#]. This mutual cyclic unfolding generates the complete C# pentatonic pitch content in terms of both the interval-2/10 and the interval-7/5 cycles (Figure 6.1a). The C# pentatonic mode is expressed in its scalar order immediately following the cyclic generation of its pitch content (mm. 5–6).

(a) mm. 1-6

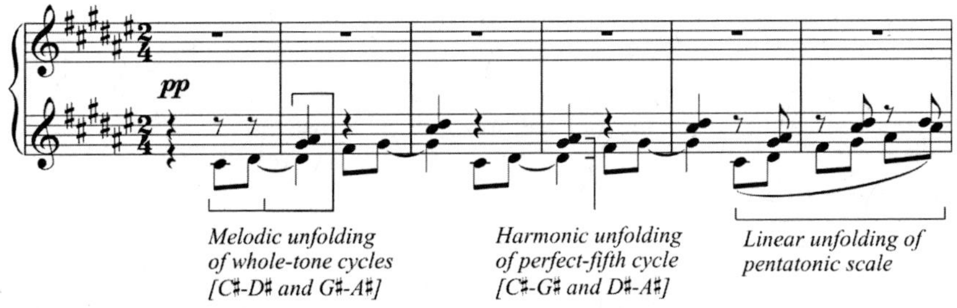

Melodic unfolding
of whole-tone cycles
[C#-D# and G#-A#]

Harmonic unfolding
of perfect-fifth cycle
[C#-G# and D#-A#]

Linear unfolding of
pentatonic scale

(b) mm. 12-13

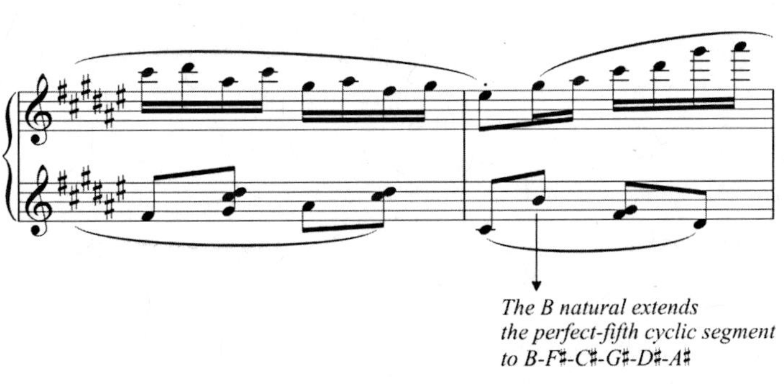

The B natural extends
the perfect-fifth cyclic segment
to B-F#-C#-G#-D#-A#

Figure 6.1a   Ravel, *Laideronnette, Imperatrice des pagodes* (mm. 1–6).
Figure 6.1b   Ravel, *Laideronnette, Imperatrice des pagodes* (mm. 12–13).

A purely pentatonic melody commences (m. 9) above the modal pentatonic accompaniment. Interestingly, the melodic disposition of the melody
creates a symmetrical pentatonic structure [F#–D#–C#–A#] that hinges on
two interlocking perfect fourths.

The complete pitch content of the entire texture remains exclusively pentatonic until cyclically extended (m. 13) by a B in the accompaniment to
generate a six-note segment of the interval-7/5 cycle [B–F#–C#–G#–D#–
A#] (Figure 6.1b). Above this new accompaniment, the pentatonic melody
is rotated downward three times. While not highly significant in the context
of cyclic generation of modes, modal rotation of this kind is one of the fundamental compositional techniques found in much 20th century music.

In the climactic measures of this passage (mm. 25–30), marked by a series
sharp dynamic contrasts and extreme changes of register in the melody, the
cyclic underpinning of the texture is made explicit. The accompaniment is
presented as descending perfect fifths [C#–G# and B–F#] while the melody
alternates grace note figures and melodic dyads consisting exclusively of
perfect fourths [G#–D# and G#–C#] and whole-tone dyads that interlock
perfect fourths [C#–D#–F#–G#].[4]

The parallel descent of the perfect fifths demonstrates that "diatonic
planning" is a cyclic rather than modal phenomenon. As soon as the melody restarts (m. 32), the accompaniment introduces the final note necessary
to complete the diatonic modal pitch content. The key signature suggests
that this note should be an E# because the key signature is that of F# major;
however, in its place there appears a continuously accented E. This unexpected occurrence marks the continuation of the extension of the cyclic
interval-5/7 segment by the accompaniment that now generates a complete
modal pitch content [E–B–F#–C#–G#–D#–A#]. The melody and accompaniment of the ensuing measures (mm. 32–37) create a bimodal texture
with C# as the new tonal center. The melody, still exclusivity pentatonic,
asserts C# at the beginning of every measure while the accompaniment
anchors the diatonic pitch content to the same pitch that now acts as a
modal tonic to the C# Dorian mode [C#–D#–E–F#–G#–A#–B].[5]

The bitonality is disrupted (m. 39) by a sudden change in the pitch content of the entire texture that renders it exclusively whole tone. This sudden and unexpected change can occur as the result of transformation from
mode to cycle, the opposite of that used hitherto in the piece. The upper
trichord of the C# pentatonic melody [F#–G#–A#] also represents a three-
note segment of the whole-tone 0 cycle. While the melody repeats these
notes in an ostinato pattern, the accompanying voices outline a whole-tone
descent that cyclically extends the pitch content of the trichord to complete
the whole-tone 0 cycle [A#–G#–F#–E–D–C–A#].

In the final measures of the first formal section (mm. 55–64), the pitch
content of the C# Dorian is rotated to finally establish the F# modal center
designated by the key signature now represented by the F# Mixolydian
mode. The cyclic origins of the mode are reasserted in an accompaniment

that cyclically reorders the modal pitch content in a series of tetrachords. These interlock interval-5 and inversionally complementary interval-7 dyads at the whole-tone in precisely the same manner used at the beginning of the piece.

In *Laideronnette, Imperatrice des pagodes*, the interlocking of simple interval-7/5 cyclic segments generates the initial whole-tone dyads as well as the pentatonic and diatonic modes. The whole-tone dyads in the pentatonic mode are then used to complete the whole-tone cycle. The bimodal texture created in the middle portion of the opening section is somewhat limited because the pentatonic mode, while expressed as an independent entity, is embedded in the diatonic mode and does not create any discrepancies between the two modes. In this piece the transformational process describes the cyclic generation of what essentially is one mode by a single simple interval cycle.

The reverse process, where single modes or modal combinations create a simple interval cycle, is also used in a great number of 20th century works. In these works, the complete or incomplete mode is outlined in its modal order before its cyclic potential is exploited to affect a transformation in which the cyclic elements are abstracted to fulfill their compositional directives. In works where the musical texture is subdivided into the traditional melody and accompaniment, the mode is often suggested by the melodic component while the accompaniment aids in establishing the tonal center and supplying modal tones absent in the melody. In works where there is no melodic/harmonic differentiation, the mode is spread over the entire texture. In both cases, nevertheless, a modal or tonal center is established at the onset of the piece.

In the third movement of Bartók's *Sonata for Piano*, the cyclic/modal relationships presented in Ravel's *Laideronnette* are reversed.[6] In the Ravel example, the cyclic accompaniment unfolds the pentatonic scale, whereas in the Bartók *Sonata*, the scale is presented first and the cyclic accompaniment is then generated. This process represents the cyclic extension of the mode. In terms of modal/cyclic relationships, the sequence in which the process begins is a relative one because both scalar pitch collection and interval cycle are one and the same.

In the opening of the movement (mm. 1–2), the principal theme immediately outlines an incomplete pentatonic collection [F#–E–C#–B–( )] and is punctuated by an accompanying chord [A–D–E] that both completes the pentatonic collection [F#–E–C#–B–A] and begins to outline a segment of the interval-5/7 cycle [D–A–E] (Figure 6.2a)

The established pentatonic nucleus is then subjected to different treatment by the melody and accompaniment. While the melody incorporates a D# (mm. 3–4), implying a modal completion, the accompaniment supplies a new chord [G–A–D] that extends the cyclic segment unfolded by the first chord [G–D–A–E] creating a D/D# modal discrepancy between it and the melody. The modal ambiguity created by the D/D# semitone does

(a) mm. 1-4

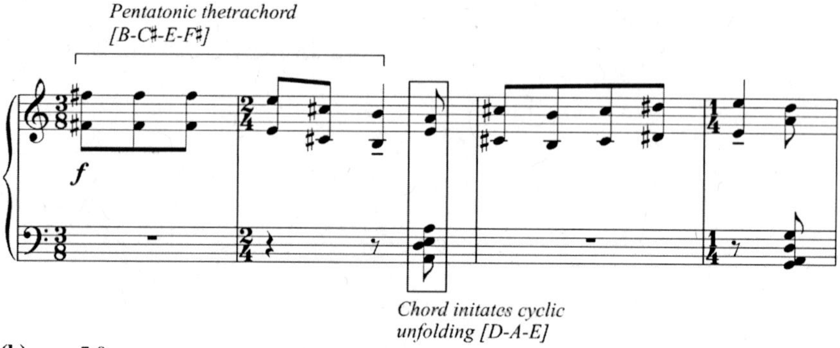

Pentatonic thetrachord [B-C#-E-F#]

f

Chord initates cyclic unfolding [D-A-E]

(b) mm. 7-8

Chord establishes E modality and extends perfect-fifth cycle to A-E-B-F#

Figure 6.2a   Bartók, *Piano Sonata*, Mvt. III (mm. 1–4).
Figure 6.2b   Bartók, *Piano Sonata*, Mvt. III (mm. 7–8). *Sonata for Piano by Béla Bartók © Copyright 1927 by Boosey & Hawkes, Inc. Copyright Renewed. Reprinted by Permission.*

not, however, disrupt the establishment of E as the primary modal center because it sounds alone on the downbeat of the last measure of the phrase. The D# that immediately precedes it further acts as a "leading tone" to the E, whereas the natural D is sounded afterward.

The abstraction of cyclic elements in the pentatonic collection is clarified as a process by the chords of the accompaniment (m. 8), which extract the principal tones of the initial thematic statement [E–B–F#], thus creates a cyclic chord that now establishes the E modality in a harmonic structure (Figure 6.2b). The interaction of melody and accompaniment generate a modal/cyclic texture in which the melody yields a non-diatonic mode, expressed in scalar order [E–F#–G–A–B–C#–D#], while the accompaniment unfolds as a seven-note segment of the interval-7/5 cycle [G–D–A–E–B–F#–C#]. These manifestations are maximally manifest as to pitch content.

The most extensive cyclic transformation of the modes used in the movement occurs in the coda of the movement (mm. 264–281). Here, both the melody and accompaniment are absorbed into a long series of cyclic chords that gradually outline a ten-note segment of the perfect fifth cycle [F–C–G–D–A–E–B–F#–C#–G#].[7] The central position of the E within this segment suggests that the E modality is established through the use of symmetry and confirmed by the E's of the final chord.

MODAL COMPLETION OF THE CYCLES

Both simple and compound interval cycles can be created by combining or interlocking two modes, where the individual modes may be from either the same or different modal families. One of the most prevalent examples of this principle occurs when two modes interlock to generate the complete interval-1/11 cycle or chromatic scale. As a general principle, the completion of this cycle indicates that it is the source pitch collection of the unordered twelve-tone continuum and most often occurs in conjunction with the completion of significant structures such as phrases, periods, and larger formal units. In many instances, chromatic completion occurs progressively and terminates in places similar to where one would find the basic cadences in traditional tonal music.

Chromatic completion by modes from a single modal family can occur in two ways. If they share a common tonic, the second of the two modes must contain the missing chromatic pitches. This allows for several combinations, two of which are shown here.

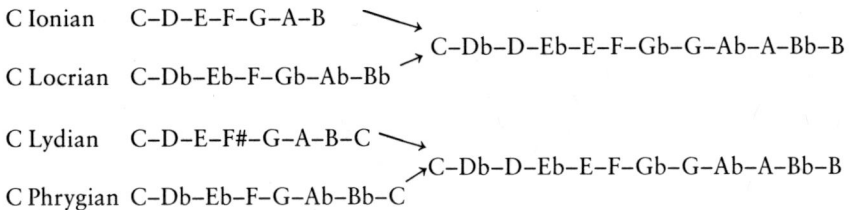

C Ionian   C–D–E–F–G–A–B
                           C–Db–D–Eb–E–F–Gb–G–Ab–A–Bb–B
C Locrian   C–Db–Eb–F–Gb–Ab–Bb

C Lydian   C–D–E–F#–G–A–B–C
                          C–Db–D–Eb–E–F–Gb–G–Ab–A–Bb–B
C Phrygian   C–Db–Eb–F–G–Ab–Bb–C

This sort of modal combination is unique in that it allows a kind of chromatic completion that retains a strong modal sense because of the shared tonic. A second way of combining two single-family modes is by using transpositions of the same or different modes. This usually results in a texture where the bimodality is easy to perceive because of the different transpositional levels of individual modes. Since the number of combinations is so vast, the following example must suffice to demonstrate the general principle.

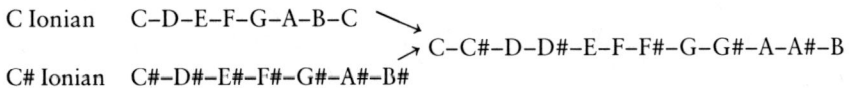

C Ionian   C–D–E–F–G–A–B–C
                          C–C#–D–D#–E–F–F#–G–G#–A–A#–B
C# Ionian   C#–D#–E#–F#–G#–A#–B#

Chromatic completion may also be achieved by using modes from different modal families. Again, the bimodality of the resulting texture is even more discernible because there are two different modes at different transpositional levels. The number of possible combinations is also so vast that one of the most favored modal combinations of this kind, that is, a pentatonic/diatonic one has been chosen to demonstrate this kind of combination.

C# Pentatonic C#–D#–F#–G#–A#

C–C#–D–D#–E–F–F#–G–G#–A–A#–B

C Ionian   C–D–E–F–G–A–B–C

In the Forest, one of Rebikov's "Trois Idylles," Op. 50, represents a developmental stage in the technique of bimodal completion of the chromatic cycle. While the bimodal combination of the "black key" pentatonic [C#–D#–F#–G#–A#] accompaniment and the "white key" diatonic [C–D–E–F–G–A–B] melody together produce a static musical texture, each part is unfolded in a series of triads that though not functional, still convey a strong tonal sense. The invariable accompaniment for the first half of this unmeasured piece is an arpeggiated F#–A#–C# triad. Against this accompaniment, the initial melodic statement, unfolded as a pair of parallel arpeggiated triads [G–B–D and F–A–C], generates a diatonic hexachord [F–G–A–B–C–D]. Together, the melody and accompaniment generate a gapped chromatic segment [F–F#–G–( )–A–A#–B–C–( )–D] that is clearly bimodal.[8]

The following long melodic ascent completes the diatonic white note collection [E–F–G–A–B–C–D] establishing what seems to be an E tonal center. The completion of the diatonic pitch collection brings the entire texture one note closer to the completion of the chromatic segment, now missing only two notes [E–F–F#–G–( )–A–A#–B–C–C#–D–( )]. A counterbalancing melodic descent establishes a new C tonal center that is confirmed in the central section. The C tonality is decipherable only by the assertion of the "tonic" at end of each melodic statement. The missing D# and G# are supplied by the accompaniment of the new middle section which points to the completion of the pentatonic black key collection laid out in scalar order [C#–D#–F#–G#–A#]. The diatonic melody is chromatically interlocked with the accompaniment to produce a series of adjacent semitone pairs that move parallel to one another, unfolding a cyclic segment in scalar order [C–C#–D–D#–E–F–F#–G–G#].

The miniature ends with the opening accompaniment while the melody unfolds the complete diatonic collection in a series of parallel triads [E–G–B, D–F–A, and C–E–G] that elucidate the C tonality. Despite the tonal underpinnings, the gradual bimodal completion of the chromatic cycle forms the compositional basis of the piece and is implemented in such a way that it helps to delineate the formal structure of the work.

The identical bimodal combination has been favored by many composers throughout the 20th century. While Rebikov's cyclic realization originates from a modal perspective, that of later 20th century composers stems from a purely cyclic perspective. In Ligeti's first piano etude *Désordre* (1983), the black note pentatonic, white note diatonic combination redefines the completion of the chromatic cycle in a context of conflicting tonal identities (C and F#) and neither pentatonic nor diatonic modes used in the combination retains a consistent tonal identity.

The formal structure of *Désordre* is based on a series of phases articulated by a gradual metric misalignment and subsequent realignment of the bar lines of the upper and lower parts. In the first few measures (mm. 1–4), the upper and lower parts are aligned note for note. At the fifth measure, the lower part adds an extra eight note while the upper part starts a new measure creating a misalignment so that the two parts are out of phase. The process is continued so that the individual parts move further and further apart only to be realigned when the process has run its full cycle (m. 33 of the upper part). The texture is arranged in such a way that the *piano* modal collections, whether complete or incomplete, are punctuated by *forte* octaves that mark the misalignment of the two parts (Figure 6.3).

The upper part consists exclusively of the white note diatonic pitch collection [C–D–E–F–G–A–B] while the lower consists exclusively of the black note pentatonic collection [C#–D#–F#–G#–A#]. Combinatorial completion of the interval-1/11 cycle occurs within the first four measures and is highlighted by the complete scalar unfolding of both modes. However, the punctuating octaves outline a series of regularly alternating tritones that disrupt any sense of tonality.

Upper octave:	B	C	B	D	C	A
Interval:	8	6	8	6	4	6
Lower octave:	D#	F#	D#	G#	G#	D#

When the modes are finally laid out (m. 4), the intervals between the notes of the two parts describe a symmetrical convergence from the tritone to the semitone that reveals the symmetrical identity of the chromatic scale rather than the tonal one.

Upper diatonic collection:	A	B	C	D	E	F	G
Interval:		6	5	4	4	3	2	1
Lower pentatonic collection:	D#	F#	G#	A#	C#	D#	F#

Further evidence that the two pitch collections are seen as chromatic subcollections rather than two individual modes is supplied by the next phrase that ends in precisely the same way as the first. The intervallic sequence described by the now misaligned octaves outlines all but one of the tritones contained in the complete chromatic cycle. The only remaining tritone [B–F] cannot be generated by the bimodal combination because it is the only tritone in which neither pitch class is contained in the pentatonic collection. The two collections are therefore linked exclusively by the interval-6/6 cycles.

Figure 6.3   Ligeti, *Désordre* (mm. 1–5). *Ligeti Études Pour Piano, Book I. Copyright © 1986 Schott Music GmbH & Co. KG, Mainz—Germany. All Rights reserved. Used by permission of European American Music Distributors LLC, sole U.S. and Canadian agent for Schott Music GmbH & co. KG, Mainz–Germany.*

```
Upper octave: A   A   D   C   E   D   G
Interval:     6   3   6   6   6   4   6
Lower octave: D#  F#  G#  F#  A#  A#  C#
```

When the two parts reach a synchronized realignment (m. 33 of the upper part), the octaves once more outline a tritone [F#–C] confirming that the completion of the chromatic scale is intended as a true transformation from bimodal combination to interval cycle.

CYCLIC TRANSFORMATION OF BIMODAL COMBINATIONS

Bimodal combinations can be used to create not only simple interval cycles such as the chromatic but also compound interval cycles such as the octatonic. The unequal interval ratios characteristic of the latter cycles are replicated in the chromatic discrepancies that arise from the combination of two different modes.

In the first movement of Bartók's *Piano Sonata*, the combination of the E Lydian and E Mixolydian modes creates a special kind chromaticism used to transform the initial bimodal texture into an octatonic one. The two lines that sound the principal motive of the first theme group present it in two different permutations, G#–A–B in the lower part, and G#–A#–B in the upper part. While the former is of interval ratio 1:2, the latter is of interval ratio 2:1 and together they articulate both octatonic interval ratios (Figure. 6.4a)

The E tonal center is asserted (mm. 2f.) by a series of E major triads that extend the pitch content to E–( )–G#–A/A#–B. In the course of the following measures, three new notes [F#, C, and D] momentarily generate a mode, *heptatonia tertia*[9] [E–F#–G#–A#–B–C–D] in which is embedded the complete whole-tone 0 cycle [C–D–E–F#–G#–A#–C]. Though not significant in the modal/octatonic transformation, it suggests that a modal/

cyclic transformation is implicit. The bimodality of the texture is confirmed (m. 7) when the principal motif is restated by the upper and lower parts, thus completing the pitch content of the E Lydian [E–F#–G#–A#–B–C#–D#–E] and E Mixolydian [E–F#–G#–A–B–C#–D–E] modes, respectively. This particular modal combination has the potential to generate several cyclic segments, among which is the octatonic hexachord G#–A#–B–C#–D–E. This bimodally generated hexachord is literally laid out in its scalar order by the top part of the first statement of the principal motif [G#–A#–B] and by the lower part in the restated version [C#–D–E] (Figure 6.4a).

The remaining two notes required to complete the octatonic compound cycle are supplied by a *sf* octave that marks the return to the original meter (m. 14). The missing E# is supplied by the accompaniment (m. 16) that underscores an exclusively octatonic-2 [G#–A#–B–C#–D–E–E#–G] texture.

The octatonic transformation of the bimodal pitch content is by no means transitory. The events that occur in the first sixteen-measure period of the *Sonata* once again demonstrate that changes of pitch collections, in this case transformational, occur at significant formal junctures. The midpoint

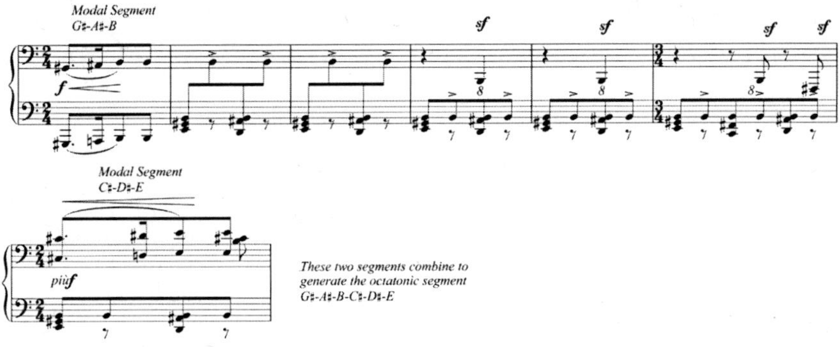

Figure 6.4a Bartók, *Piano Sonata*, Mvt. I (mm. 1–7).
Figure 6.4b Bartók, *Piano Sonata*, Mvt. I (mm. 13–16). *Sonata for Piano by Béla Bartók* © *Copyright 1927 by Boosey & Hawkes, Inc. Copyright Renewed. Reprinted by Permission.*

of a traditional sixteen-measure period would be punctuated by some kind of cadence. In this instance the cadence is replaced by the completion of the two modes. A strong cadence is also customary in the last measure of a traditional double period; here, it is replaced by the completion of the octatonic transformation of the bitonal texture.

HYBRID MODES AND CYCLES

The use of bimodal and polymodal combinations has given rise to a class of hybrid modes that contain some of the structural properties of both genitor modes. The most well known example of the hybrid modal class is the Lydian/Mixolydian mode. It contains the raised fourth modal degree of the Lydian mode and the flattened seventh of the Mixolydian mode.

C Lydian   C–D–E–F#–G–A–B
                                              → C–D–E–F#–G–A–Bb
C Mixolydian   C–D–E–F–G–A–Bb ↗

The Lydian/Mixolydian hybrid mode is also known to some as the *acoustic scale* and as *Heptatonia Secunda* to those who study Hungarian folk music. Nevertheless, it is found in an abundance of 20th century music. Like the diatonic mode, this hybrid mode can be rotated to generate a family of seven modal rotations.

Rotations of the Lydian/Mixolydian Hybrid Mode
Mode 1   C–D–E–F#–G–A–Bb–C
Mode 2   D–E–F#–G–A–Bb–C–D
Mode 3   E–F#–G–A–Bb–C–D–E
Mode 4   F#–G–A–Bb–C–D–E–F#
Mode 5   G–A–Bb–C–D–E–F#–G
Mode 6   A–Bb–C–D–E–F#–G–A
Mode 7   Bb–C–D–E–F#–G–A–Bb

Hybrid modes are special not only because of their unique modal colors but because of their potential cyclic elements. The relationship between these modes and the interval cycles is strong because the unusual chromatic alterations arising from the hybridization process often creates large cyclic segments within them. When rotated to a common tonic, the relationship between mode and cycles becomes even clearer.

Mode 1 C–D–E–F#–G–A–Bb–C   C–D–E–F# (whole tone)   G–A–Bb–C
                                                                            (octatonic)
Mode 2 C–D–E–F–G–Ab–Bb–C   C–D–E–F (diatonic)   G–Ab–Bb–C
                                                                        (octatonic)

Mode 3 C–D–Eb–F–Gb–Ab–Bb–C C–D–Eb–F (octatonic)   Gb–Ab–Bb–C
                                                       (whole tone)
Mode 4 C–Db–Eb–Fb–Gb–Ab–Bb–C C–Db–Eb–Fb (octatonic) Gb–Ab–Bb–C
                                                        (whole tone)
Mode 5 C–D–Eb–F–G–A–B–C   C–D–Eb–F (octatonic)   G–A–B–C
                                                        (diatonic)
Mode 6 C–Db–Eb–F–G–A–Bb–C   C–Db–Eb–F (octatonic)   G–A–Bb–C
                                                        (octatonic)
Mode 7 C–D–E–F#–G#–A–B–C   C–D–E–F# (whole tone)   G#–A–B–C
                                                        (octatonic)

The traditional upper/lower tetrachord breakdown shown here demonstrates how closely this mode is related to both the whole-tone and octatonic cycles. However, the pitch relationships that exist between this mode and the cycles extend beyond the traditional scalar tetrachord. The lower hexachord of mode 3 is also the lower hexachord of the octatonic-0 cycle [C–D–Eb–F–Gb–Ab], while the lower pentachord of mode 7 represents five of the six notes of the whole-tone 0 cycle [C–D–E–F#–G#]. Unlike the diatonic modal family, this mode cannot be cyclically generated using seven consecutive fifths of the interval-7/5 cycle because it contains two chromatic alterations. However, an eight-note segment of the perfect fifth cycle contains all the notes required for its generation [Bb–(F)–C–G–D–A–E–B–F#], the chromatic discrepancy [F/F#] seeming to create the only impediment.

In *L'isle Joyeuse*, Debussy uses the chromatic discrepancy to generate the Lydian/Mixolydian hybrid mode as well as both whole-tone cycles by the interlocking one of the whole-tone [interval 2] cycles of the melody and a perfect fifth [interval 7] cyclic segment of the accompaniment. The opening measures of the work consist of a trill and a thirty-second note melisma that outlines three descending interval-4 triads [B–D#–G, A–C#–F, and G–B–D#]. These inreval-4 trichords interlock to form the complete whole-tone or interval-2/10 cycle [A–B–C#–D#–F–G–A] part of which may also be interpreted as an incomplete acoustic scale [A–B–C#–D#–( )–( )–G] (Figure 6.5a). The chromatic passing tones [C, Bb, Ab] imply the presence of the other whole-tone cycle which is contained in the F#–E of the acoustic scale theme at m. 9 [A–B–C#–D# / E–F#/ G, the E–F# being the only two whole-tone 0 notes of the scale.

The scale remains incomplete for the entire introduction (mm. 1–6). The ostinato accompaniment figures of the subsequent measures (mm. 7–11) are based solely on a single perfect fifth [A–E] that almost completes the acoustic scale (m. 7) and, together with the upper part, establishes an A tonal center. The complete acoustic scale [A–B–C#–D#–E–F#–G] is then unfolded in its scalar order (m. 9) by the first real melodic statement (Figure 6.5b).

(a) m. 1

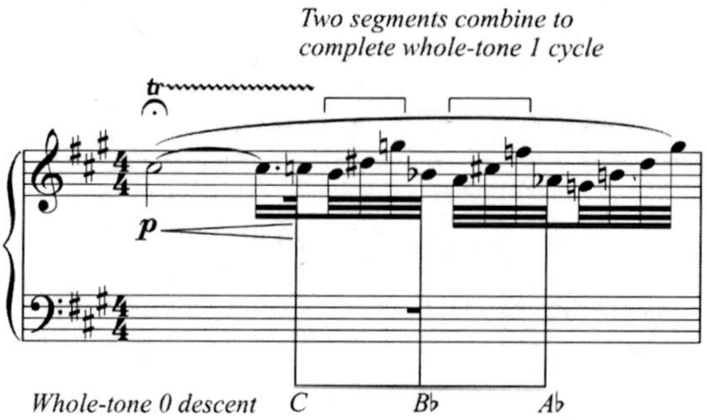

(b) mm. 8-9

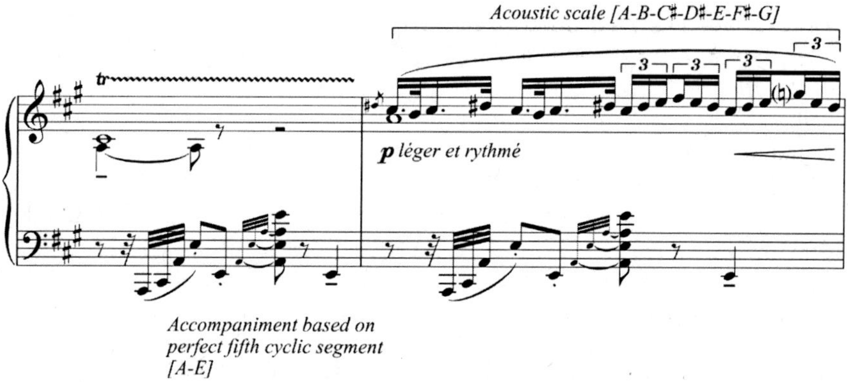

Figure 6.5a Debussy, *L'isle Joyeuse* (m. 1).
Figure 6.5b Debussy, *L'isle Joyeuse* (mm. 8–9).

However, the cyclic completion of the mode can be further clarified by investigating the relationship that exists between the initial interval-2/10 [A–B–C#–D#–E–F–G] and the systematic unfolding of the complete interval-7/5 cycle. Since this cycle can be partitioned into two mutually exclusive interval-2/10 or whole-tone cycles, the latter cycle can be mapped as a gapped six-note segment of the perfect fifth cycle [F–( )–G–( )–A–( )–B –( )–C#–( )–D#]. As the second half of the perfect fifth cycle is begins to interlock with its existing half (m. 7), it fills in all the missing notes both completing the mode as well as generating the second of the two whole-tone cycles.

Whole-tone cycle: ( )—F—( )—G—( )—A—( )—B—( )—C#—( )—D#
Unfolding P5 cycle: A—E—B—F#—C#—G#—D#—A#—F—C—G—Cx

This process occurs in the two measures that lead to the first *retenu* (ritenuto) that introduces the second statement (mm. 13–14) of the main theme.[10] In retrospect, the entire process can be traced back to the interval-7/5 cycle. The preceding example clearly demonstrates how cyclic partitioning and interlocking can generate not only diatonic and pentatonic modes but hybrid modes as well.

Since the Lydian/Mixolydian hybrid mode contains substantial whole-tone and octatonic- cyclic segments, its transformational capacity is exploited in many 20th century works. Whereas Debussy limits his exploration of the relationships between the simple cycles to the hybrid mode, in Stravinsky's "Russian Dance" from the ballet *Petrushka*, the composer uses the mode to generate not only the whole-tone cycles but also all three octatonic cycles. The process for the cyclic generation of the mode is a variation on the same technique used by Debussy in *L'isle Joyeuse* in that whole-tone dyads are used to interlock segments of the greater interval-7/5 cycle responsible for the modal generation.

In the "Russian Dance," this process is subdivided between different orchestral sections, each of which unfolds different modal segments in cyclic order.[11] The complete white note diatonic collection, sounded by the whole orchestra, forms the basic pitch content of the dance's opening measures (no. 33). The diatonicism of the opening number gives no indication of any cyclic activity. This is reinforced by traditional dominant/tonic relationships (V-I) at the end of every motivic statement. Within this diatonic texture, however, an ostinato whole-tone dyad [G–A], sounded by the brass (no. 33), is transposed to D–E by the harps and solo violins immediately following a white note glissando (No. 33, last measure). Here, the newly formed tetrachord [G–A–D–E] becomes the core harmonic structure that accompanies melodic variations of the principle motif. It also signals the cyclic reinterpretation of the diatonic pitch content of the previous number. The tetrachord, now also in the piano, can be identified as the interlocking of perfect fifth dyads that generates a five-note segment of the interval-7/5 cycle [G–D–A–E–B]. This process is confirmed by the celli of the same measure that now sound the interlocking D–A dyad. Simultaneously, the piano accompaniment adds a new perfect fifth to further extend the tetrachord [G–D–A–E–B]. On the very next beat of the same measure, the segment is cyclically extended on both ends to create a new cyclic segment [( )–C–G–D–A–E–B–F#].[12] This can also be seen as a cyclic rotation of the original modal pitch content in which the F# substitutes the F of the original diatonic pitch content.

At No. 35, the segment is once more extended by a Bb in the piano, bassoon and voile parts to generate the pitch content of the Lydian/Mixolydian hybrid mode [C–D–E–F#–G–A–Bb] and expressed in terms of both its whole-tone and octatonic qualities. The piano unfolds the whole-tone segment of the mode [F#–E–D–C–Bb] in the left hand and the voile simultaneously outline the octatonic-1 segment [E–F#–G–A–Bb–C] in a series of ascending thirds.[13]

Modal transpositions (No. 35, m. 5 and mm. 7f) ensure the completion of the original whole-tone 0 cycle and initiate a transfer to the second whole-tone cycle while simultaneously unfolding segments of the octatonic-2 and octatonic-0 cycles. Concurrent with these events, newly added black keys [F#–A#–C#–D#–G#] complete the chromatic spectrum that is once more shown to be the source of both diatonic and cyclic collections. In the "Russian Dance," cyclic/modal relationships are fully articulated in the cyclic generation of the hybrid mode that, through transposition, generates the complete range of whole-tone and octatonic cycles.

It is impossible to speak of cyclic transformation of hybrid modes without mentioning the music of Béla Bartók, not only because the composer used the latter hybrid mode extensively, but also because his transformations are among the most systematic. In *Pipes and Drums*, the first movement of the "Out of Doors Suite," Bartók uses the mode in a comprehensive set of transformations to the octatonic and whole-tone cycles as well as those diatonic modes that are closely related to the Lydian/Mixolydian hybrid mode.[14] In association with Bartók's music, the mode has been referred to as the *Romanian non-diatonic mode*. In mm. 1–10, the rhythmic dyads, which represent the drums, and the short melodic fragments, which represent the pipes, assert an E tonic. The rhythmic dyads form a ritornello that serves to depict drums; this ritornello introduces different formal sections.[15] The combined pitch content of these measures yields the incomplete third rotation of the special non-diatonic mode [E–F#–G–A–Bb–( )–D]. However, the melodic fragment that emphasizes the trichord E–F#–G (m. 10) is melodically extended downward by the whole-step D#–C# (mm. 11–12), generating a seven-note octatonic-1 segment, C#–D#–E–F#–G–A–Bb, to effect the first octatonic transformation of the non-diatonic mode through octatonic extension of the lower modal tetrachord [E–F#–G–A].[16]

This transformation coincides with the first *sf* (m. 12) that punctuates the end of the first episode. Notably, both non-diatonic and octatonic collections are missing the C that would complete them both. After a brief restatement of the drum *ritornello* (mm. 12–14), a new rotation of the mode (rotation 7), also in incomplete form, is unfolded separately (mm.19–20) by the pipes [D–E–F#–G#–A#] of the top register and drums [C#–D–E] of the bottom register. This event, also marked by a *sf*, heralds the end of the second episode. This rotation of the mode also yields the first significant whole-tone segment of the piece [D–E–F#–G#–A#].

A new drum ritornello (mm. 23–26) ushers in the third episode. The new melodic fragments of the pipes generate (m. 25) a new tetrachord [E–F#–G#–A]. This tetrachord, melodically extended to E–F#–G#–A–B (m. 26), is accompanied by a rhythmic dyad [C#–D] that yields the complete E Mixolydian mode [E–F#–G#–A–B–C#–D–E]. The melodic extension of the tetrachord continues (mm. 26–32) to generate rotation 2 of the non-diatonic mode [E–F#–G#–A–B–C–D]. Immediately following this, the dyad [C–D] that completes the non-diatonic mode (m. 33) is itself extended by whole-tones, transforming the non-diatonic mode into the complete whole-tone 0 collection [C–D–E–F#–G#–Bb].

The upper tetrachord of the E Mixolydian mode [B–C#–D–E] starts a descent in the lower register (mm. 30 f.) and is extended (mm. 32–35) by a tetrachord [A–G–F#–E] to yield the complete E Dorian mode that also marks the end of the third episode. The non-diatonic mode is thus transformed through octatonic, whole-tone, and diatonic extensions of its component tetrachords.[17]

The *ritornello* that ushers in the fourth episode (mm. 37 ff.) unfolds the original transposition of the non-diatonic mode [E–F#–G–A–Bb–C–D] in its complete form (mm. 41–43). In the lower register of the subsequent measures (mm. 45–48), the mode, spelled out in a series of descending tetrachords, is extended by a four-note octatonic segment to yield a five-note octatonic segment, Bb–B–C#–D–E, which is coupled to a three-note octatonic segment, F–G–Ab, in the upper register. The latter completes the octatonic-2 collection. The octatonic-2 tetrachord, B–C#–D–E, is transformed (m. 50) into the octatonic-0 tetrachord [B–C–D–Eb], by the lowering of the interval-3 dyad, C#–E, to C–Eb. This process is extended to a descending sequence (mm. 50–56) that transforms octatonic-0 to octatonic-1 (mm. 51–53), and octatonic-1 to octatonic- 2 (mm. 53–55).[18]

The whole-tone extension of the octatonic-0 tetrachord [C–D–Eb–F] of the top register (mm. 57–61) is completed in the bottom register of the subsequent measures (mm. 62–63) and unfolds a newly rotated transposition of the Romanian Folk mode. The drum *ritornello* (mm. 67–72), which marks the beginning of the fifth and final episode, outlines the dyads D–E and A–B. Together they outline the cycle-5/7 segment D–A–E–B. These dyads are soon (m. 73) extended by a different cycle-5/7 segment [F#–C#–G#] to generate the complete D Lydian mode [D–E–F#–G#–A–B–C#].[19]

This process is similarly repeated to generate both Bb and G Lydian modes. Bartók chooses the Lydian mode for two important reasons. First, the lower whole-tone tetrachord of the Lydian mode is structurally identical to that of the lower tetrachord of the non-diatonic mode as well as to that of the whole-tone scale. Second, the whole-tone scale as well as the Lydian mode can be systematically generated by the interval-5/7 cycle. The generation of a diatonic mode by an interval cycle that occurs at the end of *With Pipes and Drums* creates an important link to the second piece of the suite. The *Barcarolle* opens with cycle-5/7 segments that generate both whole-tone cycles. The extensive closing ritornello (mm. 89–104) is followed by a short coda (mm. 105–114), which introduces the lower tetrachord [E–F–G–A] of rotation 6 of the basic mode, followed by an octatonic segment [F#–G–A–Bb] to suggest the return of the opening rotation (rotation 3) to end the piece. In *With Drums and Pipes*, the basic mode undergoes octatonic (first episode), whole-tone (second episode), and diatonic (third and final episode) transformations by different extensions of its component tet-rachords. This specific order of transformations follows Bartók's principle of chromatic compression and diatonic expansion, moving from the more chromatic octatonic set to the diatonic Lydian mode. The transformation of the Romanian non-diatonic mode articulates the thematic development within each formal section and serves to define the formal structure of the piece. The five rotations of the basic mode represent the points of departure and arrival in the process of transformation, while serving to articulate formal structure as they are placed at significant junctures.

Nowhere is the acoustic scale/ octatonic cycle relationship tighter than in the music of Scriabin. The composer transformed the complete acoustic scale into a harmonic structure known as the *mystic chord*, which consists of a vertical series of unequal fourths created by the reordering of the scale tones.[20] The transformation of the mode into a harmonic structure allows Scriabin to use segments of the scale interchangeably between the melodic and Harmonic spheres of the texture.

Acoustic scale	C–D–E–F#–G–A–Bb
Mystic chord ordering of Acoustic scale	C–F#–Bb–E–A–D–G

Scriabin knew that by substituting one of the pitches of the acoustic scale by its upper and lower chromatic neighbors he would obtain a complete octa-tonic cycle. It is understood therefore that the process also functions the other way around. The relationship is shown in the following diagram.

Acoustic scale	C—D—E—F#—G—A—Bb
Octatonic Cycle	C—C#—D#—E—F#—G—A—Bb

In the third of his *Preludes* Op. 74, this relationship is explored in a sys-tematic manner. The pitch content of the first two measures[21] consists of the complete octatonic-1 cycle [A#–B#–C#–D#–E–F#–G–A] with the exception of one added note [G#] that appears as a passing note in the melodic line. It is precisely this note that links the octatonic collection to the acoustic scale. The latter consists of the same pitches, except where the last two pitches of the octatonic collection are substituted by the single G# just mentioned [A#–B#–C#–D#–E–F#–G#]. The second two measures are the tritone trans-position of the first two. While the octatonic collection remains unchanged [E–F#–G–A–A#–B#–C#–D#], the passing tone that appears between the last two pitches of the octatonic collection [D] generates a new transposition of the acoustic scale [E–F#–G–A–Bb–C–D] (Figure 6.6 a).

The transposition occurs three more times before the end of the first sec-tion. Two of these repeat the first two transpositions at the octave, leaving their pitch content unaltered. The octatonic collection is asserted as the exclusive collection of the B section and is unfolded in its scalar form in the final measure of the section (Figure 6.6b).

(a) mm. 1-3

(b) mm. 23-26

Figure 6.6a Scriabin, Op. 74, No. 3 (mm. 1–3).
Figure 6.6b Scriabin, Op. 74, No. 3 (mm. 23–26)

While the acoustic scale or Lydian/Mixolydian mode is well represented in many 20th century works, it is but one of a vast family of hybrid modes that continue to grow. The number of hybrid modes that can be synthesized using the seven diatonic modes alone is already great. If we then consider the cross-hybridization of the folk modes from different countries, the possibilities are even greater. The use of continuously changing modal variants is especially common in the music of 20th century Spanish, Latin American, Middle Eastern, and Hebrew composers. The reason for this is that these artists are not only influenced by western 20th century art music, but also by their own folk music, which contains strong Arab and Gypsy elements. The many non-diatonic modes and relative modal variants on which much of their music is based contain diatonic, whole-tone, octatonic, and compound interval-cycle 1:3 segments. One of the most significant of these non-diatonic modes [C–Db–E–F–G–Ab–Bb–(C)] has been named relative to its use in different parts of the world. While the term *Fregish* is used when the mode appears in Hebrew music, it has also been named *Hijaz* when used in Arabic or Turkish music and is also known as the *Spanish Gypsy* or *Phrygian dominant* mode. However, it is its fourth rotation that is most widely recognized by western musicians as the harmonic form of the minor scale [C–D–Eb–F–G–Ab–B–(C)].

Phrygian Dominant Modal Rotations
Mode 1 C–Db–E–F–G–Ab–Bb–C
Mode 2 Db–E–F–G–Ab–Bb–C–Db
Mode 3 E–F–G–Ab–Bb–C–Db–E
Mode 4 F–G–Ab–Bb–C–Db–E–F
Mode 5 G–Ab–Bb–C–Db–E–F–G
Mode 6 Ab–Bb–C–Db–E–F–G–Ab
Mode 7 Bb–C–Db–E–F–G–Ab–Bb

Phrygian Dominant Rotated to a Common Tonic.

Mode 1 C–Db–E–F–G–Ab–Bb–C	C–Db–E–F (c.c. 1:3)	G–Ab–Bb–C (octatonic-2)
Mode 2 C–D#–E–F#–G–A–B–C	G–A–B–C (diatonic)	
Mode 3 C–Db–Eb–Fb–Gb–Ab–Bbb–C	C–Db–Eb–Fb (octatonic-1)	
Mode 4 C–D–Eb–F–G–Ab–B–C	C–D–Eb–F (octatonic-0)	G–Ab–B–C (c.c. 1:3)
Mode 5 C–Db–Eb–F–Gb–A–Bb–C	C–Db–Eb–F (diatonic)	
Mode 6 C–D–E–F–G#–A–B–C	C–D–E–F (diatonic)	G#–A–B–C (octatonic-0)
Mode 7 C–D–Eb–F#–G–A–Bb–C	G–A–Bb–C (octatonic-1)	

As can be seen from the preceding table, the relationships between this modal family and the compound interval cycles are extensive. While there are no complete whole-tone tetrachords, three-note whole-tone segments are abundant, such as Ab–Bb–C in the upper tetrachord of mode 1 or G–A–B in the upper tetrachord of mode 2.

In De Falla's *Noches en los jardines de Espāna* (Nights in the Gardens of Spain, 1911–1915) interaction of the interval cycles and the different rotations of the Phrygian dominant mode effect a transformation of the latter into the compound octatonic interval cycle.[22] The modal tonality of C# minor, based on the harmonic minor rotation of the Phrygian dominant mode [C#–D#–E–F#–G#–A–B#–(C#)], is established within the first few measures of the work. The limited range of the melodic figure in the harp suggests the presence of a different rotation of the same mode [G#–A–B#–C#–D#–E–F#–(G#)] also known as the Arab variant of the G# Phrygian mode.[23] The juxtaposition of these two modal rotations creates a modal/tonal duality between the harmonic and melodic levels of introduction. However, on the harmonic level, the mode itself is generated not by a functional progression of traditional triadic structures, but by a sequence of parallel interval-7 trichords and dyads. Six of the seven modal tones are generated in this manner, the seventh being supplied by the melodic activity of the harps. The opening trichords [C#–G#–D#] of the celli and the dyads of the basses and bassoons [C#–G#], are immediately followed by a dyad [A–E] (m. 3, bassoons) to create a gapped five-note segment of the perfect fifth cycle (A–E–( )–( )–C#–G#–D#). At the first cadential point (m. 5), the addition of an F# to the C#–G# dyad of the celli extends the opening cyclic trichord to F#–C#–G#–D# and cyclically generates six of the modal tones [A–E–( )–F#–C#–G#–D#]. A dominant-seventh chord [G#–B#–D#–F#], sounded by the harps above a repetition of the original perfect fifth trichord [C#–G#–D#], supplies the last remaining modal tone, B#, which cannot be generated by the interval-7 cycle unfolding on the harmonic level. The B#, completely absent in the harp melody to this point, can be seen as a melodic filling in of the Phrygian fifth [G#–D#] that produces the Arab variant of the G# Phrygian mode.[24] The B# is even more significant in light of the imminent transformation of the Phrygian dominant mode into the octatonic cycle and the extension of the perfect fifth cycle. Two measures after its introduction (m. 7), an unexpected G is introduced into both the harmonic and melodic spheres of the piece. This might at first seem a question of chromatic color were it not for the fact that these two notes are subsequently projected as a perfect fifth dyad [C–G], which becomes the initial harmonic structure in the new combination of modal tonalities for the consequent phrase (Nos. 1–2). The initial thematic statement of the consequent phrase (No. 1), continues in the use of the lower tetrachord of the initial C# minor mode [C#–D#–E–F#], which is now circumscribed by the projected perfect fifth dyad [C–G] to extend this modal tetrachord to a six-note segment of the octatonic-1 cycle [C–C#–D#–E–F#–G]. A second perfect fifth dyad [A–E] further extends the octatonic collection to C–C#–D#–E–F#–G–A–( ), one note shy of the complete collection.

The musical examples set forth in this chapter provide concrete evidence for a significant number of relationships that exist between the interval cycles, both simple and compound, and an array of elemental modal families fundamental to so much modern music. The 20th century view, which presupposes that the pitch content of a mode is as important as its scalar ordering, generated a reversible system of transformation in which a mode may be expressed as a cycle and vice versa.

This transformational process revolutionized musical composition in the 20th century by providing composers an almost endless array of compositional possibilities with different musical outcomes. Among these are the cyclic generation of pentatonic and diatonic modes (Ravel), the cyclic reordering of modes (Bartok), bimodal combinations that generate simple interval cycles (Rebikov and Ligeti), bimodal combinations that generate compound cyclic collections (Bartok), the cyclic generation of hybrid modes (Debussy), the circular transformation from cycle to mode to cycle (Stravinsky), and the transformation of more exotic modes into cycles (de Falla). While the transformational relationships have been shown to rely largely on common elements shared by both modes and cycles, the compositional techniques used to achieve these transformations vary from one composer to another. It is because of this that the studies presented in this chapter may be considered highly representative, but by no means exhaustive. There exists an ocean of music based on these and other undiscovered transformational relationships awaiting analysis.

7   Harmonic Structures, Pitch Cells, and Cyclic Tetrachords

Music: Béla Bartók *Sonata for Piano, From the Isle of Bali, Suite* Op.14
Claude Debussy *Pour les degrès chromatiques, Pour le Piano*
Karlheinz Stockhausen *Klavierstück* IV
John Cage *In a Landscape*
Pierre Boulez *12 Notations for Piano*

FROM TRIAD TO PITCH CELL

In order to understand the role of pitch cells in 20th century music, it is necessary to understand their origins, identities, and relationships to their larger musical contexts. When we say that a piece of traditional tonal music is in the key of C major, we are stating several things at once. Firstly we are saying that pitch class "C" represents the principal tonal center of the music while the term *major* denotes the major scale as being the principal mode of the piece. Music that adheres to these precepts can only exist in either the major or minor mode at any given time. Pitch relations and tonal progression in this kind of music are controlled by harmonic function. The music is always locked into the major/minor system and anchored to a clearly defined key that is established at the outset of the piece.

Harmonic structures such as triads or seventh chords are subcollections of a major or minor scale, but in the traditional tonal musical context, however, they are more than that. They represent the vertical dimension of this kind of music. Each triad or chord, being built on a different scale degree, has a specific functional role. Individual chord tones that make up these harmonic structures move to new chord tones according to their individual function and principles of voice leading. Once a tonality or key is established by its tonic chord, any one of the seven chords represents the established key because of its function within that key. In a C major context, for example, the tonic triad [C–E–G] represents the tonal center of the key. The dominant triad [G–B–D] also represents the key of C because of its function within the key. The key can thus be recognized by the sounding of any of its constituent triads until there is a change of key. Thus, while each triad or seventh chord is a subcollection of the major or minor scale, each one is representative of the key as a whole.

In the chromatic music of the late Romantic era, the deviation from expected harmonic outcomes, which had up to then been considered exceptions, slowly became the norm. The use of an increasing amount of chromaticism and enharmonicism brought about a loosening of the strict functional roles of individual scale tones that allow for a wider palette of possible resolutions. This meant that individual chords could now be resolved in more ways than hitherto prescribed. There are a few reasons for this phenomenon. One reason was the increased use of symmetrical structures such as augmented triads and fully diminished seventh chords that could be resolved in several different ways. These chords destabilize the whole notion of an easily identifiable tonal center because they automatically allude to several keys at once. The incorporation of modes and synthetic scales that generated nonfunctional chords further weakened the entire system. During this period there was a return to the extensive use of counterpoint. In contrapuntal textures, vertical harmonic structures are generated by horizontal contrapuntal voice leading that do not necessarily conform to the dictates of harmonic function. The chord thus began to lose its identity as a purely vertical harmonic construction. Finally, the rhythm of harmonic shifts (harmonic rhythm) in the music of this period increased so much that it is often difficult to ascertain the key of a piece for any length of time. It is for all these reasons that the chord became a more malleable structure than its counterpart of earlier times. It could now be viewed as a subcollection of multiple major or minor scales. Despite the fact that the chord underwent all these changes, it was still locked into the major/minor scale system because it still, even if for brief instances, alludes to the major or minor scales from which it is extracted.

PITCH CELLS

While melody and harmony continued to play their distinct and separate roles in a good portion of 20th century works, the advent of the pitch cell changed many notions of these two musical rudiments.[1] The pitch cell can be defined as a small collection of pitches that are cast according to a specific intervallic structure, or one could say that it is a small collection of fixed pitch classes. Like triads, pitch cells are discreet fixed-interval structures. Unlike triads and chords that operate only on the harmonic level, pitch cells operate on both the harmonic and melodic levels without differentiation. Since pitch cells exist as both harmonic and melodic entities, they are not only subject to harmonic inversion and transposition but also to melodic retrograde and retrograde inversion.

While traditional triads and pitch cells have some things in common, their roles differ vastly. The triad or chord in both traditional diatonic and chromatic contexts is a non-reflexive entity. This means that it is a construct that exists prior to and independently from the composition itself. The pitch cell is instead a reflexive entity. It is a construct that does not have meaning independently from the composition itself. Its identity is determined by the immediate musical context.

The fundamental reason for this is that in contrast to the system of tonal progression of the common practice era, that is, harmonic function, the various modes of tonal progression in 20th century music depend on unique and contrasting sets of pitch relations that have little or nothing in common with those generated by tonal hierarchy of the former system. Because the major and minor scales that generated independent functional structures were replaced by the chromatic scale, all derivative harmonic and cellular structures had no identifiable functional role. That is why they rely on context. In order to understand the role pitch cells play in a musical work, it is therefore vital that their existence and purpose be regarded from a contextual perspective.

While in certain compositions pitch cells are used to generate purely cellular collections that do not belong to larger scalar or cyclic collections, in other works they are used to generate larger scalar or cyclic pitch collections. Cells can also be extracted from larger referential scalar or cyclic collections. In this case, their extraction is similar to that of triads from the major scale. The intention to generate larger modal or cyclic pitch collections in a piece based on pitch cells can only be ascertained by evaluating the musical context of the entire work. If, for example, a pitch cell generates a purely atonal texture in which the generation of a scalar or cyclic collection does not occur by design,[2] then its relationship to the larger collection is purely nominative.

THE STRUCTURE OF SYMMETRICAL CELLS

Three pitch cells, all symmetrical tetrachords, have thus far been identified as playing a significant role in many 20th century works. The first is known as cell X,[3] a chromatic tetrachord [C–C#–D–D#].[4] Because of its particular intervallic structure, it is most often found in highly chromatic textures. Its appearance may vary depending on how it is used.

In the third movement of Bartók's *Sonata for Piano*, a rondo form, the X cell both introduces and becomes the exclusive accompaniment for an entire episode (mm. 49–74). In the introductory measures (mm. 49–52), a whole-tone dyad [Ab–Bb] in the upper part is sounded together with a whole-tone dyad [A–B] in the lower part. These two dyads combine to generate X-7 [G–Ab–A–Bb]. The cell remains in its separate dyad configuration until it is projected as a complete unit into the left hand (m. 74) and becomes the exclusive harmonic accompaniment (Figure 7.1).

As its name suggests, Debussy's piano étude *Pour les degrès chromatiques* is based almost entirely on the chromatic scale. Tonal progression is most often marked by the ever-changing transpositions of melodically

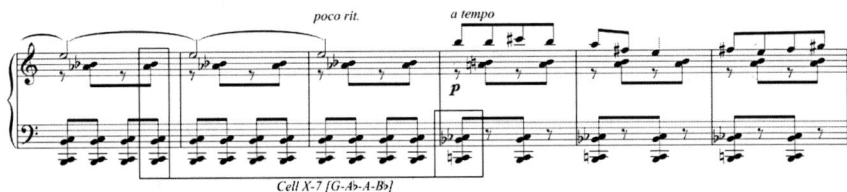

Figure 7.1   Bartók, *Sonata for Piano* Mvt. III (mm. 71–76). *Sonata for Piano by Béla Bartók © Copyright 1927 by Boosey & Hawkes, Inc. Copyright Renewed. Reprinted by Permission.*

disposed X cells. The opening measure (m. 1) consists of X-0 [C–Db–D–Eb] and X-10 [Bb–B–C–Db], which are a whole step apart.[5] While the intervallic displacement of the pair might seem inconsequential, it contains two of the three cyclic intervals fundamental not only to the tonal progression of the etude but also the intervallic structural makeup of the cell itself.

The three intervals in question are the semitone, the whole tone, and minor third (interval-3). The semitone occurs between the successive pitch classes of the cell. The whole tone occurs between alternating pitch classes of the cell, while the minor third is outlined by the first and last pitch classes of the cell.

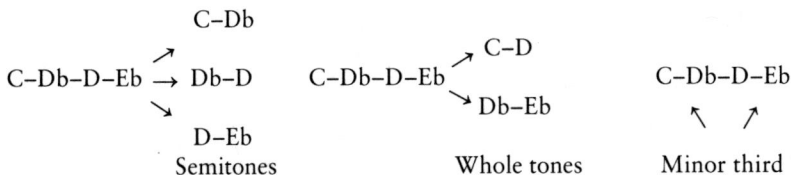

$$
\begin{array}{cccc}
& \text{C–Db} & & \text{C–D} \\
& \nearrow & & \nearrow \\
\text{C–Db–D–Eb} \rightarrow \text{Db–D} & \quad \text{C–Db–D–Eb} & \quad & \text{C–Db–D–Eb} \\
& \searrow & & \searrow \\
& \text{D–Eb} & & \text{Db–Eb} \\
\text{Semitones} & & \text{Whole tones} & \quad \text{Minor third} \\
& & & \nwarrow \quad \nearrow
\end{array}
$$

Because the X cell is a cyclic structure, any one of these structural intervals can be extracted and used to generate different and larger cyclic collections. Debussy confirms this principle by isolating the whole tone and minor third, presenting them (mm. 5–7) as foreground events.[6] By the beginning of the second half of the period (m. 5), the minor third unfolds a three-note segment of an interval-3 cycle [Bb–C#–E–( )].

The Y cell is a whole-tone tetrachord [C–D–E–F#], and except for its whole-tone rather than semitone intervallic makeup, it manifests the same set of structural characteristics as the X cell. It too operates on both harmonic and melodic levels. At the tail end of the episode used in the description of the X cell (from the third movement of the Bartók *Sonata for Piano*), the whole-tone component of the chromatic X cell is developed in order to generate a series of Y cells that transform the hitherto polymodal texture into a purely whole-tone one.

Cell Y-10 [Bb–C–D–E], representing the whole-tone 0 cycle, alternates with Y-7 [G–A–B–C#] to represent the whole-tone 1 cycle (Figure 7.2).

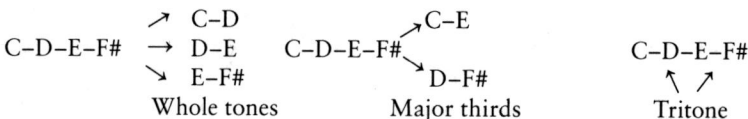

Figure 7.2   Bartók, *Sonata for Piano* Mvt. III (mm. 82–90). *Sonata for Piano by Béla Bartók* © *Copyright 1927 by Boosey & Hawkes, Inc. Copyright Renewed. Reprinted by Permission.*

After two such alternations, the whole-tone 0 representative drops out and Y-7 is extended by a whole-tone to complete the whole-tone 1 cycle (m. 90) to signal the end of the episode and heralds the return of the principal theme of the movement.

In the Prelude of Debussy's *Pour le Piano*, the composer uses a sequence of descending Y cells to usher in the recapitulation of the piece. In this example, however, the Y cells of both melody and accompaniment belong exclusively to the whole-tone 0 cycle. While the descending sixteenth notes of the accompaniment (mm. 91–96) unfold Y-2 [D–E–F#–Ab] and Y-8 [Ab–Bb–C–D] in alternation, the melody continues to outline Y-8.[7]

Just as was the case for the X cell, it is necessary to describe the intervals offered by the Y cell because these are also used to relate the cell to larger cyclic—and in the case of cell Y—modal pitch collections.

	↗ C–D			↗C–E	
C–D–E–F#	→ D–E	C–D–E–F#			C–D–E–F#
	↘ E–F#			↘D–F#	↖ ↗
	Whole tones		Major thirds		Tritone

While there are many works of the unordered twelve-tone system where pitch cells operate alongside other nonsymmetrical musical structures, the textures of a smaller number of works are based exclusively on pitch cells. In Boulez's *12 Notations for Piano* No. 4, the unfolding and interactions of four X cells completes the chromatic cycle while generating a Y cell that generates one of the two whole-tone collections.

The piece opens (m. 1) with a statement of X-4 [E–F–F#–G], which is rhythmically bound by two isolated pitches Ab and A. These two pitches form an upper extension of X-4 and begin to unfold a new and incomplete X-8 cell [Ab–A–( )–( )]. X-4 and the pitches of its chromatic extension constitute the exclusive pitch content of the unchanging ostinato of the lower part. X-11 [B–C–C#–D] unfolds over a longer period (mm. 1–3) as its two constituent whole tones [C–D and C#–B], emerging later (m. 3) in its complete form.[8] It too is extended by a single Bb, which together with its lowest pitch [B] are isolated to form a lower chromatic extension (m. 4)

The upper and lower chromatic extensions of the two cells combine to complete X-8 [Ab–A–Bb–B]. E is now the only pitch missing for completion of the entire chromatic cycle, all the other pitches being supplied by the three X cells. X-8 is also unfolded in terms of its two constituent whole tones [A–B and Ab–Bb]. The second of this pair [Ab–Bb] is immediately followed by the first whole-tone pair of X-11 [C–D] to generate Y-8 [Ab–Bb–C–D]. Y-8 is introduced by the F# of X-4 as its lower whole-tone extension and completed by the missing Eb that now forms both its upper extension and the first note of X-0 [Eb–D–C#–C]. The entire process can be visually represented.

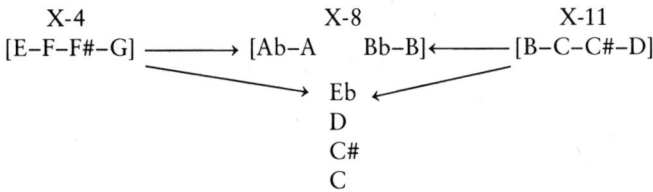

```
        X-4                      X-8                    X-11
   [E–F–F#–G] ──────────→ [Ab–A    Bb–B]←──────── [B–C–C#–D]
                    ╲                          ╱
                     ╲──────→  Eb  ←──────────╱
                               D
                               C#
                               C
```

* The pitches in bold outline the whole-tone 0 cycle.

The diagram shows that symmetry plays an important role in the tonal progression of this piece. Proof of this is that X-4 and X-11 are symmetrical around two axes of symmetry A/A and Eb/Eb. These are the dual axial intersections of the same symmetry, that is, they are the same axis. While symmetrical pitch cells can and do exist in modal musical textures, they are more likely to be associated with and generate textures in which pitch relations are based on symmetrical principles. This concept holds especially true for cell Z.

Cell Z[9] is somewhat different from cells X and Y, because it is constructed by the interlocking of two perfect fourths at the semitone. Cell Z-0/6 [C–F–F#–B],[10] for example, interlocks the two perfect fourths C–F and F#–B. Whereas cells X and Y consist of adjacent pitch classes and cannot be rearranged in any way without losing their symmetrical identity, cell Z exists in two different symmetrical permutations. Z-0/6, for example, remains symmetrical whether in its C–F–F#–B permutation or in its F–F#–B–C permutation, thus serving as a common chord between two different axes. In contrast to this, cells X and Y can only exist in a single permutation and can therefore have only one axis of symmetry.

```
B                              C
F#_____ axis at sum 11      B_____ axis at sum 5
F                              F#
C                              F
```

In their complete form, cells X and Y are representative subcollections of the chromatic and whole-tone interval cycles. In its complete form, cell Z can only be a representative subcollection of compound cyclic collections that share the compound interval ratio of its intervallic structure.

CELLS AND SYMMETRY

Like cells X and Y, cell Z is a symmetrical structure that can be readily used in musical textures where the pitch relations are governed by inversional symmetry based on an axis.

In *From the Isle of Bali* (Mikrokosmos No. 109), Bartók uses two Z cells to generate a musical texture in which pitch relations and tonal progression are based on axes of symmetry. The piece opens with a melodically disposed Z-3/9, in its G#–A–D–Eb permutation at sum 11. This is immediately followed (m. 2) by Z-0/6 in its B–C–F–Gb permutation at sum 5. The two cells are literally interlocked because they are made to overlap one another in the same register. The interlocking of these two cells generates a complete octatonic-0 scale [G#–A–B–C–D–Eb–F–Gb]. This scale is symmetrical around a C#/C# axis at sum 2, the same sum that lies symmetrically between sums 11 and 5 (Figure 7.3), that is, 11, 2(=14), 5(17) according to modulus 12.

Though the order entry of the two cells in the second phrase is reversed, the axis of symmetry remains the same to the end (m. 11) of the A section. Z-0/6 at sum 5 is melodically stated and repeated in unison (mm. 12–16) at the beginning of the B section. However, in the middle of the second melodic statement, an Abb outside the cell is stressed. While this note does

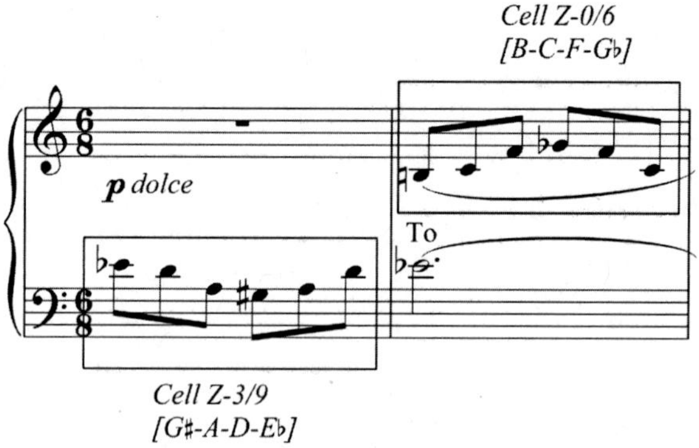

Figure 7.3   Bartók, *From the Isle of Bali* (mm. 1–2). *From the Island of Bali from Mikrokosmos by Béla Bartók.* © *Copyright 1940 by Hawkes & Son (London) Ltd.* [*Definitive corrected edition* © *Copyright 1987 by Hawkes & Son (London) Ltd.*] *Reprinted by Permission.*

not belong to the cell, its appearance serves to momentarily reestablish the principal axis of the piece at sum 2. Toward the end of the B section (mm. 23–30), two new axes are introduced by the continuing unison texture. A new melodic motive (mm. 23–24) unfolds a symmetrical tetrachord [A–Bb–D–Eb] with a C/C axis at sum 0 (Figure 7.3). The section comes to a close (mm. 29–30) on a *sf* unison D which is held as an axial pedal well into the final section of the piece. This D/D axis at sum 4 further reinforces the axial concept because it is the symmetrical complement of sum 0 when sum 2 is the principal axis.[11]

After a return of the two original cells in the final section of the piece the ending codetta (mm. 40–44) ends with a series of dyads symmetrical around the principal axis at sum 2. The first pair of dyads [G#–Eb and B–Gb] are those that outline the boundaries of the two principal Z cells. In this piece therefore, the Z cells not only generate the octatonic-0 collection, but are also responsible for establishing the system of axes that governs all aspects of the work.

Symmetrical Disposition of Axes around Principal Sum 2 Axis

↓	↓		↓		↓	↓
11	0	1	2	3	4	5
Z-3/9	A–Bb–D–Eb		↓		D/D	Z-0/6
			Principal Axis			

Like cells X and Y, cell Z contains three intervals that can be extracted and used to generate larger pitch collections.

```
                                                                   C–B
              ⟋C–F                      ⟋C–F#                      ↗ ↖
C–F–F#–B                   C–F–F#–B                   C–F–F#–B
              ⟍F#–B                     ⟍F–B                       ↘ ↙
                                                                   F–F#

       Perfect fourths               Tritones                 Minor seconds
```

Cell Z-1/7 [C#–F#–G–C] is ubiquitous throughout Stockhausen's *Klavierstück* IV. The pointillistic style of the work is the ideal medium for the compositional process of extracting and magnifying the component intervals of the cell. In the opening measures (mm. 1–2) the cell is stated a total of 229 times within a dynamic range that spans *ff* to *pppp*. Immediately following this (m. 3), the semitone component of the cell is used to generate a complete chromatic cycle over the cell itself, which is held until the completion of the cycle.[12]

Over the next several measures (mm. 4–15), the cell is inverted and repeated fifty more times before reverting (m. 16) to its original position. In the following measures (mm. 17–20), each of the component intervals (i.e., intervals 1, 5, 6, 7, and 11 of the cell) is used to generate isolated and fleeting musical gestures that cannot be regarded as being anything other than foreground events. Toward the middle of the work (m. 56), the cell itself is deconstructed into its outer and inner intervals [C#–C and F#–G] each being placed in different registers to maximize the effect of the deconstruction.

While the examples used thus far to describe the cells were based on single cell types, it is inevitable that interaction between the different cells can occur and be used to drive tonal progression not just for sections of movements, but for entire movements:[13] all three cells are different manifestations of the global network of symmetrical pitch relations that underlie so much of 20th century music.

INCOMPLETE PITCH COLLECTIONS

Bimodal and polymodal combinations are commonplace in a vast bulk of 20th century music, and composers make an ever-increasing use of diverse pitch collections such as diatonic, non-diatonic, and hybrid modes; whole-tone and octatonic scales; and interval cycles in their works. At the beginning of many 20th century works, complete modal and cyclic-interval collections are first introduced in their incomplete forms through the use of constituent subcollections. These subcollections can be melodic, harmonic, or both. Often, the subcollections of one complete collection are common to other complete collections and can therefore be used to transform the larger collections into one another. The transformation of the larger, complete pitch collections brings about a new system of tonal progression. It is this feature of 20th century music that makes possible the contrasts in the musical language in different sections of single works such as the opening *Adoration de la terre* and the tempestuous *Jeu du rapt* sections of Stravinsky's *Le Sacre du Printemps*. The former is based on a Lithuanian folk tune in the A Aeolian mode, while the latter incorporates octatonic collections. However, the cyclic intervals of the latter sections are embedded, indeed pervasive, in the folk tune of the opening. For instance, the Lithuanian tune in A Aeolian [A–B–C–D–E–( )–G] implies the presence of a six-note segment [C–G–D–A–E–B] of the 5/7 cycle, which can also be reinterpreted as a gapped segment [C–D–( )–F–( )–( )–A–B] of the octatonic-0 scale. Stravinsky uses elements common to both the Aeolian mode and the octatonic scale to transform his musical language to suit the musical ideals envisioned for the piece.

Subcollections fall into two broad categories. The subcollections of the first category are gapped segments of larger complete pitch collections, whereas those of the second are not gapped but still insufficient to define the larger collection. Both varieties bring with them a high degree of ambiguity since each can be extended or completed in various ways.

One of the fundamental considerations in a discussion of subcollections is the minimum number of pitches required to constitute an identifiable subcollection that interlocks a restricted number of larger pitch collections. Two pitches, no matter how disposed, are a subcollection of so many larger ones that they provide no real definitive information. Three-pitch subcollections are perhaps the most frequently used because they restrict the number of relationships to larger collections but still allow for a wide range of possibilities. Nevertheless, the possibilities allowed by the three-note subcollections are still too many for a practical discussion. Tetrachordal or four-note sub collections, whether contiguous or gapped, are defined enough to reduce the number of relationships to larger collections as to allow for a thorough yet concise demonstration of the concepts of completion and transformation.

Using one of the most familiar of the gapped tetrachordal subcollections, that is, the seventh chord, we can demonstrate how it can be extracted from a variety of different modal and cyclic collections. The minor seventh chord [C–Eb–G–Bb], for example, is a subcollection of the following larger pitch collections:

C Pentatonic	**C–Eb–(F)–G–Bb**
C Dorian	**C–(D)–Eb–(F)–G–(A)–Bb–C**
C Aeolian	**C–(D)–Eb–(F)–G–(Ab)–Bb–C**
C Phrygian	**C–(Db)–Eb–(F)–G–(Ab)–Bb–C**
Acoustic Scale	**C–(Db)–Eb–(F)–G–(A)–Bb–C**
Octatonic 1	**C–(Db)–Eb–(E)–(F#)–G–(A)–Bb**
C.C. 3:4	**C–Eb–G–Bb–D–F–A–C** . . . .

As seen, the seventh chord was extracted from collections that all begin on a common tonic. Even with this restriction the number of larger collections is substantial.

CYCLIC TETRACHORDS AND LARGER PITCH COLLECTIONS

Having shown that such a familiar chordal structure can create direct relationships between so many larger pitch collections—that is, the diatonic, hybrid, pentatonic, octatonic, and c.c. 3:4—it is necessary to explore the all possible compound-interval and cyclic tetrachords and show how they can be interpreted as gapped segments of larger collections and how they can be used to move between the larger modal and cyclic collections.

The most efficient and thorough way to generate all the cyclic tetrachords is by interlocking pairs of equal-interval dyads. All possibilities of interlocking will be exhausted by sliding one of the dyads against the other by the constant interval of a semitone. Some of the tetrachords obtained in this manner will at first seem to have no familiar sequential order simply because we are so used to finding scalar and tertian constructions.

In terms of interlocking dyadic pairs, the first possibility is the interlocking of two whole-tone dyads. At the semitone they will form a sequentially complete chromatic tetrachord that can only be related to the chromatic scale.

C–D + c#–d# = C–c#–D–d#

If we interlock them on the second note of the first dyad we will create the relative interval cycle but we will not obtain a tetrachord.

C–D + D–E = C–D–E

It is necessary to note that any other interval interlocked at the semitone will always create an incomplete and gapped chromatic segment. At times, the intervallic distribution of the tetrachord will make it relevant to pitch collections other than the chromatic, as is the case with our next interval.

Like the major second, the minor third (interval-3) will yield complete segments no matter whether the two dyads are interlocked at the semitone or at the whole step. At the semitone, the two dyads will create a contiguous tetrachord that can be regarded as diatonic, acoustic or octatonic.

C—Eb + C#–E = C–C#–Eb–E

As is clearly visible, a missing D would seal off this segment chromatically: C–C#–[D]–Eb–E. At the whole step, the dyads will yield a diatonic or octatonic tetrachord.

C–Eb + D–F = C–D–Eb–F

The major third (interval-4) allows for three possibilities. At the semitone separation, it will yield a gapped chromatic hexachord.

C–E + Db–F = C–Db–(D)–(Eb)–E–F

When the dyads are interlocked at the whole-step, a sequentially complete whole-tone tetrachord will be formed. From Chapter 6, we know that this tetrachord belongs to the diatonic modes as well as the acoustic scale.

C–E + D–F# = C–D–E–F#

Interlocking the interval-4 dyads at the minor third will yield a gapped octatonic hexachord.

Octatonic-1   C–E + D#–G = C–(C#)–D#–E–(F#)–G

The next interval in line is the perfect fourth (interval-5). If we interlock perfect fourths at the half step we will obtain a gapped seven-note segment of the chromatic scale.

C–F + C#–F# = C–C#–(D)–(D#)–(E)–F–F#

However, if we interlock them at the whole step, we will obtain a tetrachord that may be interpreted as an incomplete pentatonic collection or an incomplete diatonic pentachord.

Pentatonic interpretation: C–F + D–G = C–D–F–G
Diatonic interpretation: C–F + D–G = C–D–(E/Eb)–F–G

It is interesting to note that four different diatonic modes may be suggested by this incomplete segment.

C Ionian   C–D–(E)–F–G
C Dorian   C–D–(Eb)–F–G
C Mixolydian   C–D–(E)–F–G
C Aeolian   C–D–(Eb)–F–G

At the minor third, the interval-4 tetrachords may be employed in an even wider range of larger collections.

C–F + Eb–Ab = C–Eb–F–Ab.

This tetrachord would appear as gapped octatonic hexachord C–(D)–Eb–F–(F#)–Ab. Closer examination of the tetrachord reveals that it can also be interpreted as a gapped segment of several diatonic modes that share the same fundamental as the octatonic-0 scale.

C Phrygian   C–(Db)–Eb–F–(G)–Ab
C Aeolian   C–(D)–Eb–F–(G)–Ab
C Locrian   C–(Db)–Eb–F–(Gb)–Ab

This tetrachord is also common to the special Romanian non-diatonic mode.

Romanian non-diatonic mode: C–(D)–Eb–F–(Gb)–Ab

The perfect fourth may be interlocked at the major third and can really only constitute a gapped Ionian or Mixolydian hexachord.

C Ionian/Mixolydian   C–F + E–A = C–(D)–E–F–(G)–A

The next interval to be interlocked is the diminished fifth or augmented fourth (interval-6). At the semitone, the tetrachord will form a gapped chromatic segment but more significantly, it will form a gapped octatonic hexachord.

Octatonic 1   C–F# + C#–G = C–C#–(D#)–(E)–F#–G

When interlocked at the whole step, the resulting tetrachord will form a gapped whole-tone pentachord as well as a gapped non-diatonic hexachord.

Whole-tone 0   C–F# + D G# = C–D–(E)–F#–G#
Non-diatonic mode   C–F# + D–G# = C–D–(Eb)–(F)–F#–G#

The minor third interlocking can form two gapped seven-note segments of two different octatonic collections.

Octatonic-0   C–F# + Eb–A = C–(D)–Eb–(F)–F#–(G#)–A
Octatonic-1   C–F# + Eb–A = C–(C#)–Eb–(E)–F#–(G)–A

At the major third, the resulting tetrachord will form a gapped, seven-note segment of the acoustic scale, a gapped octatonic segment as well as a gapped whole-tone segment.

Acoustic scale: C–F# + E–Bb = C–(D)–E–F#–(G)–(A)–**Bb**
Octatonic-1:   C–F# + E–Bb = C–(C#)–(D#)–E–F#–(G)–(A)–**Bb**
Whole-tone 0   C–F# + E–Bb = C–(D)–E–F#–(G#)–(A)–**Bb**

Perhaps one the most significant interlockings of two interval-6 dyads is at the perfect fourth, because it yields one of two forms of pitch cell Z—the other form is at the semitone. This tetrachord forms half of the octatonic scale, its permuted minor third transposition (Eb–G#–A–D rotated to D–Eb–G#–A) forming the other half.

Octatonic-0: C–F# + F–B = **C**–(D)–(Eb)–**F**–**F#**–(G#)–(A)–**B**

The next interval in our order is the perfect fifth (interval-7). At the semitone separation of two perfect fifths, the resulting tetrachord enframes a nine-note segment of the chromatic scale.

C–G + C#–G# = C–C#–(D–Eb–E–F–F#)–G–G#

The interlocking of this interval at the whole-tone creates one of the most stable diatonic tetrachords. It can be interpreted as an incomplete, gapped pentatonic segment, four different gapped diatonic hexachords, and a gapped hexachord of the acoustic scale.

Pentatonic   C–G + D–A = **C–D–(F)–G–A**

C Ionian	C–G + D–A = **C–D–(E)–(F)–G–A**
C Dorian	C–G + D–A = **C–D–(Eb)–(F)–G–A**
C Lydian	C–G + D–A = **C–D–(E)–(F#)–G–A**
C Mixolydian	C–G + D–A = **C–D–(E)–(F)–G–A**
Acoustic Scale	C–G + D–A = **C–D–(E)–(F#)–G–A**

Interlocking the interval-7 pairs at the minor third also creates a large number of possibilities.

C Dorian	C–G + Eb–Bb = **C–(D)–Eb–(F)–G–(A)–Bb**
C Aeolian	C–G + Eb–Bb = **C–(D)–Eb–(F)–G–(Ab)–Bb**
C Phrygian	C–G + Eb–Bb = **C–(Db)–Eb–(F)–G–(Ab)–Bb**
Non diatonic	C–G + Eb–Bb = **C–(Db)–Eb–(F)–G–(Ab)–Bb**
Octatonic 1	C–G + Eb–Bb = **C–(C#)–Eb–(E)–(F#)–G–(A)–Bb**

At the major third, the possibilities are restricted to the diatonic realm.

C Ionian	C–G + E–B = **C–(D)–E–(F)–G–(A)–B**
C Lydian	C–G + E–B = **C–(D)–E–(F#)–G–(A)–B**

The possibilities allowed by a perfect fourth interlocking are more and include gapped pentatonic, diatonic, and acoustic segments.

C Pentatonic	C–G + F–C = **C–(D)–F–G–(A)–C**
C Ionian	C–G + F–C = **C–(D)–(E)–F–G–(A)–(B)–C**
C Dorian	C–G + F–C = **C–(D)–(Eb)–F–G–(A)–(Bb)–C**
C Phrygian	C–G + F–C = **C–(Db)–(Eb)–F–G–(Ab)–(Bb)–C**
C Mixolydian	C–G + F–C = **C–(D)–(E)–F–G–(A)–(Bb)–C**
C Aeolian	C–G + F–C = **C–(D)–(Eb)–F–G–(Ab)–(Bb)–C**
Acoustic Scale	C–G + F–C = **C–(D)–(E)–F–G–(Ab)–(Bb)–C**

The two remaining interlockings [C–G + F#–C# and C–G + G–D] create a new phenomenon. Both the interlocking at the tritone and the cyclic interlocking will result in a tetrachord that reaches beyond the octave. Consistency, however, requires that we examine the reordering of such a tetrachord so that it fits within the octave because in 20th century music pitch content is at times even more important than pitch sequence.

If we take the tritone interlocking of the perfect fifth dyads, C–G + F#–C#, we create the tetrachord C–F#–G–C#, which extends beyond the octave boundary. While this tetrachord could be a segment of the compound cycle that has an interval ratio of 6:1 it is not related to any of the scales or modes we have discussed so far. However, if we reorder the tetrachord within the octave, C–C#–F#–G, we will have created a tetrachord consisting of two tritone dyads at the semitone, of interval ratio 1:5. This tetrachord is identical to the one created by the interlocking of two tritone dyads at the semitone. In reordering the tetrachord, both the dyadic interval and the interval ratio of the tetrachord have been altered, transforming one compound cyclic tetrachord into another.

When the minor sixth (interval-8) is interlocked at the semitone, the resulting tetrachord [C–C#–Ab–A] cannot be related to any of the scalar sets we have referred to thus far. If, however, the interval-8 dyads are interlocked at the whole-tone, the relational possibilities are many.

Whole-tone 0	C–Ab + D–Bb = C–D–(E)–(F#)–Ab–Bb
C Aeolian	C–Ab + D–Bb = C–D–(Eb)–(F)–(G)–Ab–Bb
Acoustic	C–Ab + D–Bb = C–D–(E)–(F)–(G)–Ab–Bb

At the minor third, the interval-8 dyads can be related to the gypsy mode and octatonic scale.

Octatonic-0	C–Ab + Eb–B = C–(D)–Eb–(F)–(F#)–G#–(A)–B–C
Gypsy Mode	C–Ab + Eb–B = C–(D)–Eb–(F#)–(G)–Ab–B

When interlocked at the major third, the dyadic tetrachord can be related to the whole-tone and acoustic scales.

Whole-tone 0	C–E + Ab–C = C–(D)–E–(Gb)–Ab–(Bb)–C
Acoustic Scale	C–E + Ab–C = C–(D)–E–(F)–(G)–Ab–(Bb)–C

There are only three possible ways of interlocking major sixths (interval-9). At the semitone the dyadic tetrachord will generate relationships to the acoustic, and octatonic scales.

Acoustic	C–A +Db–Bb = C–Db–(Eb)–(F)–(G)–A–Bb–C
Octatonic-1	C–A +Db–Bb = C–C#–(D#)–(E)–(F#)–(G)–A–Bb–C

If interlocked at the whole tone, the dyads will form a tetrachord that can be related to diatonic, non-diatonic, acoustic, Gypsy, and octatonic scales.

C Ionian	C–A + D–B = C–D–(E)–(F)–(G)–A–B–C
C Lydian	C–A + D–B = C–D–(E)–(F#)–(G)–A–B–C
Non-diatonic	C–A + D–B = C–D–(E)–(F#)–(G#)–A–B
Acoustic	C–A + D–B = C–D–(E)–(F#)–(G#)–A–B–C
Octatonic	C–A + D–B = C–D–(Eb)–(F)–(F#)–(G#)–A–B–C

Finally, when the interval-8 dyads are interlocked at the minor third, the resulting tetrachord can be related to diatonic, acoustic, and octatonic scales.

C Dorian	C–A + Eb–C = C–(D)–Eb–(F)–(G)–A–(Bb)–C
Acoustic	C–A + Eb–C = C–(D)–Eb–(F)–(G)–A–(B)–C

Octatonic 1   C–A + Eb–C = C–(C#)–D#–(E)–(F#)–(G)–A–(Bb)–C

Minor seventh (interval-10) dyads can only be interlocked at the semi-tone and at the whole step. The semitone interlocking will form a tetra-chord that relates to diatonic, acoustic, and octatonic scales.

C Phrygian   C–Bb + Db–C = C–Db–(Eb)–(F)–(G)–(Ab)–Bb–C
C Locrian   C–Bb + Db–C = C–Db–(Eb)–(F)–(Gb)–(Ab)–Bb–C
Acoustic   C–Bb + Db–C = C–Db–(Eb)–(F)–(G)–(A)–Bb–C
Octatonic-1   C–Bb + Db–C = C–C#–(D#)–(E)–(F#)–(G)–(A)–Bb–C

The final interval to be interlocked is the major seventh (interval-11). There is only one possibility for interlocking the two interval-11 dyads and that is at the semitone. The resulting tetrachord C–Db–B–C can be related exclusively to the chromatic scale.

As we have seen, interlocking equal-interval dyads at fixed distances creates the complete series of gapped and contiguous compound-interval and cyclic tetrachords. These tetrachords can be completed in any number of ways to generate multiple modal and cyclic-interval collections. The musical examples in which this process takes place are so many that John Cage's *In a Landscape* will serve as a single representative case study.

With the exception of a few single-line bridge passages, the texture of this work is divided between the melody and accompaniment. For the entire opening period (mm. 1–8), the exclusive pitch content of the accompaniment consists of four pitches that spell out a major seventh chord [Bb–D–F–A]. These four notes also constitute the main pitch content of the melody, this core set shared by the accompaniment. It is the melody, however, that both establishes the modal center and supplies the first additional notes that fill in and extend the gapped tetrachord. During the opening period, the melody seems to be anchored to an A tonic because this is both the first and last pitch of the formal structure and it is visited two times in between. The melody starts the process of filling in the tetrachord so that by the period's end the pitch content [A–Bb–C–D–( )–F–G] suggests either an A Phrygian or an A Locrian mode, that is, the missing pitch either E or Eb.[14]

Immediately following this (m. 9), the accompanying tetrachord is extended by a B. This further hinders a positive definition of the mode because the pitch content now suggests the diatonic A Phrygian, A Locrian, and A Aeolian modes as well as the non-diatonic Acoustic scale. The clash between B and Bb continues until the B drops out altogether as the pitch content is rotated at the return of the original melody (m. 80) to a D modal tonic. The two suggested modes are D Aeolian and D Locrian. Cage again extends the tetrachord (m. 84), so this time the diatonic modes could be D Aeolian, D Locrian, and D Dorian. The D acoustic scale is also implied. The last remaining gap in the tetrachord is finally filled (m. 93) with an E, so the choice of modes is restricted to the D Dorian and Aeolian. The reason is that during the time the E completes the tetrachord, B and Bb are studiously avoided.

The final section of the work (mm. 180–226) recapitulates the opening in every way except at the very end where the D modality emerges as definitive. Without the chromatic alteration, the original [Bb–D–F–A] major seventh tetrachord binds together two diatonic modes, both of which are simultaneously realized to produce a bimodal combination. This shows how the tetrachords can be used as shared common elements in order to transform different larger pitch collections into one another. The extension of the original tetrachord just enlarges the number of suggested modes to generate a polymodal texture, in which even more modes can be transformed into one another.

Major and minor seventh chords are representative of the type of tetrachord that assumes symmetrical properties only when in certain rotations. If, for example, we rotate the minor seventh tetrachord into all its positions, we discover that it is symmetrical in only two of them.

rotation 1   C–Eb–G–Bb = C–Bb (0+10) and Eb–G (3+7) = sum 10
rotation 2   Eb–G–Bb–C = G–Bb (7+10) and Eb–C (3+0) = not symmetrical
rotation 3   G–Bb–C–Eb = G–Eb (7+3) and Bb–C (10+0) = sum 10
rotation 4   Bb–C–Eb–G = Bb–G (10+7) and C–Eb (0+3) = not symmetrical

While rotations 2 and 4 may be of interest in relation to a varying number of modal/cyclic pitch relations, rotations 1 and 3 are of special interest because they can just as easily be used where pitch relations are generated by symmetry.

Equal-interval tetrachords such as the fully diminished seventh chord are representative of those tetrachords that remain symmetrical regardless of their rotation. The fully diminished seventh tetrachord can be seen as an incomplete interval-3 cycle and can be analyzed in terms of its two sum dyads. These dyads, C–A (0+9) and Eb–F# (3+6), show the tetrachord to be symmetrical around the axis at sum 9—the axis being expressed by the addition of pitch-class numbers that form the dyad. If we rotate or invert the tetrachord and analyze the sum dyads of each rotation we will obtain the following:

rotation 1   C–Eb–F#–A = C–A (0+9) and Eb–F# (3+6) = sum 9
rotation 2   Eb–F#–A–C = Eb–C (3+0) and F#–A (6+9) = sum 3
rotation 3   F#–A–C–Eb = F#–Eb (6+3) and A–C (9+0) = sum 9
rotation 4   A–C–Eb–F# = A–F# (9+6) and C–Eb (0+3) = sum 3

We can immediately deduce that, because of the double tritone, this tetrachord will be symmetrical around either of two complementary axes at sums 9 and 3. Unlike the tetrachords of the former class, equal-interval tetrachords can be used in modal as well as cyclic textures.

In the third movement of his *Suite* Op. 14, Bartók uses an incomplete diminished seventh tetrachord as a common pivot to move between two different octatonic collections. The work opens (mm. 1–2) with an ostinato in the left-hand accompaniment, composed of a single contiguous tetrachord [E–F–G–Ab] that can be interpreted as belonging to a diatonic, non-diatonic, or compound cyclic collection. It is extended (m. 3) to generate an octatonic-2 hexachord [E–F–G–Ab–Bb–Cb]. The entry of the two-note melodic motive [D–Eb] (mm. 5ff.) suggests an entirely different pitch collection, because of the clash between the E of the octatonic-2 collections and the Eb of the octatonic-0 collection. However, two new melodic notes are introduced into the melody (m. 11) to create a gapped octatonic-0 tetrachord [D–Eb–( )–( )–G#–A]. The two collections are bound together by the incomplete interval-3 tetrachord [D–F–G#–( )] the pitches of which are sounded simultaneously in both collections.[15]

The tetrachords so far discussed permeate much of 20th century music, either as discrete entities or as subsets of larger scalar formations, their roles varying greatly from composition to composition. Tetrachords, no matter of what kind, tend to leave room for ambiguity. Their relational possibilities are directly proportional to the four pitches they contain. Incomplete tetrachords increase the degree of ambiguity significantly, simply because they contain a smaller number of notes and can therefore be related to a larger number of modal and cyclic collections than can their complete counterparts. When we consider all the cyclic and scalar formations discussed thus far, cell Z-0/6 in its complete form (C–F–F#–B) can only be related to a small number of compound interval cycles, c.c. 2:1, c.c. 6:1, c.c. 6:5, c.c. 6:7, and c.c. 6:11. If, however, we were to remove the F, we would create the incomplete tetrachord C–( )–F#–B. This incomplete tetrachord can be related not only to the aforementioned compound interval cycles but also to a host of new compound interval cycles—diatonic, non-diatonic, Gypsy, and Phrygian dominant modes as well as the Acoustic scale.

While it is impractical to discuss all the possibilities afforded by both contiguous and gapped tetrachords, it is apparent that the tetrachord, whether cellular or not, is perhaps the single most significant substructure of 20th century music. The reason for this is that as a structure, it binds together diverse modal, cyclic, and compound cyclic collections—all of which make up the global network of the unordered twelve-tone system.

Notes

NOTES TO THE PREFACE

1. Winthrop Sargeant, "Bernhard Ziehn, Precursor," *The Musical Quarterly*, Vol. 19, No. 2 (April, 1933), pp. 169–177.
2. David W. Bernstien, "Georg Capellen's Theory of Reduction: Radical Harmonic Theory at the Turn of the Twentieth Century," *Journal of Music Theory*, Vol. 37, No. 1 (Spring, 1993), pp. 85–116.
3. Ibid.
4. Elliott Antokoletz, *Twentieth-Century Music* (Englewood Cliffs, NJ: Prentice Hall, Inc., 1992), p. 426.
5. Henry Cowell, "Thesaurus of Scales and Melodic Patterns" by Nicholas Slonimsky, *Notes*, Second Series, Vol. 4, No. 2 (March, 1947), pp. 171–173.
6. Norman Lloyd, "Harmonic Materials of Modern Music" by Howard Hanson, *Journal of Research in Music Education*, Vol. 8, No. 2 (Autumn, 1960), pp. 128–130.

NOTES TO CHAPTER 1

1. The term *modulation* is erroneously used to describe transposition between keys of the traditional tonal system. When, for example, one moves from C major to F# major, there is no change of mode because both keys are in the same mode, that is, the Ionian mode or major scale. A true modulation occurs only when there is a change of mode.
2. In this chapter, the fundamental principles that underlie some of the most significant concept are explained in a simple and succinct manner so as to introduce them to the prospective analyst. This design will also provide the analyst with a point of departure. Comprehensive and detailed explanations of the new concepts will be found in later chapters.
3. Interval cycles have been proven to generate most of the pitch relations and tonal progression in a vast bulk of 20th century music. For a detailed discussion of intervals cycles, see Chapter 2.
4. See Claude Debussy's *La Cathédrale engloutie* (mm. 22–25).
5. See Debussy's *La Cathédrale engloutie* (mm. 41–47).
6. The whole-tone scale, constructed exclusively of a succession of whole tones, is also known as an interval 2/10 cycle.
7. This is exemplified by the last five measures of Chopin's prelude in C minor, Op. 28, No. 20. Despite the richness of its chromatic embellishments, principle tones of basic diatonic progressions leave little room for deviation.
8. See Messiaen's *Le baiser de l'Enfant-Jesus* (mm. 74–75).

9. See Chapter 7.
10. See Schoenberg's *Three Piano Pieces* Op. 11, No. 1 (mm. 46–47).
11. See Liszt's *Après un Lecture de Dante* (mm. 1–12).
12. See Liszt's *Après un Lecture de Dante* (mm. 202–211).
13. See Bartók's *Mikrokosmos* No. 121, "Two Part Study" (mm. 1–3).
14. The F# and C# are implied by the key signature.
15. See Milhaud's *Corvocado* (mm. 1–4).
16. See Bartók's *Étude* No. 2, Op. 18 (mm. 31–32).
17. See Mozart's *Sonata* K331 Mvt. I (mm. 1–8).
18. See Stravinsky's "Tilim-bom" (mm. 1–10).

NOTES TO CHAPTER 2

1. Elliott Antokoletz, *The Music of Béla Bartók: A Study of Tonality and Progression in 20th Century Music* (Berkeley: University of California Press, 1984), p. 68.
2. Ibid.
3. The complementary cycle to the interval-5/7 cycle is the interval-7/5 cycle. These two cycles can be used interchangeably to describe movement by either perfect fourth or fifth.
4. See Beethoven Sonata in C minor Op. 111 (mm. 1–5).
5. See Liszt's *Gnomenreigen* (mm. 110–121).
6. See Chapter 6.
7. Since we have adopted the numbering system where C = 0, C# = 1, etc., whole-tone 0 starts on C while whole-tone 1 starts on C#.
8. See Riegger's *The Major Second* (mm. 1–4).
9. Considering that the phrases of the opening close across bar lines, the formal structure of the opening does not deviate much from a traditional four-measure phrase structure (mm. 1–4, 4–7, and 7–13).
10. See Chapter 4 for a detailed discussion of this concept.
11. See Ligeti, *Cordes à vide* (mm. 12–15).
12. See Ligeti, *Cordes à vide* (mm. 15–16).
13. See Chapter 7.
14. See George Perle, "Symmetrical Formations in the String Quartets of Béla Bartók," *Music Review*, Vol. 16 (November 1955), pp. 300ff.
15. See Bartók's *Study* No. 1(mm. 1–2).
16. See Elliott Antokoletz, "Organic Development and the Interval Cycles in Bartók's Three Studies Op. 18," *Studia Musicologica*, Vol. 36, Nos. 3–4 (1995), pp. 249–261.
17. See n. 5, above, Perle, "Symmetrical Formations."
18. See Bartók's *Study* No. 1 (mm. 47–48).
19. See Bartók's *Suite* Op. 14 (mm. 17–20).
20. See Chapter 3.
21. See Lutoslawski, *Étude* (mm. 11–13).
22. See Lutoslawski, *Étude* (mm. 19–20).
23. Willi Apel, "Mode," in *The Harvard Dictionary of Music*, 2nd ed. (Cambridge, MA: The Belknap Press of the Harvard University Press, 1974).
24. For a detailed discussion see Philip J. Lambert, "Interval Cycles as Compositional Resources in the Music of Charles Ives," *Music Theory Spectrum*, Vol. 12, No. 1 (Spring 1990), pp. 43–82.
25. See Chapter 3.
26. See Chapter 6.
27. See Ives, *Psalm XXIV* (mm. 26–29).

NOTES TO CHAPTER 3

1. While the interval cycles are completed by the repetition of the first pitch class, compound cyclic collections must end with the repetition of the first two pitch classes.
2. See Chapter 2.
3. See Chopin's *Sonata* Op. 49, Mvt. I (mm. 89–92).
4. See Liszt's *Les jeux d'eaux à la villa d'Este* (mm. 2–3).
5. See Ravel's *Jeux D'eau* (mm. 1–4).
6. IV7 [A–C#–E–G#] followed by I 9 [E–G#–B–D#–F#] unfolds the seven-note segment in its cyclic order [A–C#–E–G#–B–D#–F#].
7. See Chapter 2
8. See Ives' *Psalm XXIV* (mm. 12–14).
9. The three octatonic models octatonic-1, octatonic-2, and octatonic-3 are so labeled in Pieter van den Toorn's *The Music of Igor Stravinsky* (New Haven, CT: Yale University Press, 1983), p. 50.

Octatonic I	E–F–G–Ab–Bb–B–Db–D
Octatonic II	E–F#–Ab–A–B–C–D–Eb
Octatonic III	F#–G–A–Bb–C–Db–Eb–E

   In this study the three octatonic models, all based on the 2:1 interval ratio, are identified by the Arabic numeral that represent the initial pitch class.

Octatonic-0	C–D–Eb–F–F#–Ab–A–B
Octatonic-1	C#–D#–E–F#–G–A–Bb–C
Octatonic-2	D–E–F–G–Ab–Bb–B–C#

10. In "Octatonicism in Recent Solo Piano Works of Tōru Takemitsu," *Perspectives of New Music*, Vol. 29, No. 1 (Winter, 1991), pp. 124–140, Timothy Koozin describes the role of octatonic trichords in the generation melodic structure and deep-level connections in *Rain Tree Sketch*.
11. See Takemitsu's *Rain Tree Sketch* (m. 14).
12. See Ginastera *Piano Sonata* No. 1, Mvt. II (mm. 1–17).
13. See Ginastera's *Piano Sonata* No. 1, Mvt. II (mm. 80–84).
14. For an in-depth explanation of cyclic/modal transformations, see Chapter 6.
15. See Ginastera's *Piano Sonata* No. 1, Mvt. II (mm. 103–106).

NOTES TO CHAPTER 4

1. Elliott Antokoletz, *The Music of Béla Bartók: A Study of Tonality and Progression in Twentieth Century* (Berkeley: University of California Press, 1984), p. 72.
2. Any sum that exceeds 12 will require the subtraction of the 12 modulus to obtain an axial sum within the octave range.
3. Elliott Antokoletz, *The Music of Béla Bartók: A Study of Tonality and Progression in Twentieth Century* (Berkeley: University of California Press, 1984), pp. 73–74.
4. See the final section of Schubert's *Wanderer Fantasy* Mvt. IV.
5. See Brahms, *Capriccio* Op. 116, No. 3 (mm. 24–28).
6. See Webern, *Fifth Bagatelle for String Quartet* Op. 9.
7. See Bartók, *The Night's Music* (mm. 18–24).
8. See Ives, *Psalm XXIV* (mm. 1–3).
9. See Ives, *Psalm XXIV* (mm. 9–11).
10. See Ives, *Psalm XXIV* (m. 12).
11. See Bartók, *The Night's Music* (mm. 41f.).

12. This mode is also known as the Lydian/Mixolydian hybrid mode or the Acoustic scale. For an in-depth description of the mode see Chapter 5.
13. See Bartók *Mikrokosmos* No. 141, *Subject and Reflection* (mm. 13–18).
14. See the performance instructions in the score of the *Threnody to the Victims of Hiroshima for 52 strings.*
15. The term *band* refers to the physical range yielded by the total number of pitches being played. If, for example, one were to press all the keys contained in a C–C octave, an octave band would be created.
16. See Penderecki, Threnody to the Victims of Hiroshima.

NOTES TO CHAPTER 5

1. The octave (C) appears in brackets to highlight the fact that each mode represents a particular octave segment. The reason is that the repetition of the tonic at the octave is a musical consideration applicable only when modal order and completion is relevant.
2. In the 20th century modal context, the tetrachord is defined as succession of four ascending or descending pitches that progress by either whole tones and or semitones.
3. The naming of the new hybrid modes follows the combination order in which the lower and upper tetrachords of the parent modes are used.
4. See Chopin, *Mazurka* Op. 68, No. 3 (mm. 42–45).
5. Please see Chapter 6.
6. Each mode discussed in this chapter is given a rotation number. The reason is that while the seven rotations of the diatonic mode—Ionian, Dorian, Phrygian, Lydian, Mixolydian, Aeolian, and Locrian—are well known, rotations of the pentatonic scale and a host of other nondiatonic modes have no names. Wherever possible, familiar appellatives will be used. Where not, rotational numbers will be given.
7. The reason for doing this is a purely practical one. It allows the analyst to know the pitch content of the entire modal family when rotated to a single tonic. It also coincides with the 20th century musical practice of simultaneously using more than one mode at the same transpositional level.
8. The concept incomplete sets as common pivots between various scalar collections and interval cycles are discussed in Chapter 7.
9. See Lutoslawski, *Melodie* (mm. 1–4)
10. This tetrachordal relationship forms the basis of the "Cycle of Fifths" used to describe the succession of keys in the traditional tonal system.
11. Note that in the comparisons all the modes were rotated to a common tonic. A bimodal or polymodal texture can be created by different modes that do or do not share a common tonic.
12. The overlapping portions of the two pentachords [G–A] outline the upper extreme of the lower tetrachord [D–E–F–G] and the lower extreme of the upper tetrachord [A–B–C/C#–D].
13. Please see the Bartók *Sonata* example in Chapter 6.
14. K. Robert Schwarz, "Process vs. Intuition in the Recent Works of Steve Reich and John Adams," *American Music*, Vol. 8, No. 3 (Autumn, 1990), pp. 245–273.
15. See Adams, *Phrygian Gates* (mm. 1–8).
16. See Chapter 4.
17. See Bartók, *Mikrokosmos* No. 12, "Reflection" (mm. 1–8).
18. For the modal/cyclic transformations of this mode, please see Chapter 6.
19. These are discussed a little later in the chapter.

20. Ann K. McNamme, in "Bitonality, Mode and Interval in the Music of Karol Szymanowski," *Journal of Music Theory*, Vol. 29, No.1 (Spring, 1985), pp. 61–84, argues that the bitonality that arises in the *Mazukas* Op. 50 are a result of perfect fifths cycles associated with the Lydian/Mixolydian hybrid mode. While this concept is demonstrated in Op. 50, No. 3, it is not shown for Op. 50, No.1. There are countless examples of bitonal combinations that are rotated to a common tonic. It must also be mentioned that there are not multiple perfect fifth cycles. There is only one cycle of perfect fifths.
21. See Szymanowski, *Mazurka* Op. 50, No. 1 (mm.1–4).
22. The fourth rotation of the Phrygian dominant mode is also known as the harmonic minor scale.
23. In western music, the harmonic minor scale resulted from the raising of the seventh scale degree to maintain leading tone function. It nevertheless exists as a non-diatonic mode in much of the music of the middle east where its different rotations are know by different names such as Nakriz, Hijaz, and Freygish.
24. For and in-depth analysis of this work, see Elliott Antokoletz, "Spanish Folk Modes and Their Transformations in the Music of Twentieth-Century Spanish Composers."
25. See Albéniz, *El Albaicin* (mm. 17–18).
26. This mode is prevalent in Spanish folk music.
27. See Albéniz, *El Albaicin* (mm. 32–36).
28. See Albéniz, *El Albaicin* (mm. 68–71).

NOTES TO CHAPTER 6

1. See Chapter 4.
2. See Mozart, *Piano Sonata in C Major Sonata* (mm. 1–8).
3. See Chapter 2.
4. See Ravel, *Laideronnette, Imperatrice des pagodes* (mm.26–27).
5. See Ravel, *Laideronnette, Imperatrice des pagodes* (mm. 31–35).
6. For a complete discussion of modal/cyclic relationships in Bartók's *Sonata for Piano*, see Paolo Susanni, "The Musical Language and Formal Structure of Bartók's *Sonata for Piano*," D.M.A. Treatise, University of Texas (2001).
7. See Bartók, *Piano Sonata*, Mvt. III (mm. 264–281).
8. See Rebikov, *In the Forest*.
9. László Somfai, *Béla Bartók: Compositions, Concepts, and Autograph Sources* (Berkeley: University of California Press, 1996), p. 152.
10. See Debussy, *L'isle Joyeuse* (mm. 12–14).
11. Elliott Antokoletz, "Interval Cycles in Stravinsky's Early Ballets," *Journal of the American Musicological Society*, Vol. 39, No. 3. (Autumn, 1986), pp. 578–614.
12. See Stravinsky, *Petrushka*, No. 34.
13. See Stravinsky, *Petrushka*, No. 35.
14. Paolo Susanni, "Modal Transformation and Axial Symmetry in Bartók's 'Out of Doors Suite'," *South Central Music Bulletin*, Vol. 3, No. 2 (Spring, 2005), pp. 11–14.
15. The formal structure of *With Drums and Pipes* is as follows: Ritornello (mm. 1–4)–Episode 1 (mm. 5–12)–Ritornello (mm. 12–14)–Episode 2 (mm. 15–21)–Ritornello (mm. 22–24)–Episode 3 (mm. 25–36)–Ritornello (mm. 37–39)–Episode 4 (mm. 39–66)–Ritornello (mm. 67–72)–Episode 5 (mm. 73–88)–Ritornello (mm. 89–104)–Coda (mm. 104–114).
16. See Bartók, *With Drums and Pipes* (mm. 10–12).

17. See Bartók, *With Drums and Pipes* (mm. 30–34).
18. See Bartók, *With Drums and Pipes* (mm. 50–55).
19. See Bartók, *With Drums and Pipes* (mm. 70–74).
20. This concept is described in connection with Scriabin's seventh piano sonata in Elliott Antokoletz, 'Transformations of a Special Non-Diatonic Mode in Twentieth-Century Music: Bartók, Stravinsky, Scriabin and Albrecht'*Music Analysis* Vol. 12, No. 1 (Mar, 1993) pp. 25–45
21. Formal Structure of Op. 74, No. 3 A (mm. 1–8) B (mm. 9–12) A' (mm. 13–20) B' (mm. 21–24) Codetta (mm. 25–26).
22. Elliott Antokoletz. "Spanish Folk Modes and their Transformations in the Music of Early Twentieth-Century Spanish Composers."
23. See Chapter 5.
24. See De Falla, Noches en los jardines de Espāna (Nos. 1–2).

NOTES TO CHAPTER 7

1. See Chapter 1.
2. If the generated collection does not itself play a significant role as a referent pitch collection of the work, then it cannot be considered significant structural determinant.
3. George Perle, in "Symmetrical Formations in the String Quartets of Béla Bártok," *Music Review*, Vol. 16 (November, 1955), pp. 185–205, was the first to use *sets X* and *Y* to describe the symmetrical chromatic and whole-tone tetrachords.
4. X and Y cells are identified by their transpositional level. The bottom note of cells X and Y are given the same numbers used to identify the pitch classes in the chromatic scale C = 0, C# = 1, etc. Cell X-0, for example, is C–C#–D–Eb, and cell Y-5 is F–G–A–B
5. See Debussy, *Pour les degrès chromatiques* (m. 1).
6. See Debussy, *Pour les degrès chromatiques* (m. 5–7).
7. See Debussy, Prelude from *Pour le Piano* (mm. 91–96).
8. See Boulez, *12 Notations for Piano* No. 4 (mm. 1–4).
9. Leo Treitler referred to this construction "cell Z" in "Harmonic Procedure in the *Fourth Quartet* of Béla Bartók" *Journal of Music Theory*, Vol. 3, No. 2 (November, 1959), pp. 292–298.
10. The unique structure of cell Z requires that we use two numbers in order to identify its transpositional level because unlike the X and Y cells, the pitch content at its tritone transposition remains the same. The pitch content of Z-0/6 [C–F–F#–B], for example, is identical to its tritone transposition, Z-6/0 [F#–B–C–F].
11. See Bartók, *From the Isle of Bali* (mm. 22–30).
12. See Stockhausen, *Klavierstück IV* (mm.1–3).
13. All three cells were first discussed in depth and shown to be part of a larger system in Elliott Antokoletz, "Principle of Pitch Organization in Bártok's *Fourth String Quartet*" (Ph.D. diss., The City University of New York, 1975).
14. See Cage, *In a Landscape* (mm. 1–10).
15. See Bartók, *Suite* Op. 14, No. 3 (mm. 8–11).

Bibliography

Antokoletz, Elliott. "Interval Cycles in Stravinsky's Early Ballets." *Journal of the American Musicological Society*, Vol. 39, No. 3. (Autumn, 1986), pp. 578–614.

———*The Music of Béla Bartók: A Study of Tonality and Progression in Twentieth-Century Music*. Berkeley: University of California Press, 1984.

———"Organic Development and the Interval Cycles in Bartók's Three Studies Op. 18." *Studia Musicologica*, Vol. 36, Nos. 3–4 (1995), pp. 249–261.

———*Twentieth-Century Music*. Englewood Cliffs, NJ: Prentice Hall, Inc., 1992.

Apel, Willi. "Mode." *The Harvard Dictionary of Music* (2nd ed.). Cambridge, MA: The Belknap Press of the Harvard University Press, 1974.

Bernstien, David W. "Georg Capellen's Theory of Reduction: Radical Harmonic Theory at the Turn of the Twentieth Century." *Journal of Music Theory*, Vol. 37, No. 1 (Spring, 1993), pp. 85–116.

Cowell, Henry. "Thesaurus of Scales and Melodic Patterns" by Nicholas Slonimsky. *Notes*, Second Series, Vol. 4, No. 2 (March, 1947).

Koozin, Timothy. "Octatonicism in Recent Solo Piano Works of Tōru Takemitsu." *Perspectives of New Music*, Vol. 29, No. 1 (Winter, 1991), pp.124–141.

Lambert, J. Philip. "Interval Cycles as Compositional Resources in the Music of Charles Ives." *Music Theory Spectrum*, Vol. 12, No. 1 (Spring, 1990), pp.43–82.

Lloyd, Norman. "Harmonic Materials of Modern Music" by Howard Hanson. *Journal of Research in Music Education*, Vol. 8, No. 2 (Autumn, 1960).

McNamme, Ann K. "Bitonality, Mode and Interval in the Music of Karol Szymanowski." *Journal of Music Theory*, Vol. 29, No. 1 (Spring, 1985), pp 61–84.

Perle, George. "Symmetrical Formations in the String Quartets of Béla Bartók." *Music Review*, Vol. 16 (November, 1955), pp. 189–205.

Sargeant, Winthrop. "Bernhard Ziehn, Precursor." *The Musical Quarterly*, Vol. 19, No. 2 (April, 1933), pp.169–177.

Schawtz, K. Robert. "Process vs. Intuition in the Recent Works of Steve Reich and John Adams." *American Music*, Vol. 8, No. 3 (Autumn, 1990), pp.245–273.

Somfai, László. *Béla Bartók: Compositions, Concepts, and Autograph Sources*. Berkeley: University of California Press, 1996.

Susanni, Paolo. "The Musical Language and Formal Structure of Bartók's *Sonata for Piano*." DMA Thesis, University of Texas, 2001.

———"Modal Transformation and Axial Symmetry in Bartók's Out of Doors Suite." *South Central Music Bulletin*, Vol. 3, No. 2 (Spring, 2005), pp.10–19.

Treitler, Leo. "Harmonic Procedure in the *Fourth Quartet* of Béla Bártok." *Journal of Music Theory*, Vol. 3, No. 2 (November, 1959), pp. 292–298.

Van den Toorn, Pieter. *The Music of Igor Stravinsky*. New Haven, CT: Yale University Press, 1983.

Index to Compositions

This index includes all music mentioned in the text. The page numbers indicate the main analyses of a given composition.

General Index